Praise for
Legacy on the Line

"With the largest wealth transfer in history underway, this book could not be more timely. My former student, Andrea Baumann Lustig, draws on decades of experience to illuminate the blind spots that derail even the most sophisticated families. This is a very useful resource for anyone determined to build and transfer their legacy."

—**Burton G. Malkiel**,
Author of *A Random Walk Down Wall Street*

"Blind spots can cost you as much as market volatility. This book shines a light on what many investors overlook—and how to fix it. If building and protecting your legacy matters to you, these insights are indispensable."

—**Stephanie Link**,
Chief Investment Strategist, Hightower Advisors & CNBC Contributor

"Building a legacy takes more than good markets—it takes strategy and planning. This book is a must-read for anyone serious about protecting their future."

—**Jamie Dinan**,
Founder & CEO, York Capital Management

"For generations, we reminded customers that 'an educated consumer is our best customer.' *Legacy on the Line* brings that same wisdom to wealth stewardship—empowering families to see what they've been missing and protect what truly matters."

—**Marcy Syms**,
President of the Sy Syms Foundation and TPD Group

Andrea Baumann Lustig

legacy
on the
line

**OVERCOME
BLIND SPOTS
TO GROW AND
TRANSFER
YOUR WEALTH**

WILEY

Copyright © 2026 by Andrea Baumann Lustig. All rights reserved.

Published by John Wiley & Sons, Inc., Hoboken, New Jersey.

No part of this publication may be reproduced, stored in a retrieval system, or transmitted in any form or by any means, electronic, mechanical, photocopying, recording, scanning, or otherwise, except as permitted under Section 107 or 108 of the 1976 United States Copyright Act, without either the prior written permission of the Publisher, or authorization through payment of the appropriate per-copy fee to the Copyright Clearance Center, Inc., 222 Rosewood Drive, Danvers, MA 01923, (978) 750-8400, fax (978) 750-4470, or on the web at www.copyright.com. Requests to the Publisher for permission should be addressed to the Permissions Department, John Wiley & Sons, Inc., 111 River Street, Hoboken, NJ 07030, (201) 748-6011, fax (201) 748-6008, or online at http://www.wiley.com/go/permission.

The manufacturer's authorized representative according to the EU General Product Safety Regulation is Wiley-VCH GmbH, Boschstr. 12, 69469 Weinheim, Germany, e-mail: Product_Safety@wiley.com.

Trademarks: Wiley and the Wiley logo are trademarks or registered trademarks of John Wiley & Sons, Inc. and/or its affiliates in the United States and other countries and may not be used without written permission. All other trademarks are the property of their respective owners. John Wiley & Sons, Inc. is not associated with any product or vendor mentioned in this book.

Limit of Liability/Disclaimer of Warranty: While the publisher and the authors have used their best efforts in preparing this work, including a review of the content of the work, neither the publisher nor the authors make any representations or warranties with respect to the accuracy or completeness of the contents of this work and specifically disclaim all warranties, including without limitation any implied warranties of merchantability or fitness for a particular purpose. Certain AI systems have been used in the creation of this work. No warranty may be created or extended by sales representatives, written sales materials or promotional statements for this work. The fact that an organization, website, or product is referred to in this work as a citation and/or potential source of further information does not mean that the publisher and authors endorse the information or services the organization, website, or product may provide or recommendations it may make. This work is sold with the understanding that the publisher is not engaged in rendering professional services. The advice and strategies contained herein may not be suitable for your situation. You should consult with a specialist where appropriate. Further, readers should be aware that websites listed in this work may have changed or disappeared between when this work was written and when it is read. Neither the publisher nor authors shall be liable for any loss of profit or any other commercial damages, including but not limited to special, incidental, consequential, or other damages.

For general information on our other products and services or for technical support, please contact our Customer Care Department within the United States at (800) 762-2974, outside the United States at (317) 572-3993 or fax (317) 572-4002.

Wiley also publishes its books in a variety of electronic formats. Some content that appears in print may not be available in electronic formats. For more information about Wiley products, visit our web site at www.wiley.com.

Library of Congress Cataloging-in-Publication Data is Available:

ISBN 9781394348824 (Cloth)
ISBN 9781394348862 (ePub)
ISBN 9781394348848 (ePDF)

COVER ART AND DESIGN: PAUL MCCARTHY

SKY10149646_031826

Legacy is not what we leave behind . . .
. . . it's what we shape forward.
—*Unknown*

To, Ivan—
Without your unwavering support, wisdom, and partnership,
our legacy would not have been created. You are the heart of
this journey and the reason it endures.

And

To our children, their spouses, and our grandchildren—
May you carry forward the values
and vision that shaped this legacy, from
generation to generation,
with purpose, integrity, and love.
You are our future, and its greatest promise.

Contents

Introduction	1
PART I WORKING WITH AN ADVISER	9
Blind Spot 1 "I Am Working with the Right Adviser"	13
Blind Spot 2 "I Have All the Advisers I Need"	37
Blind Spot 3 "I Can Implement My Plan on My Own"	55
Blind Spot 4 "It's Smart to Work with Multiple Advisers"	81
PART II DEVELOPING A WEALTH PLAN	97
Blind Spot 5 "Success Is All About Getting the Best Returns"	101
Blind Spot 6 "Not Every Asset Needs to Be in My Plan"	139
Blind Spot 7 "I Can Focus on My Wealth Planning After I Sell My Business"	159

PART III TRANSFERRING WEALTH — 187

Blind Spot 8 "I Don't Need to Share My Intentions with My Kids; It's All in My Will" — 191

Blind Spot 9 "We're Very Charitable; We Don't Need a Philanthropic Strategy" — 231

Blind Spot 10 "I Could Never Leave My Current Adviser" — 267

Conclusion — 281
Notes — 285
Acknowledgments — 299
About the Author — 303
Index — 305

Introduction

The Desire for Legacy

The desire to leave a legacy has permeated almost every culture throughout time. It can be found as far back as this tale of Ḥoni from the third-century Babylonian Talmud:

> "One day, Ḥoni was walking along the road when he saw a certain man planting a carob tree. Ḥoni said to him: This tree, after how many years will it bear fruit? The man said to him: It will not produce fruit until seventy years have passed. Ḥoni said to him: Is it obvious to you that you will live seventy years, that you expect to benefit from this tree? He said to *him:* That man himself found a world full of carob trees. Just as my ancestors planted for me, I too am planting for my descendants."[1]

Individuals and experts in nearly every society recognize the satisfaction that comes from leaving a legacy. Existential and evolutionary psychologists like Viktor Frankl (*Man's Search for Meaning*) and Michael E. Price, PhD (*Can Darwin Reveal the Meaning of Life?*), philosophers from Aristotle to Camus, and sociologists like founder-of-the-discipline Emile Durkheim, among many others, have all acknowledged and provided explanations for the human desire for our lives to have meaning.

The hope that we will be remembered and that our existence will have made a difference is deeply important to many of us. We expect that much of the mark we leave will be a values-driven legacy stemming from our ethics, character, reputation, actions, and examples set for others, most notably our family, throughout our lives. In addition, most of us (67% of investors) believe that leaving wealth to our heirs is important.[2] Many of us see the ability to grow and transfer wealth and assets to future generations and charitable causes as a direct and essential extension of our underlying values. As part of giving meaning to our lives and those of others, many of us seek to build and pass on a financial legacy. And yet, despite this enduring drive, many fail to achieve their desired goals due to avoidable blind spots. The chapters that follow seek to help illuminate the path toward a lasting and meaningful legacy.

The Impact of Transferring Wealth

The most significant wealth transfer in United States history is underway. As of 2024, Cerulli Associates projects that $124 trillion will be transferred through 2048, with 85% going to heirs and the remainder to charity.[3] The largest share of the transfer, $100 trillion (81%), will come from the Baby Boomer generation, those 74 million individuals born between 1946 and 1964.[4] Over the next 10 years, the next generation, Gen X (born between 1965 and 1980), will receive the next largest share. Still, over the next 25 years, Millennials (born between 1981 and 1996) will receive the most of any generation ($46 trillion).[5] As might be expected, wealthier households will account for a disproportionate share of the value transferred. Fully 50% of the transfer, or $62 trillion, is expected to come from high-net-worth and ultra-high-net-worth households, those with investable assets of $1 million to $5 million and more than $5 million, respectively, even though they make up only 1.5% of all households.[6]

As the wealth transfer wave continues to crest, investors are increasingly feeling the need to protect and plan for the distribution of their assets. Baby Boomers grew up in the shadow of the Depression and have lived through the stagflation of the 1970s, the stock market crash of 1987 (when the Dow Jones Average dropped 22.6% in a single day), the bursting of the tech bubble in 2000, the financial crisis of 2008, and the COVID-19 pandemic. They worry about money,[7] are increasingly looking for help from financial professionals,[8] and are willing to pay for advice.[9] Millennials, who lived through the last three crises (and hold the largest share of student debt[10]), are even more interested in receiving advice.[11]

This enormous movement of money between givers and receivers, combined with the desire for advice and the willingness to pay for it, has not gone unnoticed by financial firms. They have responded by repositioning themselves from "financial" or "investment advisers" to "wealth advisers" and are actively targeting these assets with new offerings focused on wealth planning. Industry consolidation has been unprecedented,[12] giving rise to very large firms that can leverage access to multiple products and services across investments, estate planning, and insurance.

Competition for your assets has become fierce.

With your legacy on the line in the face of this outpouring of wealth management services, it is an opportune moment to consider whether you are efficiently building the legacy you envision and effectively planning for its transfer.

What Is a Legacy Planning Blind Spot?

Over the past 30 years, I have observed that certain clients were significantly more effective than others at building and transferring their wealth. These clients worked collaboratively with their financial advisers on comprehensive, holistic wealth planning that encompassed investment management, estate planning, tax efficiency, and philanthropic strategies. The relationship with their advisers was built on a foundation of mutual respect and trust. It was deep, personal, and forthright. Discussions went far beyond simple transactions or routine financial check-ins. A profound sense of understanding underpinned every conversation. The adviser not only knew the client's financial goals and aspirations but also understood the values and motivations that drove them. Nothing was left unsaid—conversations unearthed fears, dreams, concerns, and personal challenges. Decisions were made collaboratively with the adviser offering guidance rooted in genuine care for the client's well-being, not just their portfolio. Unintended biases were brought to the surface and tackled. Most importantly, nothing was deemed out of bounds or left unaddressed by either party. Ultimately, the most productive relationships I saw were defined by knowledge, empathy, honesty, and a shared commitment to the client's long-term success.

Those who were less effective at building and transferring their wealth held fast to certain convictions about investment management, wealth planning, working with a financial adviser, and transferring their wealth. These convictions were either asserted in such a way as to indicate that the topic was off-limits or often remained unspoken, making clients reluctant to discuss specific issues, fully share information, or consider alternative lines of reasoning that could have better served their interests. These beliefs became blind spots—convictions so deeply held they couldn't be discussed, let alone dislodged. Like discussing religion or politics, these were areas that the adviser couldn't address productively head-on. They had to be side-stepped and worked around. As a result, these very convictions often stood in the way of effectively building and transferring the client's financial legacy.

I've encountered these convictions many times. The same ones continually crop up. The rationale behind each is completely understandable at first. They seem entirely logical. In most cases, however, they do not serve the investor's best interests. They may create additional risk instead of minimizing it. They may stymie growth instead of accelerating it. They may incur incremental costs instead of avoiding them. The purpose of this book is to illuminate the blind spots and offer investors a private opportunity to evaluate and reconsider their convictions. The book is meant to invite you to reflect on whether your future may be obstructed by any of the most common blind spots and consider whether it might be beneficial to discard them.

What's in This Book and How to Read It

Each of the chapters in this book covers one of the 10 blind spots most commonly held by clients that I've encountered over my 30 years of experience. The blind spots fall into three categories: Part 1, "Working with an Adviser"; Part 2, "Developing a Wealth Plan"; and Part 3, "Transferring Wealth."

PART 1: "WORKING WITH AN ADVISER"

Blind Spot 1: "I am working with the right adviser."

Blind Spot 2: "I have all the advisers I need."

Blind Spot 3: "I can implement my plan on my own."

Blind Spot 4: "It's smart to work with multiple advisers."

PART 2: "DEVELOPING A WEALTH PLAN"

Blind Spot 5: "Success is all about getting the best returns."

Blind Spot 6: "Not every asset needs to be in my plan."

Blind Spot 7: "I can focus on my wealth planning after I sell my business."

PART 3: "TRANSFERRING WEALTH"

Blind Spot 8: "I don't need to share my intentions with my kids; it's all in my will."

Blind Spot 9: "We're very charitable; we don't need a philanthropic strategy."

Blind Spot 10: "There's no way I could leave my current adviser."

Before they were addressed, each conviction potentially stood in the way of individuals or families, hindering them from opening the door to new ideas and planning strategies that could increase growth or mitigate risk. Once acknowledged and relinquished, clients were to make the most of their financial situation and build the legacy they envisioned.

What's Not in This Book

When it comes to wealth planning, most clients have some or all of the following questions, that are typically addressed in the planning process:

- Can I sustain my lifestyle in the face of inflation and uncertain markets while still leaving a legacy?
- How large a financial legacy can I truly afford to leave?
- What is the legacy I envision—and how do I maximize it?
- How do I identify and separate the core capital necessary to maintain my lifestyle from discretionary capital available for future generations and philanthropy?
- Can I balance financially intelligent strategies such as giving gifts to future generations and charities with retaining control and the ability to change my mind?

- Are there ways of structuring my legacy that will benefit me during my lifetime?
- Are there steps I can take now that will benefit my heirs later?
- What are the major risks to my legacy? What are the opportunities to grow it?

This book doesn't answer these important questions; it sets you up to understand the need to address them without blinders. Each chapter acknowledges the reasons a conviction seems so logical, asks you to consider whether your belief may actually be a blind spot that stands in your way, and invites you to reflect on whether an alternative approach might help you more effectively build and transfer your legacy. Reading it will also enable you to determine whether you are working with the right wealth adviser making the most of your relationship.

Why I Wrote This Book

My passion for helping people create and pass on their legacy runs deep. It's the result of my own very long legacy inherited and cultivated over time: I'm the sixth generation of my family to work in wealth management. My great-great-great-grandfather founded the Banque Lévy in France in 1810. That bank was passed down through the generations to my grandfather, who became president of its successor, the Banque Asch. At the time, this was the largest bank in Strasbourg, France. He and his partners led the bank, helping families build their legacies, until he was forced to flee his home at the start of World War II, when he ultimately found refuge in the United States. In the post-war era, he worked transatlantically to help families rebuild the legacies that were destroyed during the war. My father continued his father's legacy, eventually selling the bank and becoming an early partner in Stralem & Company, a wealth management firm founded in 1967.

You might think that, given my family history, I was raised to be fluent in the language of finance. However, when I was growing up, one did *not* discuss business around the dinner table. It was considered impolite—especially for a young lady. Nonetheless, I was captivated by the stories I heard about legacies that were rebuilt and transferred and what made them different from those that were lost entirely. I was endlessly curious, always urging my father to tell me more. My desire to break through the taboo surrounding discussions of money, dismantle the overwhelming sense that mastery for anyone outside the business would be unachievable, allay the fear that one could easily be taken advantage of, and help others build their futures ultimately drove me into the business.

After working at Morgan Stanley, Booz Allen & Hamilton, and Alliance Bernstein, I joined Stralem in 2003 and, following in my father's footsteps, became president in 2012. Stralem merged with Fischer & Company in 2020, and Fischer Stralem Advisers became part of Hightower Advisors in the same year. Over the past 30 years in wealth management, I've worked closely with families to develop wealth plans tailored to their specific desired outcomes and risk tolerance, enabling them to have a high probability of successfully meeting their retirement and legacy goals.

As I noticed the persistence of thought patterns that blocked clients from making progress toward meeting their financial goals, my desire to address these biases or blind spots grew. I could see how discussing money remained uncomfortable for many, enabling these blind spots to persist. Eventually, I decided that the best way to address them was to consolidate my responses into a book that investors could read and consider independently and that advisers could share with their clients. I hope reading it will enable you, your partner, and family members who are part of your legacy or building their own to avoid these 10 blind spots and build the legacy you envision.

Part I

Working with an Adviser

For most investors, building and transferring their legacy involves working with an adviser to help them maintain their lifestyle throughout their lifetimes and enhance the efficient transfer of wealth to the next generation. To accomplish this effectively, it's essential to evaluate the relationship you have with your adviser and identify any potential blind spots in your approach that may be hindering your progress. It's therefore essential to address:

Blind Spot 1: I Am Working With the Right Adviser.
Understand the standards your adviser is held to, be comfortable with their compensation, and make sure your interests are aligned.

Recent changes in access and status for investment advisers have altered the incentive structure, leading to more individuals with less knowledge claiming to perform the same job. But it's *not the same*. Understanding whether your adviser is a fiduciary who must put your interests ahead of their own and how they are compensated is crucial to determining whether their incentives are aligned with yours. This chapter will help you learn how to evaluate the landscape of professionals and decide whether you are working with the right adviser.

Blind Spot 2: I Have All the Advisers I need.
Determine whether your adviser is providing the holistic wealth management knowledge you need and effectively quarterbacking your investment managers, estate planning attorney, accountant, insurance agent, and philanthropic advisers as necessary.

You may believe you have all the advisers you need: tax, estate, insurance, and investment. But without an advocate who takes a holistic approach to your finances, you and your partner are less likely to identify the interdisciplinary risks and opportunities to grow or protect your wealth. The intersection of your overall goals and the knowledge required demands a level of vigilance and oversight, and this chapter will explain why and how to select someone for this role.

Blind Spot 3: I Can Implement My Plan On My Own.
Evaluate whether you are comfortable sharing your thinking and collaborating with your adviser instead of going it on your own.

As sophisticated as you may be financially, if you feel reluctant to collaborate with your adviser and choose not to share all your investment thoughts and intentions, you may have an underlying lack of confidence in your adviser's sophistication and understanding. This chapter will help you evaluate whether acting as your own wealth adviser serves your best interests.

Blind Spot 4: It's Smart to Work with Multiple Advisers.
Understand the potential risks and missed opportunities of working with multiple, uncoordinated financial advisers.

You may believe that you are reducing your risk by working with multiple investment advisers, and you think it's prudent to have several advisers with different approaches so that you can benefit in case one does better than the other. This chapter will help you understand why you may actually be increasing risk and how you can still utilize different investment managers while gaining the benefits of having one adviser coordinate and oversee them, helping to ensure they conform to an overall strategic asset allocation derived from your wealth plan.

The chapters that follow will help you examine whether you hold any biases that underpin these blind spots in working with an adviser. They will enable you to consider ways to overcome them, allowing you to help grow and transfer your legacy effectively.

Blind Spot 1

"I Am Working with the Right Adviser"

Most investors are very unlikely to change financial advisers in their lifetimes. Almost 70% of investors have worked with only one adviser or voluntarily changed advisers only once, according to a recent survey by Dynasty Financial Partners.[1] Investors are content overall with their advisers. More than 70% of respondents said they were "very satisfied" with their financial adviser, according to the J.D. Power 2024 U.S. Full-Service Investor Satisfaction Study,[2] which measured overall investor satisfaction with full-service investment firms.

But dig a little deeper, and you find something interesting. In a field where you would expect financial metrics to govern, investors overwhelmingly *hire and stay with their financial advisers for emotional reasons.* Figure 1.1 illustrates investor motivations.

Figure 1.1 The Top Reasons Clients Hire Their Advisors

Proportions in Each Topic

Comfort handling finances	Specific goals or needs	Behavioral coaching	Rec. by family or friends	Quality of relationship
0.32	0.32	0.17	0.12	0.1

Comfort handling finances (0.32):
- To help me better navigate the number of things available to me. To help give me a better understanding and confidence in my financial security.
- I feel more secure having a different view of my finances.
- I don't like making financial decisions.

Specific goals or needs (0.32):
- Excellent referrals with proven results. We needed some outside guidance to plan for retirements.
- For better income management.
- I wanted to start investing.
- To set up annuity.
- To see if we were on track for retirement.

Behavioral coaching (0.17):
- I lack discipline to stay invested when the market is erratic.
- He is a sane voice, and I am able to bounce ideas off of him.

Quality of relationship (0.1):
- I found an advisor who understood me, and I found to be a good fit.

■ Emotion-Based Reason
■ Financial-Based Reason

Source: Lamas et al., 2023 / Morningstar, Inc

A study by Vanguard, "Assessing the Value of Advice,"[3] found that "the emotional aspects of an advisory relationship represented nearly half (45%) of the total value assigned by those investors rating advice most highly."

"Trust" and "personal connection" create a sense of comfort and loyalty that often prevent investors from even considering switching advisers, allowing inertia to take hold. What's more, 75% of investors surveyed believe that their adviser "acts in their best interest."[4] Advisers often form close friendships with their clients. You have dinner together. You play golf together. Your husbands or wives become friends. You and your family socialize, maybe you even go on vacation together. In addition, you see that your adviser is going through or has gone through similar financial or familial milestones as you have, and you believe they can relate to your stage of life and its attendant challenges. You've had deeply personal discussions. Moreover, you've seen that they have done well financially, and their success suggests they are effective at their job. They are intelligent, well-read, and capable. You trust they have your best interests at heart. At some point, staying with them is due to much more than inertia. The idea of breaking up has become unthinkable.

Occasionally, you wonder what it would be like to start from scratch, to evaluate what services you are getting from them versus what's out there. Do they really have your best interests at heart? How are they compensated? Are you getting all the services you should be getting? Are you receiving all the services you need? What else is out there? But then you imagine the emotional cost of switching and the time it would take to evaluate, change, and build a new relationship with another adviser, and you quickly tuck the gnawing questions away. That they are the right adviser for you becomes a deeply held conviction that makes re-evaluating it completely off the table.

When a conviction is so deeply held that you can't or don't want to re-evaluate it, it is a sure sign that you've encountered a blind spot—a belief that is obstructing, rather than advancing, the vision you have for yourself and your family.

If you are concerned with building your legacy, it may be time to move beyond emotional drivers and evaluate whether you are working with the right adviser. Recognizing that your emotions may have played an undue role in the selection and retention of your financial adviser, it makes sense to reevaluate your choice based on a thorough understanding of the financial interests, regulatory standards, and growth incentives that motivate the adviser. You may find that you are working with the right advisor and discover ways to enhance your relationship, or you may find that it is in your best interests to move on. Chapter 10 will explore how to overcome any apprehension, guilt, or discomfort you may have in leaving your current adviser, so set that aside for now and consider whether you are, in fact, working with the right adviser for your needs.

Three Categories of Financial Advisers

Studies show that investors often lack a clear understanding of the differences between types of investment advisers. A study by the Rand Corporation on Investor and Industry Perspectives on Investment Advisers and Broker-Dealers concluded that "even those who have employed financial professionals for years are often confused about job titles, types of firms with which they are associated, and the payments they make for their services."[5]

Recent changes in access and status for investment advisers have shifted the incentive structure, resulting in more people with less knowledge claiming to do the same job. But roles and responsibilities do differ, often significantly. Understanding whether your adviser is a fiduciary who must put your interests *ahead* of their own and how they are compensated is critical to determining whether their incentives are aligned with yours.

The title *financial adviser* is used broadly making the landscape confusing. Advisers fall into three broad categories: Registered Representatives (RRs), Investment Adviser Representatives (IARs), and Dual Representatives (DRs), who are both Registered Representatives and Investment Adviser Representatives. Advisers in the first two categories differ significantly. Each is subject to different regulatory standards, benefits from compensation structures that create very different incentives, and offers different services. Advisers in the third category can act as either Registered Representatives or Investment Adviser Representatives (IARs), depending on the type of account in which they are dealing.

Figure 1.2 shows that of the 713,576 securities industry-registered individuals in 2023, 12% were registered representatives, 43% were investment adviser representatives, and 45% were dual representatives.[6]

Figure 1.2 Securities Industry Registered Individuals

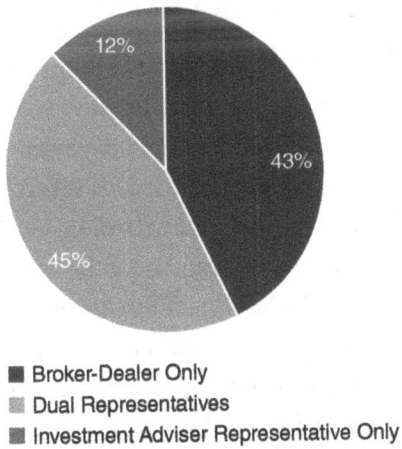

■ Broker-Dealer Only
■ Dual Representatives
■ Investment Adviser Representative Only

Source: FINRA 2024 Industry Snapshot pg. 5 / FINRA

Determining the regulatory standards to which your adviser is held will enable you to know whether your adviser is required to put your interests ahead of their own—not every type of adviser is. Knowing how your adviser and their firm are compensated will help you understand their incentives and whether they are likely to have the desire, time, and ability to dedicate themselves to working with you to help build your legacy, revealing additional incentives at work below the surface. Finally, teasing apart the different services emphasized will enable you to determine whether your needs align with the firm and adviser's focus. Taken together, understanding these differences will enable you to identify the type of adviser most likely to help you build the legacy you envision.

Let's review each adviser type in detail.

1. Registered Representative (RR)

The first type of financial "adviser" is a Registered Representative. Note that Registered Reps cannot use the word *adviser* or *advisor* unless they are dually registered as an investment adviser or supervised by one. This "financial professional" is referred to as a *broker* and is employed by a broker-dealer firm. Broker-dealers, and therefore Registered Representatives, are regulated by the Financial Industry Regulatory Authority (FINRA). This independent, nongovernmental organization writes and enforces the rules governing registered brokers and broker-dealer firms in the United States. *Broker* indicates that the firm or its employee can act as an agent on behalf of a customer, while *Dealer* indicates that it can also act as a principal on its behalf. This is your first hint that there may be multiple incentives at work—some for brokers and some for dealers.

Most accounts held with a Registered Rep/Broker are *nondiscretionary*, meaning that the broker must call you to get your permission to make a trade. The broker-dealer charges a commission on every trade you make and pays a portion of it to the broker (payout ratio). The broker-dealer is permitted to offer these brokers higher payouts for recommending specific products. This is frequently done in cases where the broker-dealer has already acted as principal—buying/acquiring third-party products for the firm to mark up and sell to you—and has inventory it wants to sell. The broker-dealer frequently increases the payout ratio to brokers when it wants to reduce its inventory of a particular product, and incent the broker to call you and suggest a trade. As long as the overall commission paid by the client does not change, the broker-dealer is generally not required to notify you about the changes to the payout grid for advisers. These are viewed as internal compensation adjustments, but they may affect you significantly.

Commission charges and broker payouts don't rise and fall in line with your portfolio—they rise and fall as a function of the trading activity recommended by the broker, so the nature of this relationship is likely to be transaction-focused. Broker-dealers have an incentive to continually offer new products, creating new incentives for brokers to recommend selling out of one investment to buy another. These products can also include proprietary mutual or other funds managed by the firm on which it earns an investment management fee as part of the fund's expense ratio. The good news is that brokers and broker-dealers are driven to find new ideas and are likely to encourage you to buy into these ideas (and, of course, sell a security to raise the liquidity to fund the transaction, creating a second round of commission charges and potential capital gains tax). This can be exciting and profitable for both you and the broker, but it is essential to understand that potential conflicts of interest may arise from the commission structure and/or the dealer's inventory, which are not required to be disclosed.

Imagine the following conversation between Jack, a Registered Representative, and Jill, the client:

Jack: "Hi Jill, I've been looking at ABC's performance lately and was thinking that you might want to add some exposure. We could sell some XYZ, which hasn't gone anywhere this year."

Jill: "Well, Jack, you're my adviser, if you think it's a good idea, let's go for it." (Jill's thinking, it was nice of him to call, but isn't this what she pays him for? Who is she to second-guess his suggestions anyway?)

Jack was obligated to call Jill because the trade was happening in a nondiscretionary brokerage account. Jill just gave Jack the order to purchase ABC, unaware that this would result in relatively higher commissions for him, as the firm had a significant amount of ABC stock in inventory and had increased the payout ratio to him. She also engendered commissions for his firm by both selling XYZ and buying ABC. Note that there was also no discussion of any potential tax implications that might arise from the sale of XYZ.

Before June 2020, brokers were held to the suitability standard, which creates a "suitability obligation," meaning they must only believe that their recommendations are *suitable* for you based on considerations such as age, investment experience, and risk tolerance. *Brokers are not required to put your interests ahead of their own.* This is why they can recommend products on which they receive higher commission payouts over ones for which they receive less, as long as both are suitable. As a result, if the firm they work for introduces new products with higher commission payouts for the "broker," you may find your broker suggesting rotating in or out of an investment and/or taking actions with tax consequences that may not be in your best interest.

Regulation Best Interest (Reg BI), which became effective on June 30, 2020, aimed to enhance broker-dealer standards of conduct when making recommendations to retail customers. It was designed to address concerns about potential conflicts of interest among broker-dealers and their associated people and to enhance the quality of advice provided to investors. Reg BI raises the standard from a suitability obligation to a "best interest standard" *but does not impose a fiduciary duty.* It requires brokers to *consider* the customer's best interests, without defining what that means, but still does not impose the same level of fiduciary responsibility as investment advisers.

Let's quickly review what a registered representative is. Table 1.1 outlines the regulatory, professional, and operational characteristics of Registered Representatives (RRs).

2. Investment Adviser Representatives (IAR)

In contrast, an Investment Adviser Representative (IAR) is employed by a Registered Investment Adviser (RIA) who is regulated by the Investment Advisers Act of 1940, a federal law that, amended as of November 2024, requires investment advisers with $100 million or more in assets to register with the Securities and

Table 1.1   Key Characteristics of Registered Representatives

Dimension	Registered Representatives (RR)
Regulatory Authority	Regulated by the Financial Industry Regulatory Authority (FINRA)
Regulatory Standards	Must meet the "suitability" standard, ensuring investments are suitable for clients
Licensing Requirements	Must pass the Series 7 and Series 63 exams
Nature of Typical Client Relationship	Transaction-based, focusing on buying and selling securities
Adviser Compensation Structure	Typically, earn a payout from the firm's commissions on the sale of financial products
Underlying firm remuneration	Earns commissions on the purchase and sale of financial products
Conflict of Interest Disclosure	Not required to disclose all conflicts of interest
Investment Discretion Authority	Generally, do not have discretionary authority over client accounts
Scope of Services	Primarily focused on investment products and transactions
Wealth Planning Focus	Low to none

Exchange Commission (SEC) and adhere to its regulations.[7] The SEC[8] places a fiduciary duty on investment adviser representatives, which is comprised of two main tenets: a duty of care and a duty of loyalty. Duty of care has three components: the duty to provide advice that is in the client's best interest, the duty to seek best execution, and the duty to act and to provide advice and monitoring throughout the relationship to act in the best interests of their clients.[9] According to the SEC,[10] "The Duty of Loyalty requires an investment adviser to put its client's interests first. An investment adviser must not favor its interests over those of a client or unfairly favor one client over another. In seeking to meet its duty of loyalty, an adviser must make full and fair disclosure to its clients of all material facts relating to the advisory relationship." The fiduciary duty moves beyond considering your best interests to placing your interests ahead of the adviser's.

Investment advisers typically charge a fee based on a percentage of assets under management (AUM). In this case, the percentage fee charged to the client first goes to the RIA. The firm then pays a portion of it to the adviser in the form of a salary or a draw against the revenue they are expected to bring in for the year. The adviser does not get compensated based on product sales or commissions. In this situation, trading commissions are paid directly to the broker-dealer that executes the trades, which may or may not be part of the same firm. The adviser's incentive is to grow the client's portfolio and attract new assets to the firm. Their interests are aligned with yours: their revenue increases as your portfolio grows and decreases if it shrinks. Typically, they do not earn commissions on trades. If compensated in this manner, they have no conflict of interest because they have nothing to gain by recommending one product over another or by making frequent trades in and out of your account to increase their fees. If a conflict of interest arises, they are required to disclose it to you.

Fees that are a percent of AUM are much more straightforward than commissions. But there's nonetheless one important aspect for you to research: the firm may pay your adviser a higher percentage of the fee on new business brought and a lower percentage on accounts already invested. Over time, the adviser (or their firm) may transfer existing relationships to a servicing team to minimize the adviser's time on existing clients. This incents the adviser to focus on new business, perhaps at the expense of servicing existing clients.

Unlike working with a registered representative, when working with an investment adviser, the client typically grants the adviser *discretion*—the ability to change, add to, or reduce investments as deemed necessary without consulting the client on every trade. This means they can change, add to, or reduce investments as advisable without obtaining your specific permission. This makes sense because your interests are aligned. The nature of this relationship is relatively more advice-based.

Now, imagine the conversation between Jack and Jill, but in this case, with Jack as an Investment Adviser rather than a Registered Representative:

Jack: *"Hi Jill, I wanted to set up a time to review the performance of your portfolio with you."*

Jill: *"That sounds great, Jack. I'm glad you called. I've been noticing how ABC has been taking off lately, and I was wondering if we should add it to the portfolio."*

Jack: *"I'm so glad you raised that, Jill. You already have significant exposure to technology in your portfolio, including ABC. When you come in, we can evaluate whether adding to that position makes sense in light of the overall concentration and risk in the portfolio."*

Whether Jill decides to add ABC or not will not affect Jack's compensation in any way. What Jack is focused on is whether the purchase is appropriate for Jill's overall risk/return profile. Will the potential for additional return outweigh the potential for additional risk? The fiduciary standard requires advisers to put your interests ahead of their own, rather than just *consider* your best interests, and the fee-based compensation structure reinforces that.

Let's review what an investment adviser rep (IAR) is. Table 1.2 outlines the regulatory, professional, and operational characteristics of Investment Adviser Representatives (IARs).

Table 1.2 Key Characteristics of Investment Adviser Representatives

Dimension	Investment Adviser Representatives (IAR)
Regulatory Authority	Regulated by the Securities and Exchange Commission (SEC) or state regulators
Regulatory Standards	Held to a fiduciary standard, legally required to act in the best interests of clients
Licensing Requirements	Must pass the Series 65 or Series 66 exams or equivalents
Nature of Typical Client Relationship	Ongoing advisory relationship focusing on investment selection and/or wealth—this change has to be made in final table that holds all three columns comprehensive planning
Adviser Compensation Structure	Receives a salary and bonus from fees based on a percentage of assets under management (AUM) or hourly rates
Underlying Firm Remuneration	Usually charges fees based on a percentage of assets under management (AUM) or hourly rates
Conflict of Interest Disclosure	Required to disclose all conflicts of interest
Investment Discretion Authority	Often have discretionary authority to make investment decisions on behalf of clients
Scope of Services	Offers a broader range of financial planning and advisory services
Wealth Planning Focus	Can be paramount. Depends on focus of the firm and individual

3. Dual Representative

Dual Representatives are held to the suitability standard on brokerage accounts, where they do not have the discretion to trade without obtaining your consent, and held to the fiduciary standard on advisory accounts, where they can make investment decisions without consulting you. Their duty is *by account* and not relationship-based. You may, therefore, have some accounts with the same adviser where the suitability/best interest standard is used and others where the fiduciary standard is applied. It is often up to you to understand which account your conversations with the adviser affect.

The firms that Dual Representatives work for are simultaneously an SEC-Registered Investment Adviser and a broker-dealer. Their compensation is a hybrid of commission payouts and salary. To the extent that the adviser invests in the firm's proprietary or private-labeled mutual funds (even if they are merely index funds), both the adviser and the firm may earn additional payout and management fee revenue. The firm owns the underlying broker-dealer, does all the trading, and may earn commissions on every transaction. Having a trading account in addition to your principal investment portfolio can be a useful or fun way to take a risk and invest in something outside your core capital. However, be aware that the funds you keep in brokerage accounts often do not count toward the size of your fiduciary, discretionary relationship with the firm. This may prevent you from reaching a higher asset level at which you might hit a lower fee breakpoint.

Dual-registered advisers can be found at what are known as hybrid RIAs or wire houses, such as Morgan Stanley and Merrill Lynch. In contrast to an independent RIA, which employs only Investment Advisers, hybrid RIAs and wire houses employ both investment advisers and registered representatives. Hybrid RIAs are typically teams of independent professionals who run their businesses and are affiliated with a broker-dealer. In contrast, advisers working at wirehouses are typically employees of the wirehouse firm, relying on its brand and resources for client acquisition and operations. Hybrid RIAs provide advisers with the flexibility to select their investment managers and products. In contrast, wirehouse advisers must adhere to firm-approved managers and products, which may be proprietary and, therefore, an additional revenue stream for the firm.

The two preceding conversations between Jack and Jill now become conflated because Jack can act as both a Registered Representative and an Investment Adviser:

> Jack: Hi Jill, I've been looking at ABC's performance lately and was thinking that you might want to add some exposure. Why don't you come in for a portfolio review, and we can see if it makes sense to add some?
>
> Jill: Sounds great, Jack! ABC's performance has attracted my attention, too. I was also wondering whether I should add some.

Jack is able to act as both Registered Rep and Investment Adviser because, depending on what decisions Jill makes, he can take action in either her brokerage or her discretionary account.

If you are working with a dual-registered adviser and have multiple accounts, some of which are brokerage while others are discretionary, you may not even be able to discern without asking which account will be affected when discussing your investments with your adviser. Since it becomes awkward and challenging to understand the financial adviser's incentives in these situations, clients often give up asking the question.

Let's review what a Dual Representative (DR) is in Table 1.3, which outlines the regulatory, professional, and operational characteristics of Dual Representatives (DRs).

Table 1.3 Key Characteristics of Dual Representatives

Dimension	Dually Representative (DR)
Regulatory Authority	Regulated by both FINRA and SEC
Regulatory Standards	Held to best interest on brokerage accounts and to fiduciary on discretionary accounts
Licensing Requirements	Differs by accounts
Nature of Typical Client Relationship	Transaction-based or advisory based on account type
Adviser Compensation Structure	Commissions on trades in brokerage accounts plus salary and bonus
Underlying Firm Remuneration	Firm earns both commissions and advisory fees
Conflict of Interest Disclosure	Not required to disclose all conflicts of interest
Investment Discretion Authority	Discretionary authority on some accounts but not all
Scope of Services	Broad range of investment, planning and other financial services
Wealth Planning Focus	Available but often not the focus of relationship

Evaluating Your Adviser Relationship

Table 1.4 summarizes the characteristics that differentiate adviser types across three areas: Regulation, Compensation, and Investments.

Sorting through these options is challenging, but once you understand the underlying dynamics outlined and consider your objectives, you can determine whether you are in fact working

Table 1.4 Comparison of Adviser Characteristics

Dimension	Registered Representatives	Investment Adviser Representatives	Dual Representatives
REGULATION			
Regulatory Authority	Regulated by the Financial Industry Regulatory Authority (FINRA)	Regulated by the Securities and Exchange Commission (SEC) or state regulators	Held to best interest on brokerage accounts and to fiduciary on discretionary accounts
Regulatory Standards	Must meet the "suitability" standard, ensuring investments are suitable for clients	Held to a fiduciary standard, legally required to act in the best interests of clients	Differs by accounts
Licensing Requirements	Must pass the Series 7 and Series 63 exams	Must pass the Series 65 or Series 66 exams or equivalents	Transaction-based or advisory based on account type
Nature of Typical Client Relationship	Transaction-based, focusing on buying and selling securities	Ongoing advisory relationship focusing on comprehensive financial planning	Commissions on trades in brokerage accounts plus salary and bonus

Dimension	Registered Representatives	Investment Adviser Representatives	Dual Representatives
COMPENSATION			
Adviser Compensation Structure	Typically, earn a payout from the firm's commissions on the sale of financial products	Receives a salary and bonus from fees based on a percentage of assets under management (AUM) or hourly rates	Not required to disclose all conflicts of interest
Underlying Firm Remuneration	Earns commissions on the purchase and sale of financial products	Usually charges fees based on a percentage of assets under management (AUM) or hourly rates	Discretionary authority on some accounts but not all
SERVICES			
Conflict of Interest Disclosure	Not required to disclose all conflicts of interest	Required to disclose all conflicts of interest	Available but often not the focus of relationship
Investment Discretion Authority	Generally, do not have discretionary authority over client accounts	Often have discretionary authority to make investment decisions on behalf of clients	Dually-registered
Scope of Services	Primarily focused on investment products and transactions	Offers a broader range of financial planning and advisory services	Regulated by Both FINRA and SEC
Wealth Planning Focus	Low to none	Can be paramount. Depends on focus of the firm and individual	Held to suitability on brokerage accounts and to fiduciary on discretionary accounts

with the right adviser. Are you looking for help executing trades? Do you want holistic investment and wealth planning advice? Or are you looking for something in between? Investors differ in the amount and type of advice they seek, although the demand for holistic wealth planning is increasing dramatically, giving rise to changes in the adviser landscape. According to McKinsey, the share of investors seeking more holistic advice increased by 79% from 29% in 2018 to 52% in 2023.[11]

Family Offices

When a family's wealth reaches a level where managing assets, tax planning, estate structuring, and governance become too complex for traditional wealth management solutions, it often makes sense for them to create or join a Single-Family Office (SFO) or a Multi-Family Office (MFO). The decision to create or join a family office is not only a financial consideration but also a reflection of stewardship—the responsibility to preserve and grow wealth for future generations while aligning decisions with family values and long-term purpose. Generally, a single-family office (SFO) becomes practical at around $100 million or more in investable assets, as operating costs can range from $1–$10 million annually for staff, infrastructure, and compliance. Families with multiple generations, cross-border holdings, operating businesses, or philanthropic goals often need dedicated governance and coordination resources, making an SFO attractive—especially for those prioritizing privacy and control. For families with $20–$100 million, joining a multi-family office (MFO) is usually more cost-efficient, offering institutional-quality services without the full overhead of an SFO. In all cases, stewardship serves as the guiding philosophy, ensuring wealth is managed not just for financial performance but for continuity, impact, and values across generations.

Family offices are not necessarily staffed with investment advisers. They differ in their approach to fiduciary standards based on their structure. Single-family offices (SFOs), which serve one family and are privately controlled, are generally not legally required to follow fiduciary standards because they are considered an extension of the family. However, many adopt fiduciary-like practices voluntarily for governance and transparency. In contrast, multi-family offices (MFOs) often operate like wealth management firms and, if registered as investment advisers, are legally bound to act in their clients' best interests under fiduciary obligations. Overall, while regulation varies by jurisdiction, many family offices implement governance frameworks—such as investment committees and conflict-of-interest policies—to maintain trust and align with best practices.

The Adviser Landscape

The breadth of adviser types persist because different needs and preferences exist. On one end of the wealth advice spectrum are the do-it-yourselfers."These investors do not work with an adviser at all. They manage and trade their accounts on their own and typically do so online. If they work with a registered representative, it is just because the representative is needed to execute a transaction. Since they are not turning discretion over to their stockbroker, they do not care that the broker doesn't put the broker's interests ahead of their own. They expect to pay a fee for trades placed. At the other end of the spectrum are those who are focused on building and preserving their legacy. They seek comprehensive wealth and investment planning advice from a fiduciary and professional who prioritizes the client's interests above their own. They expect to pay an investment management fee that fluctuates with the account's performance. Dual-registered representatives fall between these two, offering the flexibility to transfer discretion on part of the funds while keeping money in a trading account as well. Table 1.5 illustrates the range of interest in receiving advice.

Table 1.5 The Wealth Advice Spectrum

	DIY	HYBRID	FULL SERVICE
Targeted to Investors Who	Prefer managing their own investments	Seek investment management plus ongoing access to trading accounts	Seek ongoing investment and wealth management
Services Used	Online tools or an executing broker	Discretionary and non-discretionary investment management	Discretionary Investment Management and Holistic Wealth Planning
Ideal For	Those who have experience in financial management	Investors who want investment advice	Families focused on building and guarding their legacy
Provider	Registered Rep	Dual Registered	Independent Financial Adviser with Wealth Planning Focus, Family Offices

If you are a do-it-yourselfer, you may be fine with executing transactions online or with the occasional help of a Registered Representative. If, however, you are interested in building your legacy, you'll need to make sure you are working with a wealth planning professional at the other end of the spectrum.

Investor demand is shifting rapidly and dramatically toward the advisory end of the spectrum. With the largest transfer of wealth in U.S. history underway, investment firms and financial advisers have adopted a wealth management focus to align themselves with the growing need for comprehensive wealth planning. Whereas, at 45% in 2023, Dual Representatives were the largest category of the

713,576 securities industry-registered individuals, they have since been losing market share to independent financial advisers. According to Cerulli, the share of advisers in independent and hybrid RIAs is increasing at the fastest rate of all channels and has soared over the past decade, from 18% to 27%, with the share expected to reach 30% within the next five years.[12] This growth is coming at the expense of the dual-registered, wirehouse channel, which is projected to lose market share. Although wirehouses control 34% of the assets under management, they now employ only 15% of the advisers. According to Institutional Investor, "RIAs are outpacing all other channels in headcount and assets under management.[13]" In fact, the Independent RIA channel is the only one that has grown over the last decade. According to the Investment Adviser Association, the shift toward investment advisory firms and IARs has continued because investors increasingly see the value of fiduciary advice offered by investment advisers. Figure 1.3 shows that the growth in the number of Investment Advisers has been strong over one- and three-year periods.

Figure 1.3 Percentage Change in the Number of Licensed Financial Professionals

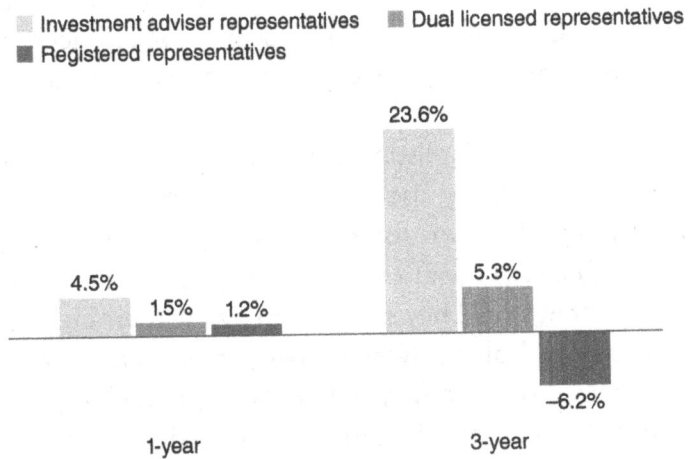

Note: Number of investment adviser representatives and dual licensed representatives includes representatives for both SEC and state registered advisers. Number of investment adviser representatives, dual licensed representatives, and registered representatives at year end.

Source: FINRA Industry Snapshot 2023 / FINRA

Legacy Building Requires a Wealth Adviser

Legacies don't happen by accident; they require focus and action. If your goal is to build and transfer your legacy, then your focus is likely to be on identifying a fiduciary-based, holistic wealth advisor. Note that there is no industry-specific recognized definition for the title *holistic wealth manager*. A holistic wealth advisor is typically an investment adviser who has chosen to incorporate or specialize in a comprehensive approach to wealth management—one that integrates financial, estate, tax, philanthropic, and life planning considerations. This type of adviser is most often found at an independent or dual-registered RIA. Not all RIAs specialize in wealth planning; most focus on investment management. Many dual-registered firms/wire houses have estate and/or wealth planning professionals that can support your financial adviser. Nonetheless, if you are concerned about building and transferring your legacy, you need to make sure your adviser is too. You'll want to narrow your search to finding an adviser who truly specializes in wealth planning and management—even if they also rely on additional in-house knowledge. Updating and refining your wealth plan should be part of every meeting you have with your adviser. You want your adviser to be deeply experienced in holistic wealth management and have the time and experience to work with you.

In contrast to a holistic wealth manager, some traditional investment advisers may use wealth models to help clients select the target asset allocation for their investment portfolio, thereby providing a first step toward wealth management. However, this is where they often stop. They simply don't view their business in the same way as the holistic wealth manager you are seeking. They don't see themselves (and may not be) compensated for developing the requisite level of interdisciplinary knowledge and spending the additional time that a holistic wealth adviser requires to provide that extra value-added needed to help plan and protect your legacy.

Moreover, traditional advisers are often evaluated and promoted primarily based on the rate and amount of new business brought into the firm. These advisers may claim to offer wealth management services in addition to investment management; the question is whether they follow through, to what extent, and with what level of experience and knowledge.

While not every adviser is motivated by financial incentives in every situation, if you are focused on legacy, not just investments, you need to find an adviser who puts your interests ahead of their own, is incented to grow your wealth, and is both psychically and financially rewarded for spending time advising you. Whether you are working with an independent RIA or a dual-registered firm, look for an adviser who is experienced in wealth planning themselves and able to call on a team. Trust and personal connection are always important, but you cannot allow your emotions to supersede making a thoughtful, well-informed choice. Finding the right match should be about much more than having a good relationship with your adviser. When your legacy is on the line, you need to look out for your own best interests.

Are You Working with the Right Adviser?

If you understand the standards your current adviser is held to, are comfortable with their compensation, and believe your interests are aligned, you may be working with the right adviser. On the other hand, if you aren't able to get a clear answer from your adviser and/or aren't comfortable with their answers, consider whether this adviser is serving your best interests. To build and transfer your legacy, you'll want an adviser who has the time, knowledge, and financial incentives to provide consistent focus on wealth planning. That adviser is more likely to be found at an independent RIA specializing in wealth management or at a wirehouse with dually registered representatives than at a brokerage firm. In either case, however, you'll need to spend time with the individual to determine whether they are a good fit for your objectives.

Key Takeaways

- Advisers broadly fall into three somewhat overlapping categories that differ according to the regulations that govern their actions, how they are compensated, and the focus of their service.
- These differences affect the nature and degree of wealth planning advice offered.
- If your objective is to build and protect your legacy, you need an adviser who specializes in holistic investment management and wealth planning.
- Fiduciary-based, holistic investment, and wealth management are primarily found at independent RIAs who specialize in wealth management, although specialists at wirehouses/dual-registered firms can also provide these services.
- To build and protect your legacy, you owe it to yourself to evaluate whether you are genuinely working with the right adviser or choosing them for purely emotional reasons.

Blind Spot 2

"I Have All the Advisers I Need"

Building on your new understanding of how advisers work and how to select one, perhaps you've determined that you *are* working with a financial adviser who will help you build and protect your legacy—one who has a fiduciary duty to put your interests ahead of their own, earns a fee that is a percentage of your assets so that your financial interests are aligned, and spends time advising you rather than being transaction-focused. You are confident that your financial adviser provides wealth management knowledge, rather than just investment management. Your adviser has asked you about your retirement spending needs and goals. You may have filled out a risk tolerance questionnaire, so they've analyzed your risk tolerance. They're aware of all your investments—even if they don't manage all your money. They've even run all the variables through a wealth forecasting model. Together, you have developed an investment plan; an asset allocation that divides your portfolio into equities and fixed income, seems to cover your spending needs, and meets your risk tolerance.

You also have a group of additional advisers who help you with specific areas of your estate. You work with an accountant whom you speak with rarely, other than during tax season. You have an estate planning attorney, although you may not have met with them since you last updated your will. Occasionally, you may hear from your insurance agent, but you politely dismiss engaging in a discussion because you assume they are just trying to sell you another product. You are confident that your insurance needs are covered since you have, or had, life insurance to cover your family during your earning years. And you are regularly approached by development professionals who suggest interesting strategies to maximize your charitable giving.

Overall, you feel pretty good about the team of people assembled over the years; you believe you have all the advisers you need. What's more, there's a lot of water under the bridge with each, and you think they understood your needs well when you consulted with them. The last thing you want to hear is that you're missing something. You've spent time and money on your estate and financial plan. The idea of doing something differently sounds a lot more time- and money-consuming and just isn't what you need.

As soon as you close a door to inquiry, you know you've encountered a blind spot. If you truly care about building and protecting your legacy, then you owe it to your family to open the door and evaluate what's behind it.

Consider Donna's situation. Her estate-planning attorney had drawn up an Irrevocable Life Insurance Trust (ILIT) so that the death benefits from her life insurance policy owned by the Trust would be outside her estate when she died. This meant that the death benefits wouldn't increase the size of her estate (or her estate tax bill) and that there would be funds for her heirs to use to cover the estate taxes without liquidating accounts or selling the property.

However, no one was ensuring that she was keeping up-to-date with ILIT regulations and requirements. The Trustee of Donna's ILIT didn't remember to write the annual IRS-mandated Notices of the Right to Withdraw, known as Crummey letters. A Crummey letter is a notice sent to the Trust beneficiaries informing them that a gift was made to the Trust (this refers to the money you contributed to the Trust so that the insurance premium could be paid) and that they have the immediate right to withdraw those funds. This notice grants the beneficiaries a present interest in the gift, thereby qualifying it for the gift tax exclusion. This may seem like a technicality, but if the estate were audited—and most large estates are—the entire ILIT could be invalidated. The death benefits that Donna thought would be excluded from her estate would actually come back into it, raising the estate taxes due, which would have caused other assets to be sold to meet these taxes, thereby vastly diminishing her legacy.

In all likelihood, Donna's estate planning attorney mentioned the need to execute annual Crummey letters and even counseled Donna to have the Trustee open a checking account in the name of the Trust from which to pay the annual premiums. However, by the time the first premium statement arrived months later, both Donna and the Trustee had forgotten all the intricacies, and, having already mentioned the needs, none of her advisers reminded her of all the required steps. Her estate planning attorney assumed she remembered and followed their advice. Her investment manager was not involved with the ILIT because there were no funds in it to manage. There was no need for Donna to have informed her accountant of the existence of the ILIT because there were no tax implications, and her insurance agent's responsibility ended with the sale of the policy. Each of Donna's advisers was doing their job, yet her legacy was on the line. As a result of professionals working in isolation, a gap of enormous consequence had emerged.

Wealth Management Isn't Just Managing Money

While you may think you have all the advisers you need (investment, tax, estate, insurance, and philanthropic), you may be missing a quarterback to lead, monitor, coordinate, and maintain momentum among the other professionals. Without such an advocate, you are likely to miss the interdisciplinary risks and opportunities to grow or protect your wealth.

Consider whether you ever met simultaneously with more than one of your advisers? If you look back on your meetings, you'll probably recognize that you've consulted with one adviser in one domain at a time.

It's relatively common to have regular meetings with your investment advisers and accountant, but what about meeting with your insurance agent, estate planning attorney, and philanthropic advisers? Most people let meetings with insurance agents and estate-planning attorneys lapse once their initial advice has been implemented. You assume you've covered your insurance needs, and you've done your will. But what about the risks and opportunities that may have arisen as your wealth has grown? And because your advisers are siloed and don't often, or ever, talk to one another, they're not going to be able to point out the gaps to you. You may have missed opportunities that could have been spotted if multiple advisers were all gathered around the same table, working together on your behalf. Some gaps may even seem counterintuitive to professionals managing specific areas of your finances.

For instance, your accountant likely approaches the situation from the standpoint of doing everything possible to help you minimize your taxes now, even if paying more in the present might result in significantly lower bills in the future. Your estate-planning attorney is likely to be focused on making sure everything is optimized if you were to die in the near future and may not realize which pockets of wealth may grow, and to what extent. This means they may not recognize the need to employ more sophisticated strategies sooner rather than later. A true wealth adviser helps you peer into the possible futures and then marshals the resources to address the opportunities brought to light.

The lack of communication that typically exists between siloed professionals often causes difficulties. Let's say you've created a revocable trust, which is a must-have for your financial situation. Perhaps the lawyer mentioned to you that you needed to retitle all your accounts and assets into the name of the trust. Did you remember to do that?

Your lawyer will likely have assumed that your investment manager has reviewed and retitled all the accounts. However, what happens if your investment manager doesn't know that the trust has been created? Since these two advisers haven't had a conversation, the reality is that there was no point in your going to the trouble and expense of creating the revocable trust. Not to mention, this means that all your assets would now go through time-consuming, costly, and public probate, simply because they weren't retitled.

Additionally, since the trust was created some time ago, your wealth may have evolved in ways that suggest some assets should be transferred out of your estate into a different type of trust, rather than being placed in the revocable trust. Without a professional wealth manager, will you conduct this analysis and have the necessary information to make a decision that enhances your legacy?

You may reach points at which you believe you've done everything you need to do, but the costs of being behind the curve could be substantial, as we saw in the previous example about Donna. If the estate were audited (and most large estates are), the entire ILIT would be invalidated, the assets returned to the estate, and the estate tax increased because of the absence of these notifications.

Working with a wealth manager means collaborating with someone who not only has experience evaluating investment managers but also has been exposed to many techniques through their connections to numerous accountants, estate attorneys, and insurance agents across their client base. This means that the wealth manager's "tool kit" for what you might be able to do, what's changing, what the new ideas are, and how to implement them is going to be much more evolved and dynamic than what you might learn from working with one investment adviser and one accountant.

The interconnected nature of your overall goals extends to each professional's area of knowledge. What you need is a guide who knows enough about each of the previous siloes to enable you to build and protect the legacy you envision. You are looking for a professional who knows where gaps are often found and has the knowledge to address them. This has become the domain of "wealth management." It doesn't mean adding another player to your team; instead, it means finding an investment adviser who is more than just an investment adviser and has the skills and incentives to be a holistic wealth manager.

What Is a Holistic Wealth Manager?

There is no industry-specific recognized definition for the title "holistic wealth manager," and any investment adviser is permitted to use the description. This makes it challenging for an investor to identify an adviser who can truly provide the necessary knowledge and skills. For our purposes, a holistic wealth adviser is a trusted professional who combines deep expertise in wealth planning, investment management, estate planning, tax strategy, and risk management with the ability to integrate multiple aspects of a client's financial life into a comprehensive and cohesive plan. Beyond technical knowledge, this adviser acts as the quarterback, coordinating among specialists—such as investment managers, accountants, attorneys, insurance agents and philanthropic consultants—to ensure decisions align with the client's long-term goals, values, and family dynamics. Their role is not limited to managing assets; it encompasses guiding governance, succession planning, and legacy strategies, delivering a comprehensive approach that balances financial performance with purpose and continuity.

Increasingly, financial advisers and the firms they work for are advertising themselves as wealth managers because clients are demanding more comprehensive advice. According to a McKinsey survey of wealthy clients,[1] ". . . in 2018, 29% said they prefer holistic advice across adjacent needs; in our 2023 survey, the figure jumped to 47%, a 60% increase." Holistic advice, in this survey, was defined "as working with an investment professional who can holistically answer my financial needs across investment, life insurance, banking, and taxes".[2] When asked to rank additional services, respondents indicated a desire for legal services (19%), tax preparation (17%), lending and banking services (10%), household saving and/or budgeting (9%), insurance products or services (9%), philanthropic planning (7%), business investment opportunities (7%), health and medical planning (6%), bill paying services (6%), other concierge/lifestyle services (6%), and real estate advice and agents (6%).[3]

The challenge is that it requires detective-like skills and a keen sense of what you are seeking to distinguish a skilled, holistic wealth adviser from a traditional financial adviser. They can and often do look exactly alike at first. Like the conventional financial adviser, a holistic wealth manager is an adviser held to the fiduciary standard and typically paid a percentage fee based on assets under management. While they may be dually registered, they rarely use nondiscretionary brokerage accounts. Many are strictly discretionary Investment Advisers. Second, while their firm may be affiliated with the broker-dealer through which they trade, they may trade through more than one nonaffiliated broker-dealer. In that case, there is no firm-driven incentive to incur commissions, as the commissions are paid to the trading firm. Finally, and most importantly, a holistic wealth adviser views their purpose much more broadly than the typical investment adviser. In addition to investment management, they collaborate with your other advisers (accountants, attorneys, insurance agents, development staff, and even other investment managers) to help you build and protect the legacy you envision—and they do this as part of the same fee percentage, in other words, for no additional charge.

Why would they provide additional services for the same fee? Essentially, firms with this philosophy believe that focusing more intensely on existing clients makes better business sense. By providing more profound, more holistic advice, they build client relationships that stand the test of time and can weather the ups and downs of life and the markets. As a result, they don't have to spend as much time bringing in new business to cover client attrition. They may even work for firms with compensation models that reward advisers equally for retaining existing business and bringing in new clients. The deeper client relationships are also the source of new, referral-based business, which tends to attract clients interested in the same type of relationship. Advisers who operate this way have both the desire and ability to spend time working with you and your other advisers on growing and protecting your legacy. Business grows; it just grows differently.

If you are looking for a broker to place trades, offer advice on investment selection, and provide a constantly changing menu of investment choices, then a Registered Representative is probably a good choice. If you have a longer-term perspective and are looking for someone to handle your investments without conflicts of interest, then a financial adviser held to the fiduciary standard is more suitable. But if you've accumulated sufficient wealth to consider growing and protecting a generational and philanthropic legacy, then you need something more. You need to find an investment adviser with *holistic wealth management experience.*

A holistic wealth manager takes a comprehensive view of your wealth, considering a wide range of personal and financial aspects of your life, including information on all your assets, not just your investment accounts. They analyze your spending needs, retirement income, cash flow, liabilities, insurance coverage, tax situation, charitable and legacy goals, and estate plan, in the context of your age and your longevity, to build a model of how your wealth evolves under different asset allocations and structures across a broad range of market and economic conditions. In conjunction with reviewing your estate planning documents and insurance structures, this enables them to see how much your assets are likely to grow over time, in which accounts specifically (taxable or tax-deferred, joint or sole, trusts, etc.), and how assets flow to beneficiaries. This, in turn, enables them to recommend insurance, tax, and philanthropic strategies that may significantly enhance your legacy.

The holistic manager then assumes the quarterback role, bringing in your accountant, attorney, and/or insurance agent and collaborating with other team members to advance your interests. Note that the holistic wealth manager may even work alongside other investment advisers, especially in cases involving pre-existing private investments, and incorporate those strategies into your overall plan. The value-added stems from the knowledge and experience the holistic adviser has in being able to identify missed opportunities or unidentified risks that could affect your future, collaborate with your tax, estate planning, insurance, and philanthropic advisers to address these gaps and chase down their resolution to maintain the momentum necessary to help reach your goals most efficiently.

What Is a Holistic Wealth Management Plan?

A sophisticated wealth forecasting model serves as the foundation for creating your wealth management plan. It generates outputs that can be reviewed for opportunities to build or protect your legacy. Figure 2.1 shows the layers of planning considerations that flow from evaluating the wealth planning model.

Figure 2.1 Wealth Planning Outputs

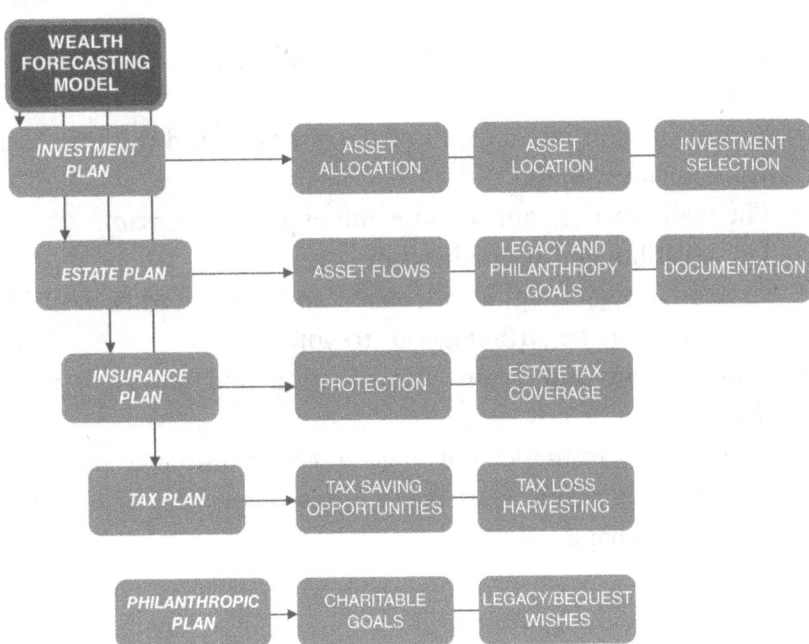

Holistic wealth management both requires and fosters a deeper relationship between you and your adviser. Conversations look at the whole picture. The model considers all your assets, including liquid and private investment accounts, real estate, partnerships, businesses, and all your liabilities. Discussions address your needs, fears, dreams, opportunities, and obstacles, often at a very personal level. Furthermore, as the relationship deepens and the value-added becomes evident, more and more assets in current and subsequent generations come under discussion. It's essential to acknowledge that a relationship of this nature may be profound, yet not emotionally driven. It's a personal relationship within professional bounds. While you may at some point become friends, the relationship is built on professional respect rather than personal ties.

How It Works

Holistic wealth planning takes a 360-degree view that considers an enormous number of personal and financial aspects of your life, including:

- Your financial and nonfinancial goals, values, lifestyle, and aspirations
- Your starting point, in terms of all your assets and liabilities, not just your investments
- The evolution of your income and expenses over time
- The volatility and unpredictability of markets
- Your estate planning, its adequacy, and what readily available structures may be advantageous to you
- Your current and future tax situation and ways to create efficiencies
- Your current insurance coverage and how insurance might be used to further your goals, well beyond income replacement or property damage

- For business owners, your desire to take care of your employees as well as yourself and your family
- Your philanthropic desires and how to maximize your impact
- Your family and how to communicate your hopes and dreams to them

Done right, wealth management goes far beyond the basic "financial planning" typically provided by investment managers. It is a personalized and collaborative approach that considers your unique circumstances and priorities and seeks to provide a comprehensive and integrated solution to help you achieve the financial legacy you envision.

Holistic wealth managers start by building a personalized wealth forecasting model in collaboration with you. This should be an in-person process guided by your wealth manager, rather than a questionnaire that you complete on your own.

Three Steps to Building the Investment Plan

If you've sent your investment account statements to be loaded into the model, you and your adviser should be able to do a first pass through and view the outcome in two hours. In my experience, most clients find that this initial meeting is much less painful and more revealing than they ever expected. The first output from wealth modelling is your investment plan. An investment plan has three components: asset allocation, asset location and investment selection. The wealth model incorporates your specific investments and their cost basis, how they are held and taxed (retirement accounts, taxable accounts, trusts, etc.), your spending needs, property ownership, retirement income, liabilities, insurance coverage, tax situation, charitable and legacy goals, and so on, looking at them in the context of your age and your longevity. Your first step will be to test the impact of different asset allocations—different percentages of your investment portfolio allocated to stocks versus bonds under a broad range of potential economic and market conditions. Will your portfolio have a high enough probability of supporting all your spending, hopes, and dreams in retirement? How will adopting a more or less aggressive asset allocation affect that? What impact are these scenarios likely to have on the size and nature of your legacy? Will you run out of money? Will you have a legacy for kids?

Once you have selected a target asset allocation, the second step will be for your wealth adviser to work with their team to develop an asset location strategy. This is a plan for migrating to the target asset allocation across all your accounts and building the asset allocation that optimizes the tax status of each account.

The third step will be for the team to evaluate your existing investments and recommend any necessary changes. Assuming your wealth manager does not work for a firm with proprietary products, they would have no incentive other than risk/return considerations to recommend any changes. Your investments can potentially be carried over in-kind, thus managing your potential capital gains costs. The asset allocation, asset location, and investment selection form the basis of your investment plan but can and are likely to evolve over time.

Beyond the Investment Plan

The investment plan, however, is not the only goal of the wealth management plan. The additional value-added stems from the impact it has on your estate, insurance, tax, and philanthropic planning.

The model will produce a chart of your estate flows, which you can view based on your life expectancy and at various points in time. This gives you an idea of which accounts will be spent down and which will grow. You and your adviser can review this together to determine if it makes sense or if it reveals opportunities for improvement. The estate flow chart will estimate your estate tax bill. At that point, your wealth adviser can help you consider estate, gifting, and/or insurance strategies to reduce it and build a legacy for your children. Your wealth adviser can then analyze steps such as implementing Roth conversions, Irrevocable Life Insurance Trusts, funding Dynasty or Descendants Trusts, establishing a foundation, etc., to help you optimize your goals. Together, you then prioritize the tasks to address. The wealth manager brings your other advisers on board to consult and implement each idea, and monitors progress to make sure the task is accomplished.

For example, consider Jennifer, a recently divorced woman in her forties, who is the sole breadwinner in her family. She and her ex-husband are the parents of three young sons. She wanted to make sure that her situation was optimized across investments, estate planning, taxes, and insurance. She met with Mike, her wealth manager, to begin building her wealth forecasting plan, including setting aside funds for her family's living expenses, high school and college tuition, weddings, vacations, retirement plans, charitable donations, and legacy desires. Using the model, Mike evaluated the probability of successfully meeting all her goals based on her investment base and projected longevity under a broad range of economic and market conditions, using different asset allocations.

From looking at the model, even with her current assets (let alone the eventual growth of her portfolio), it became clear that her assets would exceed the estate and gift tax exclusion. Mike explained that Jennifer would benefit from bringing an estate planning attorney into the conversation to protect and maximize the legacy she would leave to her sons. Jennifer gave Mike permission to work with her estate planning attorney to present the evolution of her wealth. From that meeting, they identified the need to draft a revocable trust, pour-over will, durable powers of attorney, health care proxy, and living will. They suggested gifting funds for her children into trusts for each of them with the kids as co-trustees so that those assets and their growth would be outside Jennifer's estate. The children would eventually have access to the assets but would also be protected against creditors or potential future divorces. They also noted that the life insurance policy on Jennifer was held in her name and suggested gifting it to an Irrevocable Life Insurance Trust (ILIT) so that the death benefits would be outside her estate. Jennifer agreed, and the estate attorney drafted the ILIT. Mike then arranged a meeting with Jennifer's accountant and insurance agent to gift her life insurance policy to the ILIT. The accountant filed the appropriate gift tax return in accordance with some changes to the policy recommended by the insurance agent. Even with a list of additional steps still ahead, making meaningful progress helped shift Jennifer from feeling overwhelmed and uncertain about managing her financial affairs to feeling confident and empowered. With Mike as her wealth management quarterback, she now had a team working for her, all of whom knew each other, her situation, and her goals.

Going through the planning process and reviewing the model output can help you address questions such as these:

- Is your asset allocation providing you with an acceptable trade-off between risk and return for your goals?
- How large a legacy are you likely to have at different points along the way? Given the structure of your accounts, are you likely to face estate taxes?
- After you die, is your wealth flowing as you intended, or is something thwarting your plans that you didn't realize was at work? Is it clear how income and principal flow from your estates and trusts, and does the model provide a significant opportunity to validate the flow and correct any problems?
- Is your insurance adequate and advantageously structured?
- Are there potential opportunities (to reduce taxes or grow your portfolio more effectively) and/or risks (unnecessary volatility, liquidity constraints) that can and should be addressed to maintain your lifestyle?
- Are there structures such as trusts (irrevocable life insurance, grantor retained annuity, dynasty, special needs, etc.) that could help you grow or protect your legacy or reduce your taxes to better achieve your long-term aspirations for your children, grandchildren, and philanthropic interests?
- Are there more sophisticated philanthropic structures that could also be tax-efficient?

Adapting the sample conversations from the prior chapter to illustrate the interdisciplinary nature of holistic wealth planning, the dialogue between Jack, as a wealth adviser, and Jill may now be as follows:

Jack, the adviser: *"Hi Jill. Let's set a time to catch up. I look forward to hearing what's new in your life and sharing some market, economic, and regulatory updates. It's a good time to review your portfolio performance and your wealth plan. We should discuss what might need updating to help ensure your retirement and legacy goals are optimized. It may now be beneficial to involve your accountants in the conversation and review the pros and cons of a Roth conversion strategy. Additionally, you are approaching the first premium payment for the insurance policy in your ILIT. Let's go over all the steps so we can make sure everything, especially the Crummey letters, is done correctly."*

Jill: *"Thanks, Jack, that sounds great. Yes, I've been reading about Roth conversions and wondering if it's right for me. I'm so glad you reminded me about the Crummey letters. I don't remember what they are or what I or the ILIT trustee is supposed to do. Let's go over that. I know you've been after me to create a revocable trust—can you go over that too? I think I'm ready to move forward."*

How to Draft a Quarterback

Suppose you now realize that you may not have "all the advisers you need" because your financial adviser isn't able to integrate the other members of your team and provide you with holistic wealth management services. In that case, it's time to start looking. When searching for a fiduciary, fee-based holistic wealth manager with knowledge across multiple disciplines and the ability to collaborate well with other professionals:

- Ask colleagues and friends for recommendations and try to sift through the roles, standards, and compensation structures they have experienced.
- Describe to your estate planning, insurance, and tax advisers what you are looking for and ask whom they might recommend.
- Set up informational interviews with at least three potential candidates, alerting them from the outset that you are interviewing others. In these interviews, ask them about their business, experience, and roles, all the while listening carefully for cues regarding their experience in holistic wealth management.
- Ask a few questions about the extent to which they collaborate with other disciplines and, of course, you'd end up asking them how they and their firm are compensated.

Equipped with your new understanding of the role and responsibilities of a holistic wealth adviser, you should be able to find a good match.

Do You Have All the Advisers You Need?

If your adviser offers only investment advice and isn't actively engaging in ongoing, holistic wealth planning with you and your other advisers (tax, estate, insurance, philanthropic), you may not have all the advisers you need. Ask yourself whether they are the appropriate advisor to help you build and transfer your legacy. You want a holistic wealth manager whose experience and knowledge extend beyond investments, one who possesses the interdisciplinary knowledge and personality to collaborate with your tax, insurance, philanthropic, and estate planning advisers, thereby marshaling your team's resources to identify opportunities to increase your wealth and mitigate risks that threaten it. If your adviser is more than just an investment adviser and is a holistic wealth adviser effectively quarterbacking your investment managers, estate planning attorney, accountant, insurance agent, and philanthropic advisers as necessary, then you are well set up to build and transfer your legacy.

Key Takeaways

- Wealth management is more than just investment management. Holistic wealth management takes a 360-degree view, considering a wide range of personal and financial aspects of your life, including investment strategy, taxes, estate planning, insurance, and philanthropy.
- To build and protect your legacy, you need a wealth adviser who has knowledge in holistic wealth management beyond asset allocation for your investments.
- While you may have a team of advisers (investment tax, estate, insurance, and philanthropic), you need a quarterback to lead, monitor, and coordinate among them.
- A holistic wealth manager serves as the quarterback and maintains momentum to reach closure on risks and opportunities as they arise.
- Without such an advocate, you are likely to miss both mitigating interdisciplinary risks and taking advantage of opportunities to help grow or protect your wealth.
- Interview multiple advisers to evaluate their experience and approach to wealth management.

Blind Spot 3

"I Can Implement My Plan on My Own"

In Blind Spot 1, we examined the distinctions between financial advisers and the significance of selecting the right adviser for your specific needs. In Blind Spot 2, we reviewed the differences between a holistic wealth manager and a traditional investment adviser. We discussed the fact that while you may have a team of advisers (investment tax, estate, insurance, and philanthropic), you need your professional in holistic wealth management to be skilled at taking the lead in monitoring, coordinating, and quarterbacking your other professionals. In this chapter, we address whether you can and should play that role.

You may find the idea of a closure-focused wealth adviser who knows how to quarterback opportunities across wealth management disciplines enormously appealing. The benefits of having one person coordinate your wealth management are evident to you, but you believe that no one can do that better than you. *You* are that person. *You* can implement your plan on your own—especially given advancements in technology providing greater access to research and analytic tools.

You are intelligent and analytical, perhaps even in or formerly in the financial services industry. You are facile with technology and believe that no one will ever know your situation or be able to act as quickly and as nimbly as you can. You are sure, on the deepest level, that you can, and should, act as your own wealth manager.

Convictions that are so profoundly held can be the progenitors of potential blind spots. Consider this: even though you absolutely *could* play the role, is it what's *best* for your legacy?

Acting as Your Wealth Adviser

First, consider which aspect of your wealth you want to oversee. Are you envisioning yourself as the quarterback who manages your investments or the one who oversees your entire wealth management? Let's suppose you are the former and are managing your investments, like Ben. Ben was retiring as the head of financial services at an investment bank. Although it had been some time since he had been responsible for building a model in Excel, he was deeply analytical, well-versed in investments, and immersed in financial concepts as well as economics. He felt good about the fact that he and his wife had developed their estate plan and executed their documents several years earlier. Ben allocated some investments to a financial adviser and selected others on his own as interesting opportunities arose or where he believed he could implement his own selections more economically. He had selected an overall target asset allocation and was familiar with asset location, such that he had structured his investments for tax efficiency. He also took time periodically to gather the market values of his investments, assign them to a specific asset class, and monitor the variance of his actual asset allocation relative to his target. When out of line, he would execute trades to bring his portfolio back to target. Finally, he requested and found the time to read most of the reports sent to him by the underlying investment managers in which he was invested. He believed his portfolio was comprised of conservative investments he had selected over time which would provide the growth necessary to meet his needs. What's more, once he retired, he expected he would have time on his hands and would monitor and tweak his investments as necessary. Nonetheless, wanting to ensure that he was doing the best for his family, as he approached retirement, he began working with a wealth adviser. Having prepared a personal net worth and income statement, including a deep dive into his annual expenses, he was confident that he and his wife would be able to cover their spending needs for what he estimated would be more than their likely life expectancy. His goal was to have this advisor "run his case through" their model just to confirm his thoughts. He didn't think he was missing much that could be relevant. Implementing his plan on his own seemed perfectly doable to him. After all, what more was there for Ben, or you, to consider?

Portfolio Construction

It turns out you could be missing a lot. Portfolio construction involves numerous steps that subsequently need to be continually reviewed and adjusted. Figure 3.1 illustrates the three basic phases of portfolio construction and some of the factors that require evaluation.

Portfolio construction begins with determining the appropriate asset allocation for your plan, which is more nuanced and complex than simply selecting a stock-bond mix. Determining an overall asset allocation requires wealth modeling *tailored to your unique family circumstances* (ages, children, starting assets, state and local taxes, spending needs, etc.) to enable you to view potential trade-offs between risk and return over the long term. Once decided, the asset allocation isn't simply replicated inside each

Figure 3.1 Portfolio Construction Phases and Considerations

PORTFOLIO CONSTRUCTION		
ASSET ALLOCATION and ASSET LOCATION		
Stocks	Bonds	Alternatives
Global Allocation	Duration Taxable vs. Tax-free	Private Equity or Credit Hedge Funds, etc.
Steady Growth: Taxable	Volatile Growth: Tax-Deferred	Ordinary Income: Tax-Free
SPENDING ORDER		
Taxable	529 Savings Plans	Tax-free
Tax-deferred for client, no penalty	Inherited Roth	Roth no penalty
Inherited Traditional IRA	Inherited Traditional IRA	Qualified no penalty
Tax-deferred with penalty	Roth with penalty	Qualified penalty
MANAGER SELECTION		
Separately Managed Strategies vs. Mutual funds and EFTs	Active vs. Passive	Investment Style Growth, Value, Core
Performance Volatility vs. Return	Manager Tenure	Turnover/Tax Efficiency
	Fees and Lockups	Asset Class Conformity

account. Instead, an asset location strategy is developed that seeks to improve tax efficiency. It involves allocating dollars assigned to specific asset classes (as a result of your asset allocation work) across taxable and tax-deferred accounts to address volatility and improve tax efficiency. Once asset location is fixed, the appropriate spending order from your accounts (i.e., how, when, and from which account you raise your monthly spending needs so that you meet all regulatory requirements and continue to grow tax-deferred accounts as well as those targeted for your heirs) needs to be developed. This not only requires initial analysis but also needs to be revised as accounts are spent down. Moreover, the portfolio needs to be monitored and rebalanced in light of market fluctuations and/or spending to help ensure it remains aligned with the overall asset allocation. Finally, selecting and monitoring investment managers to fill each asset class requires knowledge beyond simple performance analysis. It includes evaluating the following:

- The use of separately managed portfolios versus mutual funds or ETFs
- The allocation across investment styles (value, growth, core)
- Investment-specific criteria such as manager tenure, asset class conformity, performance, fees, turnover, investment style, historic style drift, and volatility
- The use of passive (index) investments versus active managers

Asset Allocation Is Nuanced

First, let's examine how you may have shortchanged yourself by adopting an asset allocation without thorough analysis of the trade-offs between growth and capital preservation that underlie any selection. The implications of different asset allocations should be derived from a model tailored to your specific situation. The types of accounts you hold, your retirement spending needs, the spending order in which you deplete them, your longevity outlook, inflation, taxes, and your legacy goals should all be evaluated when considering your risk tolerance and subsequent choice of asset allocation. Investment firms will typically ask you to complete a brief risk tolerance questionnaire to select an appropriate asset allocation. While you may believe this will result in a well-thought-through asset allocation recommendation tailored for your situation by your advisor, the process is simply part of a regulatory requirement for investment firms. The Know Your Customer (KYC) Rule is a regulatory requirement of the Financial Industry Regulatory Authority (FINRA) for financial institutions and investment firms to verify the identity of their clients before engaging in financial transactions. As of 2025, KYC remains a cornerstone of global financial compliance, particularly in the fight against money laundering, fraud, and terrorist financing. As part of their KYC compliance, investment firms are required to conduct customer due diligence by assessing the risk level of customers based on factors like investment experience, occupation, income, and source of funds. The result is a broad-based, generic recommendation rather than one tailored to your specific circumstances.

Perhaps you decided to use one of these questionnaires to determine your risk tolerance and the appropriate asset allocation on your own. A Google search for "investment risk tolerance questionnaires from U.S.-based investment firms" returns 371 million results. Perhaps you found one that seemed workable, or maybe you were overwhelmed by the choices available. Alternatively, after viewing a few, you may have been disappointed by their simplicity and lost confidence in their value, so you've decided to select your allocation based on what you have heard or read.

Perhaps you felt you were, moderate risk investors like Marc and his wife. They gravitated to a 60% stock/40% bond allocation because they heard it was the most popular asset allocation and provided a "safe" mix of stocks and bonds. They had read lots of articles in the popular press exhorting the benefits of a mixed portfolio offering growth, stability, diversification, and moderate risk.

Or perhaps you identified with Connie, a very conservative investor, who followed the adage that "you should own your age in bonds." A long-standing rule of thumb in personal finance, this rule is often attributed to John Bogle, the founder of Vanguard, and is sometimes referred to as the Bogle Asset Allocation Rule.[1] Connie has continually been increasing her allocation to fixed income, believing that the safest portfolio is ultimately 100% fixed income. Risk-averse Connie believed that if she confined her spending to the coupon percentage on her bonds, they should provide her with enough income for the rest of her life.

Or perhaps you are a risk-taker like Rick, and you believe that 100% equities is the most logical asset allocation. As a risk-oriented investor who knows that stocks have historically outperformed bonds over time, you want to maximize your return.

These are all understandable possibilities. However, it is essential to understand that your asset allocation or how you construct your portfolio has enormous implications for your legacy. It is a major driver of your portfolio's long-term performance and one of the most important decisions you make about your investment portfolio. Asset allocation accounts for *approximately 90% of your return* over time.[2] Furthermore, portfolio construction has implications for wealth preservation and growth, risk management, tax efficiency, and legacy planning.

Harry M. Markowitz, PhD, won the 1990 Nobel Prize in Economics for his work on portfolio construction, which began in the 1950s. He is known as the founder of modern portfolio theory. His analysis led to the widely accepted concept of the efficient frontier.[3] This curve delineates the set of asset allocations (or portfolios) that offer the highest expected return for a given level of risk (or the lowest risk for a given expected return[4]). The curve enables one to evaluate whether a portfolio, as it is currently structured across asset classes, has too much risk for the return it is receiving or whether, given the portfolio's risk level, it should be receiving a higher return. Among other concepts, his work provides what is almost a "menu" of asset allocations, enabling us to see the trade-offs among them. From this menu, one can evaluate whether the additional return from moving up along the curve requires taking on additional risk or not and whether the incremental return justifies it.

Since it's proffering, the efficient frontier has been both supplemented and adapted to accommodate additional real-world complexity stemming from market dynamics (changing correlations and return distributions), behavioral factors (investors' concern for liquidity, taxes, etc., not just risk and return), and new frameworks such as post-MPT approaches, factor investing, goals-based investing and dynamic optimization. Still, it remains a useful theoretical foundation and helpful in conceptualizing asset allocation choices.

Figure 3.2 illustrates the optimal investment portfolios at each level of risk, or, in other words, the combination of stocks and bonds that offer the highest expected return for a given level of risk or, conversely, the lowest risk for a given level of expected return. Portfolios below the curve are suboptimal—they either take on too much risk for their return or offer too little return for their risk. Portfolios on the curve are ideal choices for investors depending on their risk tolerance. Figure 3.3 illustrates three different investors and their options.

Figure 3.2   The Efficient Frontier 1970–2023

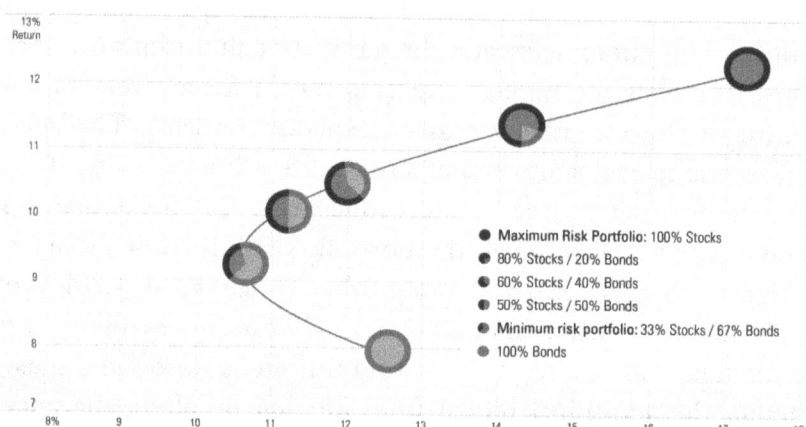

Past performance is no guarantee of future results. Risk and return are measured by standard deviation and arithmetic mean, respectively. This presentation is for informational and illustrative purposes only and is not financial advice or indicative of any investment. An investment cannot be made directly in an index. iGrad, LLC is not a financial adviser. If you want financial or other professional advice, then you should consult with a qualified professional. Source: Morningstar. The reproduction of this chart without prior consent from iGrad, LLC is prohibited. All Rights Reserved. About the data: About the data: Stocks in this example are represented by the Ibbotson® Large Company Stock Index and bonds by the 20-year U.S. government bond. Risk and return are based on annual data over the 1970–2023 period and are measured by standard deviation and arithmetic mean, respectively. Standard deviation measures the fluctuation of returns around the arithmetic average return of the investment. The higher the standard deviation, the greater the variability (and thus risk) of the investment returns. An investment cannot be made directly in an index. The data assumes reinvestment of all income and does not account for taxes or transaction costs.

Figure 3.3 The Efficient Frontier 1970–2023 With Investor Mapping

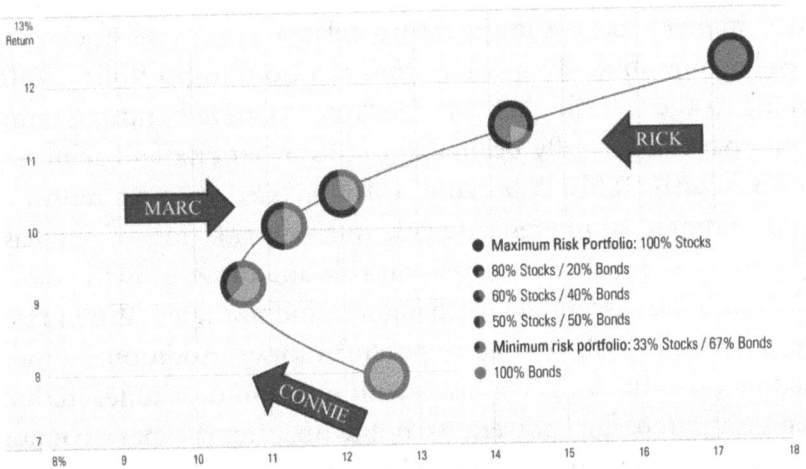

Past performance is no guarantee of future results. Risk and return are measured by standard deviation and arithmetic mean, respectively. This presentation is for informational and illustrative purposes only and is not financial advice or indicative of any investment. An investment cannot be made directly in an index. iGrad, LLC is not a financial adviser. If you want financial or other professional advice, then you should consult with a qualified professional. Source: Morningstar. The reproduction of this chart without prior consent from iGrad® LLC is prohibited. All Rights Reserved. About the data: About the data: Stocks in this example are represented by the Ibbotson® Large Company Stock Index and bonds by the 20-year U.S. government bond. Risk and return are based on annual data over the 1970–2023 period and are measured by standard deviation and arithmetic mean, respectively. Standard deviation measures the fluctuation of returns around the arithmetic average return of the investment. The higher the standard deviation, the greater the variability (and thus risk) of the investment returns. An investment cannot be made directly in an index. The data assumes reinvestment of all income and does not account for taxes or transaction costs.

Using this efficient frontier curve as a guide, let's revisit risk-taking Rick, who wants to be 100% in equities. The efficient frontier would show that for an investor as aggressive as Rick, it may make sense to be 80% in stocks instead of 100%. By moving from the highest circle above (100% stocks) to the next lower one (80% stocks/20% bonds), he would have historically been able to lower his portfolio risk by a greater amount (4%) than his return (1%), resulting in a positive overall trade-off. Adding a small percentage of bonds provides a slight cushion against downturns, potentially preventing Rick from having to sell stocks during a downturn should he need funds.

The efficient frontier also shows that Connie's 100% fixed-income portfolio was not, in fact, the most conservative portfolio. The 100% fixed income portfolio has historically provided higher risk *and* lower return relative to a 33% stock/77% fixed income mix. By moving from the bottom portfolio (100% bonds) to the next higher one (33% stocks/67% bonds), Connie would have historically been able to lower her risk and achieve a higher return. This is because a 100% fixed-income return is highly exposed to interest rate risk, inflation risk (loss of purchasing power), reinvestment risk, credit risk, and lower growth potential. Bonds are susceptible to changes in interest rates. When rates rise, bond prices fall, leading to potential losses. Additionally, their fixed income may not keep pace with inflation over time, eroding Connie's purchasing power. As bonds mature, the new coupon may be lower than what she had been counting on (reinvestment risk). And there is always exposure to credit risk in a nongovernment bond. Stocks have historically provided higher long-term growth due to capital appreciation. A portfolio with 33% stock exposure benefits from this upside while maintaining stability with 67% fixed income.

The efficient frontier suggests that Marc and his wife's choice of a 60% stock/40% bond portfolio might also be optimized by exploring the impact of slightly higher and lower risk/return portfolios. Those risk/return trade-offs within the "middle" allocations can have a significant impact on the probable size of your legacy and the probability of meeting all your spending needs without running out of funds. Moving up along the curve by adding equities may provide the growth needed for them to successfully accomplish their spending and legacy goals. Alternatively, they may be able to achieve their goals by moving down along the curve, reducing their risk, and enabling them to have a less volatile experience. Depending on the initial portfolio's size and spending demands, it is possible to see a multimillion-dollar increase/decrease in the expected-return legacy value with only a 1–2% advancement/decline in an already high probability of successfully meeting spending goals as a result of increasing one's allocation to equities.

To properly determine your risk profile, it's essential to test whether and why increasing your exposure to equities or fixed income affects your probability of accomplishing your goals. Rather than "picking" an asset allocation, using a sophisticated wealth planning model to test the impact of different asset allocations on your future is one of the most important steps you can take to protect your legacy.

Asset Location and Spending Order Affect Outcomes

Ignoring the future impact of spending order, the sequence in which different types of accounts (taxable, tax-free, tax-deferred, Roth, Qualified, 529 Plans, etc.) are spent during both your working and post-retirement lives is another risk you face by acting on your own. The order in which assets are spent down determines tax efficiency and can significantly impact portfolio longevity. Typically, you would want to spend from taxable accounts first (such as investment and savings accounts) to minimize taxable income early in retirement. Next, you would draw from tax-deferred accounts (Traditional IRAs and 401(k)s to delay taxes on distributions and benefit from tax-deferred growth). You would try to spend last of all from tax-free accounts (Roth IRAs and other tax-free investments) to enable further tax-free growth.

Without understanding spending order, you would miss the benefits of structuring your overall asset allocation among taxable, tax-deferred, and tax-free accounts to help enhance your legacy. Rather than mimicking your overall asset allocation in each subaccount, your asset allocation should be tailored to the type of account. For example, you would typically want to tilt your tax-deferred and tax-free accounts to hold more volatile assets such as equities and use your taxable accounts for relatively more fixed income, potentially obtaining even more tax efficiency by investing in municipal bonds[5].

Let's suppose you understand asset location strategy and have organized your holdings to be tax-efficient across accounts. By not modeling the effects of spending, taxes, growth, volatility, and inflation over time, you are likely to miss the impact of your spending order on your legacy. The decision to spend from certain accounts and not others will reduce those accounts and impact the amount available for your children and grandchildren, as well as the type of account, thereby affecting whether it is taxable to them in the future.

For example, after inheriting a large Traditional IRA from his wife, Robert assumed that since he was required to take required minimum distributions (RMDs), the optimal move was to shift the IRA asset allocation to hold fixed income. He believed this move would reliably generate income for the RMD, support his spending, mitigate his risk, and extend the account's longevity. He assumed his children would inherit what was left in his brokerage accounts, which were invested for growth, in addition to his homes. After working on a detailed wealth and estate plan, his adviser, Jane, found he could maximize what he was leaving his children by converting the majority of the Traditional IRA to a Roth, paying the taxes up front from his taxable account, and investing the Roth aggressively for growth so that his kids were likely to benefit over time. Jane then reduced the allocation to equities in his taxable accounts using the additional fixed income to support his spending goals. This would not have been evident without the sophisticated analysis provided by the wealth management model and process.

Dynamic Rebalancing Is Beneficial

Next, let's address monitoring and rebalancing your asset allocation. Rebalancing means realigning your investments in the portfolio to adhere to your target asset allocation as they fluctuate in value.

It almost always involves selling what has appreciated and reinvesting the proceeds in what has lost value. Let's assume you've set yourself up so that it isn't that cumbersome to integrate all your accounts, their holdings, and their market values by asset class each time you evaluate whether you need to rebalance. You have even decided on tolerance bands around each asset class target (threshold deviations) so that you are acting only when an asset class's market value deviates from the tolerance band, thereby reducing your trading costs.

It's essential to consider how often you'll be able to examine your situation and whether you have the self-discipline to follow your own rules, especially in light of the benefits offered by advances in technology. Historically, rebalancing was done on a periodic (calendar) basis. Advances in software over the past 15 years have enabled this to be done dynamically (in real time, typically daily). Studies have shown that periodic (calendar-based) rebalancing is inferior to dynamic, threshold-based rebalancing[6] in terms of reducing risk and enhancing return. In dynamic rebalancing, guardrails, or thresholds (+/−), are established around each asset and subasset class in the portfolio construction process, and the software flags all instances where the market value has deviated from the threshold. This is manageable for investment managers who review the output daily. It immediately alerts investment managers to situations where portfolio realignment for return or risk control warrants further action. Great news, right? However, since you probably lack access to this technology, even if you are vigilant and manually analyze your data monthly, you may be shortchanging yourself in terms of your risk/return targets.

Investment advisers who are experienced in wealth management make use of this software to keep the most crucial decision you've made about your portfolio on track. While they may give the markets a few days to see if the deviation from the threshold endures, they rarely allow the overweight or underweight position to persist. This is because they understand the importance of your asset allocation selection to your long-term success and do not want the portfolio to take on more risk or be under-positioned for return. Individual investors are often tempted to "let top performers run." It's tough to have the self-discipline to sell what is doing well and buy into what isn't when markets are calm, let alone when they are volatile.

Manager Selection and Monitoring Require Time and Effort

Finally, unless you are invested only in index funds, the question you face is whether you have the knowledge and the time to research and monitor your specific underlying investment managers and or individual security holdings (especially if they carry additional risk from being concentrated.) Even if you understand portfolio construction and have diversified across styles within each asset class, your active managers still require regular monitoring, and new additions need research and due diligence. You need to be able to evaluate their performance relative to their strategy. While it's natural to want to move money to whoever is performing best, especially if it has been over a long period, you need to be able to distinguish whether underperformance is manager-driven or a function of a style or sector being out of favor. In the latter case, you may want to retain relatively underperforming managers who are in line with their style benchmarks, as they provide diversification benefits. Rather than timing the market, you will benefit significantly from having these investments when the market style shifts. It's not just the performance record that is important; you need the time to evaluate elements such as the fund's degree of asset class conformity, investment style, risk-adjusted performance, volatility, costs, management fees, investment minimums, size, length of time the fund has been in existence, manager turnover, and experience. Due diligence requires a great deal of skill and effort, which is why investment firms have dedicated research departments.

Privacy and Independence Can Be Accomodated

Perhaps you recognize the value of having an investment professional involved in many of the aspects outlined—asset allocation, asset location, spending order, rebalancing, and manager selection—and that's why you work with a financial adviser for some or most of your assets. Yet you haven't shared the complete picture with them. You may have informed the adviser that you have additional assets and even broadly shared the asset classes and investments with them, indicating that you prefer to manage them on your own. Your motives are varied. You may not want or care about the adviser's opinion on certain private or alternative assets to which you have access. You want to keep those confidential. You may feel the adviser will talk you out of certain investments because they can't get compensated for them. You don't want to be constrained. You don't want to miss out. You may be working with another adviser whom you selected for their experience with a different asset class, such as fixed income, and again, you don't want to hear all the reasons why consolidating at the first adviser might make sense because you suspect they would be doing so to convince you to bring the assets to them. Ultimately, you value your privacy and independence.

Ben felt this way, which is why, even though he was going to work with an adviser to confirm his own wealth forecast, he had not included all of his holdings on his net worth statement. By his calculations, removing those assets would still enable him to meet his goals, leaving him with a cushion not shared with the adviser. What's more, he was adamant that no one would ever have his whole picture. It wasn't necessary for wealth management, and he valued his privacy. Privacy and independence are essential, and they can be respected if you are working with an adviser whom you truly trust. Your reluctance to share information may suggest that you don't have confidence in your adviser. Like Ben, perhaps you are just using them for tasks that you need accomplished. Perhaps you believe they don't have the skills, experience, or intelligence you need or expect. It's possible that your adviser hasn't insisted on incorporating all your investments into your plan, even if they are held away from their firm and/or not part of the fee base. If you haven't been pressed to be complete, that could be a red flag about your adviser's experience and comfort level in handling held-away assets without fearing they look like they are trying to grab more of your net worth. At the least, held-away investments can be manually assigned to one or more asset classes using overall values and growth assumptions, ensuring they are incorporated into your plan. That way, you would be able to estimate the impact of their evolution on your plan and your legacy. Better yet, they can be digitally linked to your plan even if they are held outside your adviser's program so that their values are automatically updated. In any case, you want to feel you are working with an adviser who understands that the investment world is larger than just their firm, that you may have access to investments they don't, and that these investments need to be incorporated into your plan for you to receive the best advice possible. You are not asking your adviser to research the investment. Simply incorporating held-away investments into your plan for tax, estate and legacy planning purposes is essential. If you don't have the confidence to share with them, consider whether they are sufficiently knowledgeable and experienced to serve your best interests. Rather than accept your reluctance to share, think of it as a potential indicator of the quality of your relationship. Chapter 6 explores this issue in greater detail.

Acting as Your Own Wealth Adviser

In contrast to overseeing your investments, perhaps you envision acting as the second type of quarterback. In other words, you view your role acting as your own wealth manager, overseeing the holistic plan, and integrating the advice of your investment managers, tax professionals, estate planning attorneys, and insurance agent(s).

In this situation, there are even more considerations to evaluate. Here it's important to consider whether you can play two roles. The first is driving closure: following up on ideas, tactics, and projects to advance your legacy by maintaining the momentum needed to reach closure. The second is focused on identifying opportunities to enhance your legacy by identifying and deploying key tactics.

The Closure Role Requires Ongoing Attention

If you have the time, inclination, and self-discipline, you likely have the talent to play the role of following up on an idea that requires coordination across your investment adviser(s), accountant, estate attorney, and/or insurance agent. You are the client, after all, and as long as you stay focused, you can command the attention necessary to make sure the project reaches closure. There are, nonetheless, a few questions to consider. First, is this how you *want* to spend your time, especially given your other priorities? Wouldn't it be more satisfying—and perhaps even more efficient—to have a trusted adviser maintaining momentum and reporting to you?

Second, what happens as you age or if you slow down? Will you be able to be, and still want to be, vigilant on these issues? If, at some point, you choose to hand the integration role over to a wealth adviser, will you be able to accurately recount all the considerations and justifications for essential actions you have taken? Might it have been better to have that adviser on board from the beginning so they already would have a clear understanding of how and why you've set your estate up the way you have and be much more effective going forward? What if something happens to you before you've had a chance to pass the baton? Involving a wealth manager in your life well before you step back from that role means there will be someone who can continue along the path you have forged—someone who can implement what you've set up, who can continue to address your needs and wishes, and, after you pass, who is committed to helping ensure continued protection for your spouse and the next generation? Might that person have been better informed because they've worked with you over the long term?

Edith was an elegant and independent businesswoman. She had managed her investments her entire life and had been particularly successful. A widow who had never had children, Edith, at the age of 87, finally agreed to meet with her wealth adviser and estate planning attorney to update her estate documents. A revocable or living trust was put in place, naming a family friend as successor trustee. All her assets were retitled into the revocable trust, and Edith maintained complete control. Over the next five years, the successor trustee worked closely with Edith and her financial adviser to understand her financial situation, expenses, standards, and care objectives. A thorough wealth planning effort reassured Edith that she was unlikely ever to spend all her funds and helped her decide on her bequests. As she reached the age of 92, her energy and memory began failing. She was delighted to hand over all bill paying and investment oversight to the successor trustee in whom she had by then developed tremendous confidence. As a result of having been brought into the situation with plenty of time, the successor trustee was familiar with Edith's preferences and approach and was able to continue to support Edith's lifestyle in the manner to which she was accustomed. When Edith passed away two years later, the trust was converted into Edith's estate. The successor trustee became the executor and because they had been involved for such an extended period of time, was able to carry out Edith's wishes seamlessly.

Married couples often face a different situation. It's common in client/adviser relationships for one spouse or partner to be less involved. It can happen due to a longstanding division of labor within your relationship or because your partner does not want to participate. Perhaps your partner initially met with your adviser and felt excluded or disrespected. Or perhaps, they believe they have nothing valuable to contribute or may not be interested in finance. All in all, it has just become easier for you to be the point person. But what happens when you die? Will you bring your spouse along on your journey so that they can continue? Will your partner have the talent, inclination, self-discipline, and desire to take this on?

As common as this disparity in involvement is, it severely reduces the odds that all the planning done by the "financial" spouse will survive that person's death. If that spouse dies first, the "nonfinancial" spouse can be left ill-equipped to carry on alone. Although this is changing, even today, the "financial spouse" still tends to be the man in heterosexual couples. According to TransAmerica,[7] whereas *80% of men die married, 80% of women die single*. This means that it's more likely for the woman to be responsible for overseeing her wealth management once widowed. It is also worth noting that 70% of women switch advisers[8] within the first year after their husband's death. Having little or no part in the planning leaves them in the dark about how to manage their financial life and family legacy; they have a steep learning curve at the most difficult time in their life. Imagine the challenge if the inherited portfolio is "complex" with various private investments, various liquidity profiles, and various advisors, with no one other than the deceased able to see the whole picture.

Starting over with a new adviser often entails costly changes, including taxes and commissions, to both the investments and the overall strategy that were previously in place. When both spouses or partners are involved in planning conversations as early as possible, each can contribute to developing the plan, setting goals and building a relationship with the adviser. A longstanding relationship with the right adviser makes it easier for the other person to understand why things have been set up the way they have and to continue taking advantage of what has been established.

The risks associated with a "non-financial spouse" suddenly becoming responsible for wealth management—often due to death, incapacity, or divorce— are significant. Proactive planning, organization and communication can help reduce them. Consider:

- Maintaining a clear, accessible record of all accounts, advisers, estate documents, passwords, and key contacts,
- Simplifying financial structures wherever possible by consolidating accounts and reducing unnecessary complexity,
- Involving the non-financial spouse early—inviting them to periodic meetings with advisers to build familiarity and confidence,
- Creating a concise "wealth roadmap" that outlines the family's financial structure, goals, and decision-making process and can serve as a practical guide if the non-financial spouse ever needs to assume responsibility.

Advisers play a critical role in bridging the gap. They can facilitate education through tailored financial literacy sessions. They can make joint meetings standard practice to ensure both spouses are engaged and build trust so the non-financial spouse feels increasingly comfortable reaching out independently. Your adviser can help develop a clear transition plan for scenarios where the non-financial spouse becomes responsible, including coordinating all specialists and simplifying complexity to ensure continuity and confidence during any transition.

If the "non-financial spouse" feels they don't understand what's being discussed, then perhaps the fault lies with the adviser, not the client. If the adviser can't explain a strategy in simple terms, it may mean that the adviser isn't able to take enough time with the client or perhaps doesn't fully understand it themselves. Or it could mean that the adviser is not showing the necessary respect for the importance of involving the other partner. At this point, you may want to evaluate whether this is the right adviser to help you build and protect your family's legacy.

Jim would always bring his wife, Anne, to wealth planning meetings and performance updates. Although he led the discussion and questioning, he was solicitous of Anne's involvement. She agreed with his comments and decisions when asked, but remained quiet otherwise. After taking her to lunch on her own a couple of times, her adviser realized that she had had no financial or investment education or experience on her own. Now that the kids were grown, she had more time and was interested in better understanding her financial situation, especially since Jim was 10 years older than she was. The adviser suggested they meet once a month, just the two of them so that Anne could gain an understanding of how and why their estate was structured and invested. She would have the time to ask questions without worrying that she was wasting Jim or the adviser's time. A quick study, she mastered a great deal of information, which enabled her to participate more fully in the regular meetings with Jim. He was proud that his wife knew so much, pleased that Anne and the financial adviser had bonded, and comforted by the fact that the planning they had put in place would continue after he passed.

While you may be perfectly capable of playing the closure role, consider whether this is how you want to spend your time, the benefits of working with an overall wealth adviser sooner rather than later, and the importance of having your spouse or partner build a relationship with someone they trust. Your legacy is likely to benefit from working with a trusted adviser.

The Opportunity Identification Role Requires Interdisciplinary Knowledge

Acting as your own wealth adviser by assuming the role of identifying opportunities to enhance your legacy raises the stakes. Believing that you can identify significant opportunities across investment, tax, estate planning, insurance, and philanthropic disciplines presumes that you have experience and knowledge in each area. Although it is possible, you would need to have the ability to know the intricacies of techniques that might be appropriate to increase your return, reduce risk, reduce taxes, and preserve wealth for future generations. What's more, the law changes, the market changes, the environment changes, and your life changes, and there are always trade-offs in taking any steps. Without a guide who has experienced them before, who has seen others make similar trade-offs, and who can counsel you on the process and outcomes, you are likely to shortchange yourself. Even doctors consult other doctors when it comes to their own health.

Regulatory Environment Constantly Changes

The regulatory environment is constantly evolving. Federal and state governments modify the tax code on an annual basis. As of the start of 2025, there have been at least 12 significant tax law changes since 2010. Your accountant will keep up with the effect of tax-law changes on your tax returns, but are you keeping up with their effect on your wealth plan? What about the impact of the Secure Act 2.0 on your retirement accounts and permitted distributions? How about the significant evolution that's happened in the insurance market? Could you enhance your coverage and reduce costs in ways that improve your plan or enable you to make more gifts? What about the impact of higher estate tax exclusions no longer sunsetting in 2025? Have you taken advantage of what is permissible? Do you understand the impact of these gifts on your lifestyle now and into the future? You may have an excellent plan, but the reality is that you can't just "set it and forget it." Your plan needs to be updated continually. Working with a wealth adviser whose responsibility is to stay up-to-date with these changes can meaningfully contribute to growing and guarding your wealth.

Personal Life Continuously Evolves

Finally, your situation also evolves. New spouses or children may come into the picture. Some of your children may have children, while others don't. Some of your children may have substantial financial success, while others struggle. Divorce or death may impact family members and alter the overall landscape. You may develop new passions or find new causes you want to support.

Having frequently postponed reviewing her estate plan, Sarah came in to set up educational savings accounts for her grandchildren. The discussion naturally led to a broader discussion of her family's wealth management plan. After reviewing her estate planning documents, including her beneficiary forms, will, healthcare proxy, testamentary, and other trusts, it became clear that the documents were markedly out-of-date. Her children were now married with children of their own, and many of the named guardians, executors, agents, and/or beneficiaries had passed away or become incapable of acting. Charitable donations were being made to organizations that she no longer wanted to support. Moreover, should she become incapacitated, no one had the authority to act on her behalf to make financial decisions or even pay her bills. Had something happened to her before she reviewed the plan, not only would the estate have been tied up potentially for years in court, but also funds would not have flowed to the desired beneficiaries in a tax-efficient manner as she had intended. Working with her estate attorney, her wealth adviser was able to model the evolution of her wealth, enabling the preparation of appropriate estate planning documents to protect her and ensure that her wishes were fulfilled.

You may be fluent in investing, possess a great analytical mind, and have excellent people-management skills. But when it comes to being your own wealth manager, it's important to consider whether that is enough. Many investors underestimate the amount of unglamorous and labor-intensive minutiae that are crucial for long-term financial health. Do you have a cost-effective and efficient way to keep up with interdisciplinary techniques for advancing your wealth and protecting your interests in light of ongoing regulatory changes and developments in your personal life, all while considering the opportunities and risks that arise as you age? Working closely with a wealth adviser whom you and your partner trust is likely to preserve and enhance your legacy through your lives and those of future generations.

Can You Implement Your Plan on Your Own?

If you are sophisticated financially and have the time and energy to dedicate, of course, you could implement a plan on your own. However, given the complexities and ongoing demands of doing so, it's essential to determine whether it is in your best interests. Can you really stay on top of all the elements as your portfolio fluctuates, regulations change, and your personal life evolves? Do you have the energy and the knowledge to play the role fully? Can your need for privacy be addressed? If you feel reluctant to collaborate with your advisor and share all your investment thoughts and intentions, evaluate whether this may be due to a lack of confidence in the sophistication and understanding on the part of your advisor. Perhaps the reason you aren't fully collaborating is really because you haven't found an adviser with the degree of sophistication you need. It's like going to see your doctor but not telling them what is really concerning you. It's understandable to hold back, but ultimately you know the advice you receive won't necessarily address your situation. Whether your physician or wealth adviser, you want to work with a person with whom you truly feel comfortable collaborating.

Key Takeaways

- You may be competent and want to act as your own wealth adviser without considering whether it is in your best interests.
- Whether you view acting as your own wealth adviser as overseeing your investments or coordinating your entire financial life, each role comes with distinct responsibilities and risks.
- When you are primarily managing your investment portfolio, consider whether you have the time and technology to source, vet, monitor and research multiple aspects of portfolio management, including asset allocation selection, asset location strategy, rebalancing, and manager selection.
- When you are considering managing your entire financial life, evaluate whether you have the time and skills to identify, integrate, and follow through on opportunities and tactics to enhance your legacy.

Blind Spot 4

"It's Smart to Work with Multiple Advisers"

You've learned how to identify the "right" adviser for your needs and, more importantly, how to distinguish between an investment adviser and a holistic wealth manager. The idea of a quarterback who knows how to identify and maximize opportunities across wealth management disciplines makes a lot of sense. The fact that this person can be counted on to follow up with your other advisers to make sure each task reaches closure is enormously appealing.

But there's still something bothering you: the idea of giving all your money to one adviser to manage. You know about the importance of diversification. Working with one manager would be too risky. What if the firm goes out of business? You want to have different approaches to managing risk and return so that you can benefit in case one adviser does better than the other. You want to compare performance and service levels. Finally, you want to benefit from different views of the markets. You would *never* "put all your eggs in one basket!"

That kind of certainty is a sign that you've come up against another blind spot. It's worth evaluating the perceived risks more closely if your goal is to build and transfer a lasting legacy.

Risk of Institutional Failure

Let's start with the risk of firm failure or bankruptcy. The key concept to understand is that advice (who delivers recommendations) and custody (where your assets are held) must be provided by two distinct types of entities. A foundational principle in financial regulation and industry best practices, the separation of asset custody from asset advice, is rooted in investor protection, risk mitigation, and maintaining trust in the financial system. The amended SEC's Custody Rule (Rule 206(4)-2) of the Investment Advisers Act of 1940 requires Registered Investment Advisers (RIAs) to hold securities through "qualified" custodians. RIAs provide advice; they do not hold assets unless they are also a custodian. Custodians hold assets. The separation of advice and custody helps safeguard client assets by reducing the risk of fraud and misappropriation, enhancing transparency and accountability, and ensuring compliance with regulatory standards.

When you invest, your assets are electronically or physically held by a custodian and not by your investment adviser. When your adviser wants to make a trade, they contact the custodian who processes the trade and keeps a record of the cost basis and execution price. The fastest way to see who your custodian is, is to look at your statements. Providing monthly statements enumerating what is in your account is the principal responsibility of the custodian.

Custodians are independent financial institutions that have a fiduciary duty to safeguard and protect assets (e.g., stocks and bonds) from theft or physical loss (not loss of value) and manage processes such as transaction settlement, record-keeping, and reporting. They are required to ensure they are held in the client's name and are not commingled with their own institution's balance sheet. Institutional consulting firm Callan LLC explains: "A custodian is a specialized financial institution (typically, a regulated entity with granted authority like a bank) that holds customers' securities for safekeeping in order to minimize the risk of their misappropriation, misuse, theft, and/or loss."

According to Callan LLC, a custodian has three primary responsibilities:

- **Safekeeping of assets:** Maintaining proper indicia of ownership, valuation, accounting, and reporting of assets owned by a plan/fund sponsor or an institutional investor
- **Trade processing:** Tracking, settling, and reconciling assets that are acquired and disposed of by the investor, either directly or indirectly, through delegated authority with an asset manager
- **Asset servicing:** Maintaining all economic benefits of ownership such as income collection, corporate actions, and proxy issues[1]

When you invest, your assets are electronically or physically held by a custodian and not by your investment adviser. When your adviser wants to make a trade, they contact the custodian who processes the trade and keeps a record of the cost basis and execution price.

Custodians are regulated by the SEC in the case of securities, the Commodity Futures Trading Commission (CFTC) in the case of commodities and derivatives, and the Office of the Comptroller of the Currency (OCC) for derivatives. These regulatory bodies supervise compliance with licensing and registration, as well as anti-money laundering, suspicious activity, Know-Your-Customer, and other crime prevention provisions.

The separation of roles means that should your investment adviser encounter financial difficulties as a firm or even go bankrupt, your assets remain safe and unaffected because they are held at the custodian. Could a custodian fail? It's possible but rare. Not only do custodians maintain insurance policies to cover losses from errors, but since they are also required to segregate their business assets and balance sheet from client assets, even in the event of bankruptcy, client assets would be protected from creditor claims. Bear Stearns and Lehman Brothers went bankrupt in the 2008 financial crisis, but brokerage clients did not lose their shares of securities, mutual funds, or bonds.[2] Thanks to the separation of investment advice and custody, the institutional risk of adviser firm failure or bankruptcy is, therefore, not a compelling reason to have more than one adviser.

Four independent firms control an estimated 84% of custodial assets.[3] Schwab Adviser Services is the largest independent custodian, followed by Fidelity, Pershing, and LPL Financial. Independent RIAs tend to use the big four and, as fiduciaries, are required to conduct ongoing operational due diligence on their custodian of choice to make sure they have the proper structure and controls in place to ensure safekeeping of the client's assets.

Although broker-dealers principally facilitate the buying and selling of securities, they may also act as custodians. Dual-registered firms, by being registered as an adviser and a broker-dealer, may also act as custodians through their broker-dealer side or a subsidiary. Morgan Stanley, for example, a dual-registered firm, offers custody services through its subsidiary, Morgan Stanley Trust National Association (MSTNA), an independent organization. Institutions where "self-custody" is the case typically conduct internal and external audits to make sure the client's assets are safe.

This separation of roles, advice versus custody, is foundational for the safety and protection of your assets. Before 2009, although not required to, most advisory firms used separate custodians.

Madoff Securities did not. Madoff was acting as his own custodian, facilitating his ability to co-mingle investor funds with those of Madoff Securities and giving rise to one of the greatest Ponzi schemes in financial history. The absence of a qualified, independent custodian was a critical red flag for investors who didn't succumb to the apparent "guaranteed returns." In 2009, the SEC adopted rules for the first time *requiring* investment advisers to use a qualified custodian to ensure the separation of advice and custody and eliminate the risk that your assets could be intermingled with your adviser's business operations. According to the SEC, "The rules provide greater assurance to investors that their accounts contain the funds that their investment adviser and account statements say they contain."[4]

Currently, digital assets such as cryptocurrencies are not subject to the custody rule. After Sam Bankman-Fried was found guilty on November 2, 2023,[5] of defrauding investors in FTX Trading Ltd., specifically by commingling customer assets at Alameda Research[6] among other charges, the SEC proposed expanding custody rules to require the use of qualified custodians for digital assets. However, as of March 2025, the SEC is reconsidering this proposal and may withdraw it.

Diversifying Your Advice

Next, let's address the idea that you want to have different approaches to managing risk and return so that you can benefit in case one adviser does better than the other. Suppose you are working with Jennifer, a holistic wealth adviser, and have gone through an in-depth wealth forecasting model. In that case, one of the most important decisions you've made is your target asset allocation: the percentage of your investment assets that you are going to allocate to different asset classes such as U.S. equities, developed foreign world equities, emerging market equities, fixed income, and alternative investments. Together, you've made this decision by testing the impact of the risk/return characteristics of different asset allocations on the probability of successfully meeting all your spending needs and the size of your legacy under various market conditions throughout your lifetime. But now, you've heard from friends that Carl is getting great results for his clients, and you are considering allocating some of your assets to him to manage. You are now faced with a few choices when it comes to diversifying your eggs. You can give Carl a slice of the overall pie and (1) allow him to "manage how he sees fit" and depart from your target asset allocation or (2) instruct Carl to "manage to your target" and maintain your target asset allocation. What's more, you've also long had the desire to (3) allocate a specific dollar amount to Jim, who specializes in a particular asset class, to "manage just this investment" because you've heard he's a great manager. Each has its considerations.

1. "Manage How You See Fit": Allow Departures from Your Target Allocation

Allowing Carl to manage your assets according to a different asset allocation means the asset allocation you targeted in your wealth management plan will not be adhered to. This will cause your portfolio to drift from its target. It can introduce additional risk if Carl tilts toward equities or potentially reduce returns if he emphasizes fixed income. Giving him free rein to "adapt to what he sees in the markets" means that he will be more focused on outperforming the markets than managing to your long-term needs as outlined in your wealth plan. While you may benefit from possible short-term outperformance by Carl, if he makes the wrong call, your legacy could be at risk. An overallocation (relative to your target) to equities in a down year could mean a loss from which you'll have to spend time recovering. An overallocation to fixed income in an increasing interest rate environment could do the same. The primary objective of sophisticated wealth management forecasting is to estimate the likelihood that your asset allocation will successfully meet all your spending goals across a wide range of market conditions over time. It doesn't make sense from a legacy point of view to depart from that.

If you believe it's important to make use of different views of the markets, you are essentially making the same harmful decision—allowing Carl to manage to his view of the markets rather than to your risk/return target. Yes, since you've given discretion to your Carl to manage your portfolio, you'll hear his views on the economy and the allocation moves he's made in response. It's informative to understand different points of view, but it's not very actionable from your standpoint. Yes, you could agree or disagree and possibly affect his positions, but then you would be second-guessing him. If you are trying to understand why Carl holds a different view from the Jennifer, then, while it may be intellectually interesting, you are back to allowing Carl to pursue an asset allocation potentially different from the one in your wealth plan. Rather than allowing your overall portfolio to drift from the target you've evaluated in terms of the probabilities of meeting your needs and building your legacy, it's far better to stay focused on your primary asset allocation.

2. "Manage to This Target"—Maintain Target Allocation

Now, let's say you ask Carl to adhere to the target asset allocation in your model with Jennifer. This approach makes more sense from a wealth management perspective, as it provides an understanding of the service levels offered by both teams. However, in this case what you are doing is allowing Carl to choose the same or different underlying managers/investments with which to construct your target asset allocation.

While that seems diversifying at first glance and it can protect somewhat against Jennifer making a poor pick, it can also work against your best interests. First, Carl's investments and/or their underlying holdings could be duplicative of Jennifer's. Where you thought you were diversifying, you were actually increasing your risk by accidentally owning more than you realized, increasing your concentration risk. One hand doesn't know what the other is doing, thereby creating additional risk for you.

Second, Carl may sell a security at a loss to have that loss available to offset a gain they want to realize in another security, only to have you find that Jennifer bought the same security within 30 days of the other's sale, thereby negating the tax loss (known as a wash sale rule violation). Carl could also have simply "used up" the loss that Jennifer thought was available by selling something at a gain that they owned. Again, one hand doesn't know what the other is doing, thereby creating tax inefficiencies for you. Rather than benefiting from one outperforming the other, having two advisers may end up costing you. Finally, performance comparisons, unless they are very different, are hard to make once taxes are taken into account.

3. "Manage Just This Investment"—Allocate a Specific Amount to a Specific Class

Lastly, you could allocate a specific dollar amount to Jim known for his private equity fund or perhaps you've already invested in his fund and are reluctant to sell it. You may think Jim is uniquely talented, or your funds may be locked up and unable to be sold for a certain period of time, or perhaps the lockup period has expired but your investments have appreciated so much that selling would incur a substantial capital gain tax. As long as you communicate what you own to Jennifer, this investment can be incorporated into your overall plan. Jennifer should be able to review the investment for you, taking into account both its performance, adherence to its asset class, lockup, and unrealized capital gains. Rather than sell it, she should be able to incorporate it into your overall plan and help you make the most of your existing holdings. While not increasing your diversification or necessarily reducing your risk, this can be an efficient way to incorporate an investment or manager outside those used by your wealth adviser.

Working with a Single Holistic Manager: Portfolio Construction

With the understanding that pre-existing investments may need to be incorporated into your new strategy, working with a single, holistic wealth adviser can and should provide diversification in the structure and selection of the underlying investments for your portfolio. Your adviser's explanation of the principles underlying their portfolio construction process will enable you to understand whether they do so.

Consider Max's situation. Max approached his first meeting with Emily with the intention of "trying you out by giving you some money to manage and see how you do." Sensing that this wasn't the first time he had done this with advisers, Emily decided to take him through a simplified wealth management process. Even without loading all of his holdings, asking where the assets were managed, asking what their cost basis was, or asking how much he needed to spend to support his retirement, they built a "preliminary" wealth management model using gross numbers simply so he could see the impact of different asset allocation choices on his legacy. Max explained, using round numbers, how much each of his advisers managed and what they invested in. A very astute man, when he compared his current blended asset allocation—the result of each of his managers pursuing their own strategy—against several other asset allocations that were constructed using risk-return management principles, he quickly realized the downside of having multiple advisers each going in their own direction with no cohesive strategy. "But I have no strategy," he exclaimed. Once he realized the impact an overall asset allocation strategy could have on his probability of successfully meeting his goals and the size of his legacy, it became easy to point out the potential concentration risks from overlapping holdings, the tax inefficiencies from uncoordinated trading, the complexities of disaggregated reporting, and the potential for higher fees. At that point, he said, "I'm in. Let's do this right. I'll send you all my statements. We'll do the plan in a detailed fashion and move forward from there. I'll move everything that makes sense over to you."

To understand the principles underlying the portfolio construction process and evaluate the extent of diversification provided, begin by asking who is making the portfolio construction and investment selection decisions. Is it the adviser or their team, and is it centralized at the firm for all clients or outsourced? Each model has its pros and cons, but what is most important is that you find it to be research-driven and evidence-based. As shown in Figure 4.1, portfolio construction has three components: asset allocation, asset location, and investment selection.

Asset Allocation

Your adviser should be able to outline and demonstrate the importance of asset allocation. As mentioned earlier, approximately 90% of your return over time is a function of your asset allocation.[7] That doesn't mean other factors, such as investment selection, aren't also important—even small percentages add significant dollars to your portfolio over time. It just underlines the importance of focusing on thoroughly evaluating the impact that your asset allocation choice has on the probability of meeting your needs. This is why holistic wealth management begins by modeling the impact of different asset allocations on your likelihood of meeting your goals. Does your adviser understand this? Do they believe that modeling different asset allocations is so important in the first place because

Figure 4.1   Portfolio Construction Process

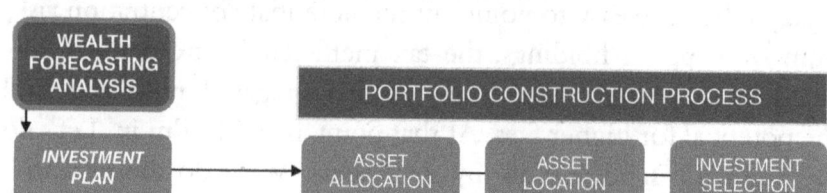

of the underlying differences in diversification benefits? It is also essential to understand the adviser's rules for rebalancing the portfolio when it drifts, how often actual versus target differentials are monitored, and at what point action is taken to bring the portfolio back to target. Allowing your actual allocation to drift too much from your target essentially moves you toward a new target—one you haven't modeled and one the impact of whose risk/return trade-off you haven't evaluated on your probability of success.

Asset Location

Second, your adviser needs to present the rationale underlying their asset location strategy. The ability to hold tax-inefficient assets in tax-deferred accounts can significantly reduce the cost of taxes (tax drag) on your portfolio.[8] What types of investments do they believe should be held in tax-deferred accounts versus taxable accounts, and why? Tax-inefficient assets include assets that generate taxable income, such as high-yield bonds or REITs, as well as those that may be more volatile, such as emerging market funds, and would generate capital gains upon rebalancing. The benefits of locating assets in tax-deferred accounts need to be balanced against other concerns, such as the fact that required minimum distributions may place you in a higher tax bracket than otherwise would be the case, as well as your liquidity needs.

Investment Selection

Lastly, your adviser should explain how investments are selected. Within equities, the portfolio construction principles should cover the following:

- The rationale for their percentage allocation of equities to global subasset classes (U.S., Developed Foreign World, and Emerging Markets)

- The use of separately managed portfolios versus mutual funds
- The allocation across investment styles (value, growth, core)
- Investment-specific criteria such as manager tenure, asset class conformity, performance, fees, turnover, investment style, historic style drift, and volatility
- The use of passive (index) investments versus active managers

Portfolios are often constructed using a combination of index funds and active managers, who research and select securities that do not mimic the index for their respective asset class. Risk budgeting provides a disciplined approach to adding/removing and sizing investments in your portfolio. Systematic risk, the risk inherent in being invested in a specific asset class, is beyond the manager's control. However, active risk, the risk that the manager takes on by departing from the index, arises from active portfolio management itself and can be measured and monitored. Utilizing a risk-budgeting framework, the adviser can construct a portfolio that spreads active risk among managers in each asset class. Understanding and tracking the source of active risk can spread it among managers in the same asset class, for example, by owning both growth and value managers simultaneously. By ensuring that no single style dominates, overall risk can be constrained within a "budget" that provides risk "worth taking" to achieve above-index returns.

Within fixed income, the portfolio construction principles should explain the following:

- The duration strategy (how the portfolio is positioned across different length bonds) and how it changes
- The use of passive (index) investments versus active managers
- The use of separately managed or laddered portfolios versus mutual funds
- The allocation across different types of bonds
  - Within municipal: In-state versus national
  - Within taxable: Government, versus corporate, versus high yield

Finally, the portfolio construction principles should outline the criteria for utilizing alternative investments:

- What percent of your portfolio are they permitted to represent?
- How are they sourced?
- What are the liquidity constraints?
- What is the risk/return history?
- What is the fee structure?

By reviewing the portfolio construction process in detail, your adviser should be able to demonstrate a deep understanding of the principles of diversification, such that it gives you confidence that you are *not sacrificing the diversification that matters, even though you are working with a sole adviser.*

Having one quarterback also provides benefits beyond the fact that, as a holistic wealth adviser, they integrate estate, tax, insurance, and philanthropic planning into a cohesive strategy tailored to your specific situation. A single adviser can provide you with centralized reporting that can be most helpful in monitoring performance against your wealth plan and communicating tax, insurance, and philanthropic actions to your tax preparer. Consolidating your assets can reduce fees and increase tax efficiency. Best of all, working with one overall quarterback reduces complexity and simplifies your life.

Once you, like Max, consider that the risks of consolidation are not what they appear to be at face value and that the benefits of working with a holistic wealth adviser might outweigh them, you may no longer be concerned about consolidating your assets. Rather, you may appreciate the opportunities to build your legacy that come from working with a single adviser.

Is It Smart to Work with Multiple Advisers?

Working with multiple advisers may provide you with a false sense of diversification. If you consider the potential risks and missed opportunities of working with multiple, uncoordinated financial advisers you may find it to be counterproductive to building your legacy. While it makes sense that different investment managers are likely to manage your underlying investments, you want a single wealth advisor to coordinate and oversee your investments so that they conform to an overall strategic asset allocation derived from your wealth plan. Your adviser should be able and willing to consolidate investments across multiple investment managers—whether sourced by them, brought over by you, or offered in your 401(k) or other employer-related retirement accounts. Building and transferring your legacy is likely to benefit from consolidating oversight with your advisor, who can track adherence to your wealth plan by monitoring your asset allocation, rebalancing as necessary, managing concentration risk, and supervising the performance of your investment managers across your overall portfolio. If your adviser is reluctant to do this, assess whether they have the wealth planning focus, portfolio construction knowledge, research capabilities, technology, and flexibility to serve your best interests.

Key Takeaways

- Investment advisers are required to use independent, qualified custodians—regulated institutions that safeguard your assets separately from the adviser's business operations—to safeguard your assets in the event of adviser bankruptcy.
- Splitting your assets among multiple advisers to increase diversification can mask deeper inefficiencies and risks that undermine your long-term legacy planning.
- Giving multiple advisers discretion over your portfolio may seem like a way to hedge risk, but it often leads to conflicting strategies that dilute the effectiveness of your carefully constructed asset allocation and wealth plan.

"It's Smart to Work with Multiple Advisers"

- There are different ways to divide responsibilities among multiple advisers (giving them full discretion, asking them to follow a shared allocation, or assigning them a specific investment), but each approach introduces coordination challenges, potential inefficiencies, and risks that can compromise the integrity of your overall wealth plan unless carefully managed by a central adviser.
- A single, holistic adviser can deliver meaningful diversification and incorporate held-away assets through disciplined, research-driven portfolio construction while also balancing asset allocation, asset location, and investment selection.

Part II

Developing a Wealth Plan

P art 1 of this book invited you to consider whether you hold any blind spots that might interfere with getting the full benefit of working with an adviser. We reviewed the ins and outs of adviser compensation, standards and incentives, the characteristics of a holistic wealth manager, the benefits of having them as your quarterback, the risks of not fully collaborating with your adviser, and, finally, the trade-offs in working with multiple advisers rather than consolidating the supervision of your portfolio with a single wealth management adviser.

Part 2 addresses blind spots that arise in connection with developing your wealth plan. Wealth planning is the foundation of identifying and sizing opportunities and risks you may face in building and transferring your legacy to the next generation. In developing and working with your wealth plan, it's important to:

Blind Spot 5: Success is All About Getting the Best Returns.
Understand how to evaluate performance for the long term.

Many investors equate success with maximizing returns and/or outperforming benchmarks. While important, too narrow a focus can obscure long-term goals, introduce unnecessary risk, and take your eye off the ball that really matters—assessing whether you are on track to achieve your lifestyle and legacy goals. This chapter will help you understand the nuances of performance evaluation, address rules of thumb such as the 4% spending rule and a laddered bond strategy, and explain why Monte Carlo–based wealth planning done in collaboration with a skilled wealth adviser can help you stay focused on building your legacy.

Blind Spot 6: Not Every Asset Needs to Be in My Plan.
Consider whether and how to include "outside" investments you may have sourced on your own in your wealth plan.

While many investors understand the benefits of wealth planning, they also believe that keeping some investments outside their plan will not negatively affect their legacy. However, omitting certain investments from your wealth plan may expose you to unforeseen risks. It may also mean missing opportunities to enhance your legacy through planning techniques that emerge only when all assets are considered together. This chapter will help you understand how bringing your adviser into the conversation can assist in assessing whether and how to include these investments in your plan to unlock strategic advantages that may better support your legacy goals.

Blind Spot 7: I can focus on my wealth planning after I sell my business.
If you own a business, learn how important pre-sale wealth planning is and the potential costs of postponing it.

Small business owners can often find themselves in one of two situations: (1) postponing wealth planning because juggling daily operations with complex planning feels overwhelming or (2) moving ahead too quickly when a purchase offer arises without taking the time to lay the strategic wealth planning groundwork that may help them grow and transfer their legacy. However, delaying wealth planning can have significant costs for you and your heirs. This chapter will help you understand how and why developing a wealth plan with an experienced wealth adviser as early as possible can help enhance and protect your legacy.

Each of the chapters that follows will help you consider whether you may be subject to blind spots associated with developing your wealth plan. They will enable you to evaluate ways to overcome these blind spots, allowing you to grow and transfer your legacy more effectively.

Blind Spot 5

"Success Is All About Getting the Best Returns"

You've learned a lot about the importance of finding and working with the right adviser to build and transfer your legacy. You know you want to work with a fiduciary who is holistic in their approach and goes beyond investment management. You expect them to add value by marshaling your tax, insurance, estate, and philanthropic advisers around your wealth management plan to help you grow and guard your legacy by identifying opportunities and mitigating risks. As financially sophisticated and analytical as you may be, you've come to recognize the ongoing benefits of working with professionals, and although you may continue to be invested with multiple investment managers, you understand the benefits of consolidating the oversight of these accounts with one quarterback.

You are also quite confident about how to measure success. Ultimately, you believe, it all boils down to "getting the best returns." While you expect excellent service, appreciate the role of wealth planning, and value periodic market updates, you believe that, at the core, portfolio performance is the most critical factor in building your legacy. In your view, building your legacy means taking every step possible to maximize your wealth by closely monitoring your investments to ensure that your managers consistently outperform the asset-specific benchmarks applicable to each investment. You expect your U.S. equity managers, for example, to outperform the S&P 500 Index (the bellwether index for U.S. stocks, which contains 500 of the largest publicly traded companies in the United States), your developed foreign world equities to outperform the MSCI EAFE Index (the stock market index tracking performance of developed, foreign-world, large and mid-cap companies in Europe, Australasia and the Far East), and your fixed income to outperform the Bloomberg Aggregate Bond Index (the broad, market-weighted benchmark that tracks performance of the investment-grade, fixed-rate, taxable bond market in the United States).

Outperforming benchmarks is a tangible measure of success. You intend to focus on this metric each time you meet with your adviser. After all, you believe the investment managers chosen by the adviser should have an investment outlook, manage your investments accordingly, and be held accountable for the accuracy of their strategies. If the underlying investment managers are professionals, then you believe they should be able to outperform or at least match the markets when there is an upswing and protect your capital by minimizing your losses when markets decline. You not only accept that discarding poor performers and switching to better-performing investments is needed to deliver strong returns, but also expect that your adviser is continuously monitoring performance and implementing any changes needed to upgrade your portfolio's performance.

Wealth planning may be a valuable exercise, but deep down, you are somewhat skeptical of its reliability. You wonder how accurate or complete any projections can be. Planning may be useful, but you want to make sure that it does not overshadow the focus on performance. As long as you keep the pressure on your financial adviser to select managers who consistently deliver strong returns, you think you will be doing your best. After all, what more can you do? You can't change the markets, so you must ensure your adviser is getting you the "best" performance.

When something feels so unquestionably true, it can be helpful to consider alternative perspectives. It could be that you've run into a blind spot. Sometimes, the things we're most sure of are precisely where our blind spots can be found. We may have limited our own understanding because we've failed to take into account the nuances involved. This is especially true of a "returns-focused mindset." Of course, it is crucial to have a metric against which to measure progress in building and maintaining your wealth. However, a single-minded focus on relatively short-term investment performance relative to an asset class benchmark can be one of the most insidious and well-entrenched blind spots standing in the way of growing and guarding your legacy. Legacy goals are long-term by definition. Short-term performance is not. Short-term performance may be driven by investment skill or lack thereof, warranting a change, but it can also be underpinned by temporary market trends, volatility, or luck. Chasing short-term outperformance can lead to taking on increased risk, substantial tax and trading costs, market timing that results in lower long-term returns, and inefficient wealth transfer. Understanding the nuances of performance evaluation and how they relate to wealth planning is crucial in avoiding these obstacles and building your legacy.

Performance Evaluation: Relative to Benchmarks

Benchmarks are important. It is essential to have a benchmark against which to monitor, understand, and evaluate performance. Asset class indexes, like those mentioned, serve an important role as useful benchmarks against which you can evaluate whether, *for a specific period of time*, your investments have out- or underperformed the market.[1]

Many clients meet with advisers annually to evaluate the performance of their portfolio. Together, you may review performance over various time periods, such as year by year, annualized over one-, three-, and five-year periods, and since your account's inception. These results for each investment are typically compared to its corresponding asset class index.

This information is almost universally included in advisers' performance reports. Measuring whether a manager outperformed or underperformed relative to the relevant asset class benchmark for their investment provides important information about the performance of individual managers. When you meet, your adviser typically explains which managers outperformed or underperformed their benchmarks, why they performed the way they did, and how that contributed to the overall result. Sometimes, a detailed attribution report is included, which shows the exact contribution or detraction made by each position due to its performance and weight in the portfolio, whether it is a mutual fund, individual bond, or equity. In any case, the standard performance report typically provides overall portfolio performance over the specific period you are analyzing relative to your asset class benchmark. Asset classes may also be blended using a weighted average to compare the overall portfolio's return to an overall portfolio benchmark for each period.

Let's take a very simple example. You own only two mutual funds: 60% of your investments are in the "Fabulous Fifteen" actively managed U.S. stock fund, which was up 12% this past year, and 40% are in the "Supremely Safe" actively managed taxable bond fund, which was up 6%. The benchmark for the Fabulous Fifteen, the S&P 500 Index, was up 10%, while the benchmark for the Supremely Safe, the Bloomberg Aggregate Bond Index, was up 8%. Multiplying the percent ownership times the percentage performance for your portfolio $(0.6 \times 12 + 0.4 \times 6)$ provides an overall return of 9.6% compared to 9.2% $(0.6 \times 10 + 0.4 \times 8)$ for the blended benchmark. Congratulations, you outperformed the benchmark portfolio.

That is one measure of success. However, since one active manager, the Fabulous Fifteen, outperformed its individual benchmark, while the other, the Supremely Safe, underperformed, does that mean you should jettison Supremely Safe, add more to Fabulous Fifteen, or just be satisfied that the overall portfolio outperformed? Should you give Supremely Safe more time? Were there other reasons that Supremely Safe underperformed that might benefit you in different markets? Might Fabulous Fifteen have run up and become too expensive? Is it time to trim, add to your investment, or do nothing?

The Nuances of Performance Relative to Benchmarks

Measuring success can be complicated and layered. The desire to chase good performance is something almost everyone experiences. It's natural to value and want to maintain an investment when it outperforms. It's also human nature to consider abandoning an investment if it underperforms. When an investment manager disappoints or an asset class languishes, it's easy to simply change investments, managers, or asset classes to something or someone that has just performed better. It feels good to have taken action. Moreover, switching behavior can be subtly encouraged by financial advisers who earn commissions based on your decisions to buy and sell securities, as well as those who have products for which they receive compensation to promote, and those who don't want to disagree with you, the client.

However, performance-chasing behavior may work against your best interests. It can be akin to "driving using only the rear-view mirror." We all know that relying solely on your rearview mirror can be the fastest way to drive off a cliff. Your eyes aren't on what's ahead. You're not looking at the long-term. You're not focused on where you are going. You are focused on the past, and there is no guarantee that it will be like the future. It's precisely to prevent undue reliance on what has happened that the following warning is required to appear on every investment manager's performance report: "Past performance is no guarantee of future results."

On the surface, making a change may seem sensible. However, abandoning an investment, manager, or asset class that has underperformed—or piling into one that has just outperformed—can often be the wrong move at the wrong time. You may be penalizing a manager who has had the discipline to stick to their long-term strategy, even if the tide is going against them in the short term and may soon reverse.[2] Or you may be over-rewarding a manager who has been lucky to benefit from the recent market environment but can't navigate the potentially choppy waters ahead. Continually jettisoning investments that performed poorly in the prior year for those that outperformed may be the fastest way of permanently harming your capital. Disciplined, long-term capital allocation, coupled with a fundamental understanding of market cycles developed through years of investing experience, can help separate signal from noise and help achieve lasting, risk-adjusted outperformance. Slow and steady often wins the race. Underperformance over a few years may be more than compensated by outperformance from those very same funds in other years. Piling into investments that have just outperformed means buying them at a higher price and potentially taking on more risk. Selling investments that have recently underperformed incurs taxes and transaction costs. These nuances are why it is useful to consider what distinguishes performance chasing from performance analysis that underlies thoughtful changes.

There are at least six key factors to consider when contemplating a performance-driven investment change: the active versus passive choice, market conditions, skill versus luck, risk management, market timing, and taxes and transaction costs.

Active versus Passive Management

Active managers believe they can outperform the passive indexes which represent a market through research, security selection (which securities and when to purchase/sell them), and portfolio structure (over/under weighting investment themes, sectors, and/or factors, among other emphases). The active versus passive debate dates back to at least 1974. Paul Samuelson, the first American to win the Nobel Prize in Economics, in an article entitled "Challenge to Judgment," which appeared in *The Journal of Portfolio Management* in 1974, was the first to argue that active managers could not consistently outperform the market. The article, among other developments, served as the inspiration for John Bogle, founder of Vanguard, to create the first index mutual fund available to retail investors in 1975. Bogle's famous quote, "Don't look for the needle in the haystack. Just buy the haystack,"[3] summarized his belief that passive index funds were far more beneficial to investors than actively managed funds. While it is not possible to invest directly in an index, index funds mirror the holdings of their index and, as a result, benefit from expense ratios that are significantly lower than actively managed funds, which require more research and trading. Through lower costs, less trading and broad diversification, and index funds, Bogle and others have argued, result in better returns, greater risk reduction, and participation in the market's overall upward trend if held for the long term.

The debate rages on today, 50 years later, with numerous organizations annually analyzing what percentage of actively managed mutual funds outperformed their indices. The latest data (2024) on Large-Cap US equity funds from SPIVA (S&P Indices Versus

Active), "the de facto scorekeeper of the long-standing active versus passive debate . . . states that . . . 65% underperformed the S&P 500, worse than the 60% rate observed in 2023 and slightly above the 64% average annual rate reported over the 24-year history of our SPIVA Scorecards . . . underperformance rates typically rose as time horizons lengthened.[4]" Over 15- and 20-year periods, 90% and 92% of all U.S. Large-Cap funds underperformed the S&P 500 Index.[5] Even Warren Buffett in his 2013 shareholder letter, instructed that his wife's inheritance be invested "10% in short-term government bonds and 90% in a very low-cost S&P 500 Index fund.[6]" The fact that expense ratios for some of the largest S&P500 funds are so low, ranging from 0.03% (Vanguard S&P 500 ETF) to 0.15% (Fidelity 500 Index Fund), plays a significant role in this.

To many, the idea that a majority of managers don't outperform the index means that they will be better off investing passively. To others, the fact that 36% of all active large-cap U.S. equity funds did so on average over 24 years means it's worth hunting for the needle. Many advisers create portfolios that are entirely passive, believing it is not worth taking on the risks and costs associated with active management. Other advisers combine active and passive funds to try to outperform the indices overall. Some asset classes may be inherently less suitable for passive investment, such as those with highly volatile or opaque assets (e.g., emerging markets, small-cap stocks, junk bonds, loans). Other asset classes, like U.S. government bonds, are so large, efficient and transparent and offer so few degrees of differentiation that they lend themselves more readily to passive investment. Keep in mind that when you allocate to active managers, you take on the potential for both out- and underperformance. Understanding the active versus passive choice is essential because it shapes not only the cost structure and expected returns of your portfolio but also how effectively it aligns with your long-term risk tolerance, investment philosophy, and confidence in market efficiency. As you measure your success, consider the role of the actively managed funds in your portfolio and their contribution over time to your overall risk/return objectives before deciding to replace or add to a position.

Market Conditions

Second, it's essential to understand the market conditions that characterized the period being evaluated to understand how they may have contributed to or detracted from the investment's performance. The investment landscape varies significantly over time, with different economic cycles, market trends, and geopolitical events influencing performance. An investment manager who outperformed benchmarks over the past several years may have benefited from specific market conditions that may not persist in the future. Similarly, one who underperformed may be better positioned to capitalize on potential market developments. It's essential to consider how a manager's strategy performs in various market environments, such as high- and low-interest-rate environments, recessions versus expansions, periods of high versus low geopolitical risk, and so on. Understanding which market conditions favor a specific manager is not about switching strategies in an attempt to predict which one will perform best under those conditions. but rather, first to identify investments that are truly representative of each environment, so as to hold a collection that provides true portfolio diversification by balancing each other out, and second to identify the root causes and address an investment underperforming in an environment that should favor them.

It is essential to remember the challenges of predicting a transition from one environment to another. This is why intelligent portfolio construction maintains exposure to multiple investment styles simultaneously, as outlined in Chapter 2. Maintaining exposure to investments that perform well in various environments—rather than trying to predict the future and invest accordingly—is part of what underlies a well-diversified portfolio. Diversification can ultimately yield better long-term returns by mitigating risk and reducing volatility. Allocating to two opposite investment styles, such as Value and Growth, for example, can smooth out short-term fluctuations that occur when one outperforms the other. Value investors seek to buy companies at levels below what their analysis suggests is the fair market value of the company. Value as a style tends to perform well in high-inflation and rising-interest-rate environments. Growth investors seek to purchase fast-growing companies whose valuations are typically higher than the overall market's, reflecting their future long-term growth potential, Growth, as a style, tends to do well when economic growth is moderate, inflation and interest rates are low, and/or innovation is occurring in a particular sector. Value and Growth indices are constructed so that, when combined, they reflect the entire market. Therefore, by definition, when growth outperforms, value underperforms, and vice versa. It's not possible to have both Value and Growth outperform at the same time. Since predicting which style will outperform is almost impossible, having both styles means your portfolio may be better able to weather different economic and market cycles and provide steadier returns over time.

Let's look at the following example. You, Joan, and each have $100 cash to deploy in your portfolios. Joan adds her $100 to her Fabulous Fifteen holdings, which had just shot up in the strong growth environment. David puts his in Supremely Safe, thinking Fabulous Fifteen has gone up too much, and Growth, as a style, is going to fall out of favor. Having read about diversification, you put $50 into each. Joan turns out to be right in year 1. The Fabulous Fifteen increases by 30%, while Supremely Safe remains at 0%. Joan now has $130, while David remains at $100. You have $115 because 50% of your original value increased by 30%, while the other half remained constant. In year 2, each of you remains steadfast in your thinking—but this year, Growth and Value rotate,

Fabulous Fifteen goes nowhere, and Supremely Safe increases by 30%. At the end of year 2, Joan and David each have $130, but you actually have $132.25—more than either of them. This is because, at the end of year 1, you rebalanced your $115 portfolio—another important principle of portfolio management covered in Chapter 2—allocating 50% ($57.50) to Fabulous Fifteen and 50% ($57.50) to Supremely Safe. The half you invested in Supremely Safe increased by 30%, giving you $74.75. When added to the $57.50 in Fabulous Fifteen, this leaves you with $132.25. As Table 5.1 illustrates, not only did you end up with more money at the end of the two years, but you experienced lower volatility. Rather than increasing by 30% or 0%, your portfolio grew by 15% each year.

Understanding the market conditions at play can also help you focus on considering what the relevant time horizon is for evaluating investment performance. Performance reports typically present performance over annual and annualized periods. They present what happened from January to December or through the most recent quarter end. Market conditions, movements, and phases, however, do not follow the calendar. The mismatch can mean that in reviewing your performance, you may conflate under- or outperformance with a change in market conditions and perhaps unduly penalize or reward the manager.

There are times when it is necessary to sell an investment, particularly if it is underperforming in an environment that should be favorable or if security selection has repeatedly been poor. In these cases, the situation warrants further analysis to understand and evaluate the cause of the deviation. It is important to be able to distinguish whether underperformance was due to something more than market conditions, and the investment should therefore be further analyzed and perhaps sold. Relying on the analytical prowess of your research team is critical here to help tease apart the factors underlying performance.

Table 5.1 Sample Diversification

	Start	Year 1	End Year 1	Rebalance	Start Year 2	Year 2	End Year 2	Total
Jenn	$100 in FF	+30%	$130 in FF	No	$130 in FF	+0%	$130 in FF	$130
Carl	$100 in SS	+0%	$100 in SS	No	$100 in SS	+30%	$130 in SS	$130
You	$50 in FF	+15%	$65 in FF	Yes	$57.50 in FF	+15%	$57.50 in FF	
	$50 in SS		$50 in SS		$57.50 in SS		$74.75 in SS	$132.25

For Illustrative Purposes Only

Luck or Skill?

Performance relative to a benchmark can be a function of luck—good or bad—instead of skill. It's essential to delve deeper into the reasons behind the out- or underperformance and assess what drove the results. Even the best research teams can get caught with a poor-performing stock or sector—and sometimes the less-skilled just happened to catch the wave for what caught the public's eye but may not be fundamentally supportable. Skill can sometimes take time to be validated. Perhaps an investment underperformed because the manager had the discipline to stick to their strategy, even when the market was going against them in the short term. This could well have contributed to the strong performance record on which they were initially selected. Conversely, perhaps the investment or asset class that has been rising is already overvalued, based on hype or a fad rather than fundamentals. Are you buying in at a high? Is the performance justified by the additional risk you are taking on? What happens when that investment ceases to perform? Are you chasing risk rather than fundamentals? Will you know enough to exit before it's gone down? Will you be exiting at a loss, and searching for the next "new, new thing"? Rather than acting emotionally based on short term out- or underperformance, a strong research team will have clear, unemotional metrics for evaluating performance over the longer term.

Of course, there are times when it makes sense to change an investment manager within your portfolio—when you are not performance chasing but rather conducting thoughtful analysis that leads you to believe a change is warranted. Repeated underperformance that can't be explained—management team turnover, a change in investment style, firm ownership, asset class, geographic focus, volatility, or expense ratio—are all important red flags that require additional due diligence and research to determine whether it makes sense to move on from the selection. Knowing that your adviser's research team is analyzing the issues to make a thoughtful decision on whether to hold or sell/reduce your exposure can reassure you that they are focused on your best interests. Furthermore, working with a wealth adviser who themself is invested alongside you in the same products can enable you to take comfort in the fact that these issues will also be important to them.

Risk Management

Fourth, underperformance may be both useful and justified because an investment carries lower risk than the benchmark itself. Perhaps your adviser has considered your sensitivity to losing money and has employed an investment manager with a more conservative strategy who is likely to persistently trail their benchmark. Investors who have insisted on wanting a conservative portfolio often don't realize that taking less risk may mean underperforming the benchmark in certain years and are nonetheless disappointed at underperforming. Or, conversely, perhaps the outperformance has been due to the manager taking on more risk than you had realized. What if an adviser gives in to your desire to outperform and puts you into a higher-risk investment? It performs well for a while, but when it declines, as higher-risk investments typically tend to do, it will eat into your principal going forward. It's easy to forget that investment risk and return are correlated, especially when something captures the public's imagination. Investors have been hurt dramatically by bubbles bursting ever since and even before the well-known tulip mania of the 1630s. Remembering that scenario can quickly temper your urge to outperform.

Improving your performance may actually mean reducing the volatility in your portfolio to achieve steadier returns, rather than constantly shifting to recently higher-performing investments. Steadier returns mean that the portfolio is continually compounding on a higher base. Remember, if you start with $100, all invested in one security, and it loses 50%, a 50% increase will not return you to $100. Your portfolio would need to increase by 100% to return to its starting value. If by having two equal but opposing investments in your $100 portfolio, you are able to reduce the portfolio decline to 30% ($70—because while one investment declined by 50%, the other rose by 40%), your portfolio would only need to increase by 43% instead of 100% to return to its starting value of $100. Moreover, subsequent returns will be based on the higher portfolio ($70 instead of $50). A 10% return would be $7 instead of $5, adding $2 more to the portfolio. Steadier returns enable compounding to take greater effect.

By declining less when the market drops, you're starting from a higher base when the market turns around. This means you can get back to where you were, with less of an increase and in a shorter time, than someone whose investments went down further. This is why risk management is so important when managing wealth for the long term.

Market Timing

Fifth, consider the following: if performance chasing is your approach, are you essentially trying to time the market? Market timing has seduced many investors but has not consistently worked for anyone. It requires you to make two decisions correctly: when to exit and when to re-enter. Since returns often come in dramatic spurts, investors who exit an investment after it has declined, often don't enter another one until after it has already risen. That's the opposite of buying low and selling high. And since investors want to be certain a bad period is truly over, they often delay until the pickup in return is over. This creates even more long-lasting damage to portfolios.

As you can see in Figure 5.1, missing only the 10 best days in the market over the past 20 years would have cut your return in half compared to staying invested. Moreover, seven of the 10 best days occurred when the market was in bear market territory.[7]

Figure 5.1 Value of $10,000 Invested in the S&P 500

	10 Best Days	
	Date	Return
	10/13/2008	11.58%
	10/28/2008	10.79%
	04/09/2025	9.52%
	03/24/2020	9.39%
	03/13/2020	9.32%
	03/23/2009	7.10%
	04/06/2020	7.03%
	11/13/2008	6.93%
	11/24/2008	6.47%
	03/10/2009	6.37%

- Invested All Dates: $75,297
- Missed 10 Best Days: $33,498
- Missed 20 Best Days: $19,458
- Missed 30 Best Days: $12,367
- Missed 40 Best Days: $8,222
- Missed 50 Best Days: $5,611
- Missed 60 Best Days: $3,954

Source: Bloomberg, S&P 500 Index Total Returns 12/31/1999–12/31/2025; Fischer Stralem Analysis as of 1-13-2026

Taxes and Transaction Costs

Finally, keep in mind that making changes usually incurs costs. Taxes and transaction charges (commissions) can eat into the returns of the new investment. In the heat of performance chasing, they are sometimes forgotten. Even if your investment underperformed or declined over the past year, if it has appreciated since you originally purchased it, you will be subject to federal and possibly state and local capital gains taxes. There may also be commissions charged for the purchase and sale transactions. With each investment change, you are likely to have reduced your capital available to deploy. In some cases, it may be worth it—you don't want tax considerations to overwhelm investment directions and cause you to hold onto a nonperforming investment. Capital gains taxes may be among the lowest taxes you are exposed to. However, it's important to remember that frequent changes for the sake of chasing performance can eat away at your capital.

Table 5.2 summarizes the analytical focus, key considerations, and implications for each factor.

Performance Relative to Plan

If the nuances of performance evaluation lead you to understand that chasing short-term outperformance relative to benchmarks can be risky, costly, and unproductive, and may result in lower long-term returns, then how else might you measure success?

One of the most significant pieces of information your wealth management plan gave you was the probability of successfully meeting your goals based on achieving the *hypothetical average portfolio return* over the remaining planning horizon for you and your partner. In other words, as long as your performance achieves the average hypothetical return in your wealth plan, there is a high probability of achieving all your goals. *Focusing on your performance relative to the hypothetical average portfolio return is a far more crucial benchmark for evaluating progress toward your legacy.* This is the benchmark that really matters. While almost all advisers will provide you with a standard performance relative to benchmarks report, a wealth adviser focused on building your legacy will concentrate on how the overall portfolio is performing relative to the target in your wealth plan.

It's worth highlighting that measuring performance against a unique, situationally-derived target is how sophisticated institutional managers allocate and benchmark their portfolios. Institutional investors benchmark performance against custom targets tied to their obligations rather than market indexes. Pension funds aim for returns aligned with actuarial assumptions for future liabilities, insurance companies set goals based on expected claims and premium

Table 5.2 Summary of Investment Performance Evaluation Factors

Factor	Analytical Focus	Key Considerations	Implications for Evaluating Performance
Active vs. Passive	Management style and its impact on performance relative to benchmarks.	Active managers may outperform but often don't; passive funds offer lower costs and broad diversification.	Evaluate whether performance is due to strategy or market exposure; consider cost and consistency.
Market Conditions	Influence of economic and market environments on performance outcomes.	Style performance varies across cycles; diversification and rebalancing help manage volatility.	Assess whether performance aligns with expected behavior in current conditions; avoid misattribution.
Luck vs. Skill	Distinguishing randomness from repeatable expertise.	Short-term results may be misleading; long-term discipline and fundamentals are more telling.	Use deeper analysis to determine if performance is sustainable or circumstantial.

Factor	Analytical Focus	Key Considerations	Implications for Evaluating Performance
Risk Management	Relationship between risk exposure and performance variability.	Lower risk may trail benchmarks; higher risk may inflate short-term gains but increase downside.	Consider volatility and drawdowns alongside returns; steadier performance may compound more effectively.
Market Timing	Attempting to enhance returns by predicting entry and exit points.	Timing is notoriously difficult; missing key days can drastically reduce returns.	Avoid performance chasing; evaluate consistency and discipline in staying invested.
Taxes & Transaction Costs	Hidden costs that erode net performance.	Gains may trigger taxes; frequent changes reduce capital and may not justify the performance improvement.	Factor in after-tax returns and trading costs when assessing manager or portfolio performance.

dynamics, and endowments target returns that cover inflation and spending needs to preserve long-term capital. This liability-driven approach ensures portfolios are evaluated on their ability to meet specific financial commitments, not just beat a market index. In reality, households are no different—their true benchmark is meeting personal wealth planning goals such as retirement and legacy planning, not simply outperforming an asset class.

Let's address your potential skepticism about the reliability of wealth planning. Unpacking some of the plan's modeling and understanding how significantly it has evolved from what was used in the past may alleviate some of your concerns.

The Better Benchmark: The Wealth Plan Return

The hypothetical average portfolio return in your wealth plan underlies all scenarios in your wealth modeling. It's important to understand how it is calculated and why it is so useful. The return is typically derived from a Monte Carlo–based simulation of the possible returns for your customized asset allocation across a broad range of market conditions. Monte Carlo–based simulation is a statistical technique used to model and predict the potential outcomes of a portfolio's performance under uncertainty. It randomly generates numerous portfolio performance scenarios over time based on underlying asset class index returns, standard deviations (risk), and correlations.

The wealth management plan model will enable you to look at your probability of success under any of the 1000 returns and, most importantly, will provide the hypothetical average return across all scenarios for your selected asset allocation.[8] The hypothetical average return is typically provided both nominally (including inflation) and on a real basis (without inflation).

The returns, standard deviations, and correlations are typically based on historical data but can also be modified by the adviser to project, for example, lower and/or more volatile returns. In other words, your adviser could adjust all the futures you are modeling to be lower and/or more volatile than the past to be extra conservative. Most models generate at least 1,000 scenarios for how your specific portfolio might perform under different market conditions over your lifetime taking into account how your portfolio is structured (how much is in taxable versus tax-deferred accounts, spending needs, taxes, inflation, Social Security, required minimum distributions, gifting, etc.). Your probability of success is based on the percentage of those 1,000 return scenarios in which you do not run out of funds before the plan ends. For example, if you are able to meet all of your needs without depleting your funds in 980 out of 1,000 scenarios, then you have a 98% probability of success.

Is that good enough? The model further provides what's known as a confidence interval for you to evaluate the percentage from the model so you can understand what percentage constitutes a good result for your age.[9] Figure 5.2 shows that in the particular scenario presented, 98% of all market scenarios (individual lines) are light gray (successful) and result in the ability to successfully meet all goals over your lifetime and leave a legacy to the next generation. A 98% probability of success puts you in the dark gray zone, exceeding the light gray confidence zone. This suggests that if maximizing your legacy is not a priority, you could be spending more than you currently are during your lifetime. If you had fallen into the medium gray zone, a probability of success less than 75%, then it meant you were facing too much uncertainty and would need to examine the impact of changing your asset allocation or reducing your spending. If your probability of success had landed in the light gray zone, it would have meant that you face a good balance between your current and future lifestyle. (See Figure 5.2.)

Modeling 1,000 different outcomes makes the conclusion statistically significant or, in other words, reliable for planning purposes. It's as if you were assessing how your portfolio holds up under almost all possible futures you could experience in the markets based

Figure 5.2 Current Scenario Probability of Success

You have a simple question: "Can I fund all my goals without running out of money?"

Current Scenario

Unfortunately, because no one knows what the future returns will be, there's not a simple Yes or No answer.

That's why we run 1,000 trials of your plan using 1,000 different return possibilities to calculate the probability your plan will be successful.

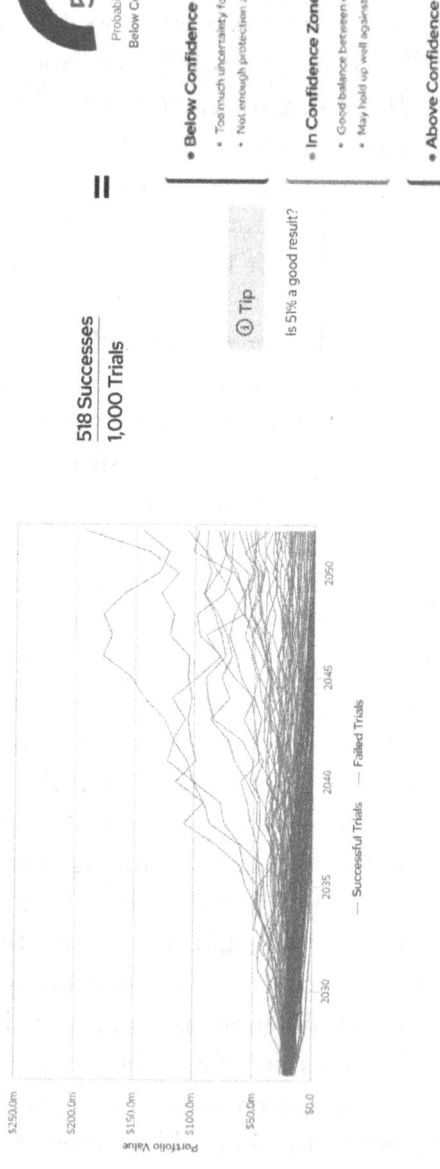

Source: MoneyGuidePro, Envestnet.

on your asset allocation and determining in what percent of them you are able to meet all your goals without depleting your funds.

Performance Since Inception

Just like in the earlier discussion about measuring your performance against benchmarks, your choice of time periods is again important. Taking the figures in your standard performance report, you will want to compare annual, annualized, and, most importantly, since-inception-performance against the Monte Carlo–based hypothetical average return in your wealth plan. To determine whether your portfolio has been performing well enough to achieve the probability of success you are targeting, you need to understand whether your return since inception is keeping up with the hypothetical average Monte Carlo–based portfolio return in your plan. It's tempting to want to compare each year's performance to the wealth plan average—and even to think you can spend a little more if your results exceeded the wealth plan average in a particular year. However, one year of performance close to the target does not mean your portfolio has been growing at that rate on average over time; that can be concluded only using performance since inception. There will be years when your portfolio underperforms the wealth plan average, and you'll be happy you "banked" the excess returns from prior years.

Before Monte Carlo: Expected Return

Prior to the widespread adoption of Monte Carlo–based simulation software in the 1990s and early 2000s, financial advisers relied on simple arithmetic calculations to estimate the return of a portfolio. The process was straightforward: multiply the expected return of each asset class by its portfolio weight. Consider a classic 60% stock/40% fixed income portfolio. If stocks had a long-term average return of 10% and government bonds averaged 5.2%, the expected return would be $(0.6 \times 10\%) + (0.4 \times 5.2\%) = 8.08\%$.

This 8.0% served as your benchmark. Each year, you would evaluate your portfolio's performance against the expected return—before accounting for taxes or inflation.

Without more sophisticated models, advisers turned to heuristics. A common adjustment deducted 2% for taxes and 2% for inflation from the expected return, leaving a "safe" withdrawal rate of 4%. The thinking was simple: as long as you spent no more than 4%, you could preserve your principal in real terms indefinitely.

Popular discussions of the "4% spending rule" for retirement persist today. The 4% spending rule was developed by William Bengen in 1994.[10] Based on historical analysis of returns over the prior 75 years, it posited that 4% of the portfolio, increased by inflation, could be withdrawn from their portfolio annually without running out of money over a 30-year period, assuming a 50–60% stock/50–40% bond allocation.

Over 30 years later, this rule continues to be used despite significant risks arising from assuming constant annual withdrawals (when actual behavior seems to rarely correspond to reality), the impact of poor market returns early on (which can deplete the portfolio even if followed by stronger returns later), the 30-year time horizon (when retirement can be longer), ignoring taxes and fees (which eat into returns further), and the potential for future returns to be lower than historical.[11] These criticisms have undermined consensus on the usefulness of this rule, yet it still often remains top of mind for investors.

The Limits of Arithmetic Planning

Rules of thumb can be useful for quick and relatively unimportant calculations. However, relying on them when your future is at stake is unwise. Although easy to use and intuitive for clients, the expected return method and corresponding spending rule have limitations. They fail to take into account several risks:

- Sequence-of-returns risk: Poor returns early in retirement can permanently erode your portfolio—even if strong markets follow.

- Volatility and unpredictability: Arithmetic assumes stable conditions, but markets rarely behave that way.
- Single-point estimation: An average (or mean) return tells you nothing about the range of potential outcomes—or what happens if your actual return falls below the mean.
- Complex personal variables: From changing tax rates to evolving health needs, your life introduces factors no simple formula can capture.

Take John, a retired engineer who followed conventional wisdom and used the arithmetic expected return to guide his withdrawals. Everything looked fine—on paper. But in the first few years of retirement, the market tanked. John withdrew the same fixed amount from a shrinking portfolio, and those early losses were never fully recovered. His subsequent earnings were compounding on a significantly diminished asset base. Even when the markets rebounded, his portfolio couldn't catch up.

Had John used a Monte Carlo simulation, he'd have seen how vulnerable his plan was to poor early returns. He might have adjusted his withdrawals, buffered risk, or built more flexibility into his spending.

Monte Carlo: A New Lens for Real-Life Planning

Monte Carlo models revolutionized financial planning by simulating thousands of market scenarios. Instead of aiming for a single expected return, they illuminate:

- The probability of success over time
- How variable factors interact (inflation, taxes, sequence risk, mix of taxable/tax-deferred assets)
- When and how your portfolio might fail to meet your goals

It's like trading a compass for a GPS—with Monte Carlo–based modeling you're no longer just pointing in the "right" direction; you're able to almost pre-experience the terrain ahead.

The arithmetic techniques—however intuitive—are more of a trial-and-error method. They don't account for:

- Dynamic tax and inflation rates
- Account-specific tax treatments
- Shifts in health, longevity, or spending
- Market booms, busts, and behavioral shifts
- The unique patterns of your life

Relying on them alone can be risky. Monte Carlo modeling provides a fuller picture—one calibrated to uncertainty, time, and possibility.

Relying on Bond Coupons?

Taking the lead from the "4% spending rule," some investors take an inverse approach to performance. Let's take John again as our example. He can't let go of the 4% rule, and he thinks he can achieve 4% without taking on any equity risk. John's thinking is as follows: "If I can lock in a 4% municipal (muni) bond coupon from a laddered bond portfolio and keep my spending to less than 4% of my portfolio, I should be able to support my spending for the rest of my life." John's calculation, for example, would be that if he invests a $20 million portfolio 100% in laddered municipal bonds with a 4% coupon, he will not run out of money as long as he and his wife confine their total spending, including any taxes, to $800,000 a year. Given that they are 100% invested in municipal bonds, the tax bill should be minimal, especially if the bonds are triple tax-free (exempt from federal, state, and local taxation.) Moreover, John fully expects that he will then be able to leave the full $20 million to their heirs, solidifying their legacy. The strategy sounds prudent with stable income, tax efficiency, and low volatility. But once again, the reality is more nuanced.

First, John hasn't factored in inflation. He is either assuming that inflation will be 0% over the next two decades or low enough so that, if he spends only the interest income from the portfolio, his principal will remain roughly around $20 million at the end of 20 years. Based on historical data, this assumption is unlikely to be realized and may lead to two unfortunate surprises summarized in Table 5.3. The 20-year monthly rolling inflation over the past 80 years has averaged 3.5%. Over the last 80 years (the post-WWII era), there have been only two periods in which the 20-year rolling average inflation dipped as low as 2%: in 1968 and in 2020—all other periods have been higher.

The first surprise is the extent of principal erosion. Even if John had been swayed by the prevailing moderate inflation regime in 1968, for example, and had allocated 100% to bonds (also yielding ~4% back then) for the next 20 years and lived off the interest income, his $20 million principal would have lost *70%* of its purchasing power over the ensuing 20 years when inflation actually averaged 6.3%. Ignoring taxes, fees, and credit/default risk, the portfolio passed on to his heirs would have had the purchasing power of $6 million. Even if inflation had averaged the rare rate of 2%, the purchasing power of his principal would have been reduced to $13 million.

The second surprise is the impact of inflation on the purchasing power of his income. John also overlooked the fact that inflation will mean that his interest income won't go as far in terms of purchasing power each year. Even at a modest 2% inflation, the real value of his initial $800K annual income drops by nearly one-third to $549K over two decades. He will either have to cut back his spending to stay within the confines of the interest income or use some of his principal to cover his spending.

Table 5.3 Inflation Impact on Principal and Income Over 20 Years

Item	Nominal Amount	Year 1 Purchasing Power (Year 1 $)	Year 20 Purchasing Power (Year 1 $)	Change Over 20 Years (%)
Principal	$20,000,000	$20,000,000	$13,728,615	−31.36%
Annual Interest Income	$800,000	$800,000	$549,145	−31.36%

Assumptions: Inflation = 2% per year; Horizon = 20 years; Interest spent; Principal remains $20M nominal.

For Illustrative Purposes Only

Had John included equities in the portfolio, a meaningful portion of the loss of purchasing power could have been mitigated. If you think back to Chapter 3, you'll recall that a 100% bond portfolio was less efficient than a 33% stock/77% bond portfolio, which historically offered both a higher return and lower volatility than the 100% bond portfolio. Overexposure to inflation and interest rate risk in the 100% bond portfolio underlies this relative inefficiency. Adding a strategic allocation to equities can provide the growth needed to offset inflation and help maintain your legacy.

Second, John hasn't factored in the fact that since interest rates in the bond market are constantly changing, the actual return realized from holding a municipal bond is rarely the bond's current yield. This concept is called "yield to maturity (YTM)." Whereas current yield is a simple measure of the annual coupon payment divided by the current market price, YTM represents the total return an investor can expect if the bond is held until maturity, assuming all coupon payments are reinvested at the same rate, and the issuer does not default. YTM accounts for coupon payments, premium to par amortization (or discount to par accrual, conversely), and the time value of money. For purposes of marketability, liquidity, and structural flexibility, municipal bonds are issued with a 5% coupon. While John may focus on the 5% coupon and think that is what he is earning, the actual YTM will depend on the price he pays for the bond, not just the coupon. For instance, suppose John purchases a municipal bond maturing in 10 years with a 5% stated coupon and is aware that his financial adviser had to pay $125 per par value ($100). If he had done the calculation, he might have already seen that 5% coupon ($5 on a $125 principal) would provide a 4% current yield. However, because John will only receive $100 (par value) back when the bond matures, he may not have taken into account the impact of amortizing the $25 premium over the 10-year term ($2.50 per year).

When this amortization is included, what he really earned over the period wasn't the coupon yield of 5% or even the current yield of 4%, he received the YTM, which was 2.2% (annualized). YTM is the relevant number John should use to evaluate his portfolio against his spending and legacy goals. It's interesting to note that many investors don't look for or consider the market prices their financial firms pay when purchasing a passive ladder of individual bonds, and so are unaware of the YTMs. Clients experience a healthy 4% tax-exempt cash yield but do not see the offsetting amortization, since this is not a cash line item. In addition, each time a bond matures or is called, John faces reinvestment risk. Each time a bond matures or is called, another bond needs to be purchased, raising inflation, interest rate, premium, credit quality and liquidity issues.

Return calculations are made even more complex when the "callability" of municipal bonds is factored in. When a bond is callable, the issuer has the right to redeem it before its stated maturity date, usually at a predetermined call price (often at or slightly above par). Callability is where the bond issuer can "call" their bond back at par irrespective of the price the client paid for it. This tends to happen when the market value of the bond is above par (an issuer voluntarily calling a bond at par that is trading below par wouldn't make economic sense). Approximately 75% of municipal bonds are callable, and the non-callable portion trades at a substantially lower yield, making it challenging to avoid callable bonds. In these cases, John would lose the higher coupon payments he was expecting for the remaining years. If he had purchased the bond at a premium (e.g., $125 for a $100 par bond), and the bond was called at $100, he would have lost the premium paid. This can significantly reduce or even wipe out the expected yield. This is why the convention in the municipal bond market is to quote the Yield to Call (YTC), which would show that a premium bond called away soon has a lower YTC than the YTM.

Understanding these dynamics is complex, especially in a market with constantly shifting interest rates. Furthermore, the municipal bond market is relatively illiquid. There is no centralized exchange (as there is for equities), so all trading is done on a bilateral basis, with thousands of issuers and millions of different bonds. There isn't a single quoted price in the market; instead, pricing results from continuous competitive bids from many market participants trading with one another. This process is called price discovery, and it reflects prevailing interest rates, credit risk, liquidity, and investor sentiment. The bid-ask spread summarizes what bidders are willing to pay relative to what sellers are asking. Investment management firms often purchase large quantities of municipal bonds to put in their clients' portfolios. While the financial adviser is not *technically* charging a management fee to the client, the purchase price of the bond is typically marked up when it is added to a client's portfolio to compensate the firm. This markup, driven by the bid-ask spread, is entirely invisible to the client because the (often large) markup is not required to be disclosed.

Over-reliance on Individual Bonds

Let's summarize why John's strategy may not be optimal for building and transferring his legacy.

First, there is inflation risk:

- To his principal: Even moderate inflation erodes principal over time.
- And to his spending power: Coupon income may feel sufficient today, but inflation erodes purchasing power for spending needs.

Second, he's overlooking the fact that he's not actually locking in 4%:

- He needs to take into account the impact of paying a premium and calculate YTM.
- The actual return realized from holding a municipal bond is rarely the bond's current yield.
- Callability increases the chance of losing higher coupon payments and the initial premium paid.

Third, he continually confronts reinvestment risk:

- As bonds mature or are called, he'll need to reinvest proceeds.
- If rates fall, he'll reinvest at lower yields, reducing future income.
- If rates rise, his other longer dated premium bonds' prices will fall in value, limiting the ability to sell and reinvest at higher market rates.

Finally, he has less flexibility and this isn't cost-free

- A passively managed ladder doesn't adapt to changing needs, market conditions, or tax laws.
- He may miss out on better opportunities—e.g., active muni strategies, ETFs, or tactical credit exposure.
- Although not being charged a fee, there is a markup applied to each bond.

Rather than using a passive bond ladder strategy, actively managed mutual funds or ETFs can offer higher yield, better liquidity, and active management to opportunistically trade relative value as well as avoid onerous call risks, often making them a more flexible and potentially more sustainable income vehicle. See Table 5.4 for a comparison of features. Mutual funds do not charge a markup based on the bid/ask spread because the bonds are going into the overall portfolio thereby enabling the mutual fund shareholder to receive the benefit of their trade execution.

Table 5.4 Premium Muni Ladder vs. Actively Managed Muni Fund

Premium Muni Ladder vs. Actively Managed Muni Fund

Feature	Premium Muni Ladder (4% Coupon)	Actively Managed Muni Fund
Yield (Net of Premium)	Lower effective yield than coupon—requires calculation	Standardized metrics that comply with SEC rules to ensure transparency and comparability
Trade Execution	Small scale purchases and sales increase bid/ask spread	Economies of scale minimize bid/ask spreads
Liquidity	Low (individual bonds can be difficult to sell)	High (daily liquidity via fund shares)
Diversification	Limited (20 bonds)	Broad (hundreds of issuers, sectors, geographies)
Active Management	None	Yes—managers adjust duration, monitor credit, and call risk
Tax Efficiency	High (tax-free income)	High (funds are also tax-exempt)
Reinvestment Risk	High (as bonds mature)	Lower (fund managers reinvest automatically and constantly monitor market for relative value)
Fees	None ongoing but typically subject to markup by adviser	Typically in the range of 0.22–0.44% expense ratios

The Importance of Measuring Relative to Monte Carlo–Based Average Return

Advisers understand that clients are typically focused on returns relative to benchmarks. They know that that is the conversation clients seek and expect. In wanting to meet those expectations, advisers typically begin by reviewing the standard performance report that presents results relative to benchmarks. Conversations can become detailed, and often there is little time left to address performance relative to the Monte Carlo–based average return in the client's wealth plan. This means that conducting the performance comparison, that is a much more relevant measure of success often gets overlooked.

In addition to the client's predilection for benchmark performance comparisons, some advisers also prefer to remain focused on relative performance rather than spend the time and risk the outcomes from discussing topics that could arise in a wealth planning conversation. Updating your plan in real time and comparing your portfolio's performance to the Monte Carlo results can engender conversations that are much more sensitive and often challenging for the adviser.

June met with her adviser, who began their meeting by confirming and updating the assumptions in her wealth plan. June had been frequently requesting additional distributions over and above her monthly payout. There had been several extra vacations and substantial redecorating. These unplanned expenditures occurred in 2022, a period marked by surging inflation due to post-pandemic supply chain issues, labor shortages, and energy shocks. The war between Russia and Ukraine broke out, adding geopolitical uncertainty and disrupting energy and commodity markets. The Fed raised rates seven times in 2022, increasing borrowing costs and causing high-growth tech stocks to plummet. The S&P 500 declined by 19%. Rather than offsetting the decline in equities, as was often the case, bonds fell as well. It was, in fact, the worst year for bond market since the Great Financial Crisis in 2008–2009. When the results were run, June's probability of success had decreased and was now approaching the low end of the confidence zone. June was embarrassed, and her somewhat inexperienced adviser felt awkward about telling her she "overspent."

An experienced adviser knows that June's situation is far from unusual. Rather than static scorecards, wealth plans are meant to be constantly evolving. They are there to support your aspirations rather than constrain you. Working with a skilled adviser can enable you to test and evaluate opportunities to help improve your plan.

Many investors have withstood an extended period of below-average market performance in one or more asset classes due to developments such as a recession, black swan event,[12] scandal, or policy changes. Some have been affected by unforeseen tax law changes, or inflation. Many clients spend more than they anticipated (job loss, over indulgence, additional heirs, unanticipated charitable donations, etc.) or didn't receive the expected payout from the sale of their business. Some overestimate the amount of an expected inheritance. In any case, if your probability of success falls below the confidence zone, focusing on outperformance relative to a benchmark could lead you to take precisely the wrong actions. Without a sophisticated wealth planning model, you might independently try to increase your return by taking on a more aggressive asset allocation by shifting a greater percentage of your portfolio into equities or adding higher-risk investment managers. Taking on more risk could be necessary, but it also could ultimately reduce your probability of success even further. Instead of focusing on short-term performance or relying on rules of thumb, conducting a deeper analysis using a Monte Carlo–based wealth model can be informative and lead to more effective actions.

In such a case, your adviser can work with you to run different scenarios that test the impact of changes to, for example, your retirement age, spending level, gifting strategies, and overall asset allocation. While adjusting your asset allocation may not be a sensitive issue, reducing your spending, working longer, or lowering the size of a gift or bequest is likely to be a more challenging conversation for your adviser to have with you. You need to make space for this conversation. Missing the drop in your probability of success because you were focused on outperforming a benchmark instead of comparing returns since inception to your composite plan return could have a lasting, negative impact on your legacy.

June's adviser used her situation to help her understand that, rather than spending without planning for it and risking the impact to her portfolio, working together to test and incorporate expenditures into the plan ahead of time could mitigate the impact of withdrawals on her overall probability of success. No adviser wants to act as a gatekeeper. And no experienced adviser is likely to reprimand you for overspending. Wealth advisers who are focused on helping you build your legacy look for ways to help you meet all your spending goals without significantly lowering your probability of success.

Stay the Course

It's hard to accept that as long as your average return meets your hypothetical average return target in your wealth management plan, underperforming in a particular year or in an individual investment will not matter for your long-term success. Following a prudent course requires self-discipline and self-awareness not to chase what's going up. Self-awareness is necessary to develop a comprehensive wealth management plan, and self-discipline is required to stick to it. The right wealth manager is there to remind you of the importance of both and to counsel you through difficult decisions.

There are times when circumstances like job loss or significant unexpected expenses make it necessary to adjust course, whether by cutting spending or revising your asset allocation. However, chasing returns will move you to take on more risk than you might need to—and may embed a degree of cost and volatility that undoes the probability of meeting your goals. Human nature is often the driving force behind the chase. We are easily captivated—along with everyone else—by whatever seems to be the golden goose. We are afraid of missing out. Despite caution from our advisers, we may truly believe that "it's different this time" and feel that we must get in on the action. However, those of us who have been in this business for decades know that "it's different this time" may be the four most dangerous words in investing. It may be "different" for a short moment, but the fundamentals of valuation—economic growth and corporate efficiency—typically return. What really matters is meeting your wealth management plan's long-term return goals. Your wealth manager should be someone who helps you remain focused on your plan while the market winds blow asset classes to and fro in the short term.

Is Success All About Getting the Best Returns?

Many investors equate success with maximizing returns, but this narrow focus can obscure long-term goals, introduce unnecessary risk, and take your eye off the ball that really matters—assessing whether you are on track to achieve your lifestyle and legacy goals. After all, we are not in a race with the benchmarks; we're trying to help ensure that the strategy we have in place meets your particular goals. A singular focus on returns can lead to harmful behaviors, such as performance chasing, excessive risk-taking, and, ultimately, inefficient wealth transfer. These actions may undermine long-term goals and undo your legacy planning.

True success lies in achieving the long-term objectives outlined in your personalized wealth plan. Measuring performance relative to standard benchmarks, such as the S&P 500, can be useful for understanding the underlying drivers of performance and identifying potential disappointing investments that may need to be replaced. However, the more meaningful benchmark is the hypothetical average return derived from a Monte Carlo simulation tailored to your specific assets and how they are structured, your time horizon, spending needs, legacy goals, and risk tolerance. This approach accounts for uncertainty, taxes, inflation, and life changes—offering a more reliable path to building and preserving wealth.

Monte Carlo–based simulations revolutionized the probability-based reliability of plans. However, like any tool, its value stems from the skill of the one who holds it. Fully blending the insights derived from performance measurement into action requires working with an adviser skilled in wealth planning with whom you are ready to fully collaborate.

Key Takeaways

- While benchmarks are useful, they tell only part of the story; performance must be assessed in context and over time. Evaluating performance solely against market indices misses the bigger picture of how investments align with your goals and time horizon.
- Chasing recent performance can be harmful. Switching investments based on short-term outperformance often leads to higher risk, unnecessary costs, and lower long-term returns.
- A more nuanced understanding of performance is useful. Thoughtful investment changes should consider factors like market conditions, manager skill, risk, and costs—not just recent returns.
- The more meaningful performance benchmark is the hypothetical average return in your wealth plan, which reflects your personal goals and risk profile. Monte Carlo simulations offer a more realistic and dynamic view of future outcomes than outdated arithmetic rules or "confine your spending to your income." These strategies may seem appealing, but inflation, premium costs, and other risks can erode principal and reduce real returns over time.
- Staying disciplined and aligned with your wealth plan helps avoid costly detours driven by short-term market movements.

Blind Spot 6

"Not Every Asset Needs to Be in My Plan"

You are a sophisticated and experienced investor who often encounters interesting investment opportunities through your own connections that you would like to consider for your portfolio. Through friends, your business network, or other advisers marketing to you, intriguing investment opportunities often come your way. You want the ability to invest in compelling new investments, especially if you are in the deal flow and continually presented with interesting options. Or perhaps, like many of us who have attended cocktail parties where people have discussed their successful investments, you want to preserve the ability to act on what you hear. While you understand that there are benefits to wealth planning, you fundamentally believe that keeping some investments outside your plan will not negatively affect your legacy.

As a result, you play some of your cards close to the vest when meeting with your financial adviser. You don't quite share everything you own or are considering investing in with them. While you feel you've been forthcoming enough by telling them you have some small outside or additional investments, you nonetheless keep details like amounts, asset class, and tax nature to yourself. You believe your adviser should focus on what you've given them to manage. You've presented them with what you consider to be your core capital. They don't need to know about what you have kept on the side or how it's invested. As long as they manage the core of your wealth, you are convinced that it doesn't matter if your wealth plan excludes a few assets. After all, you want to preserve your independence and flexibility and keep costs low. You never know what investments may capture your attention, and you want to have some capital available to deploy. You want the freedom to take action independently.

Deep down, you suspect your adviser may discourage you from making certain investments or they may share them with others. In some cases, you may doubt your adviser would be able to understand the complexities of the investment itself or why it appeals to you. On one hand, you believe they may try to disrupt your intentions—perhaps because something wasn't their idea or maybe because they won't be compensated for it. On the other hand, if your adviser accepts incorporating investments that they haven't sourced into your portfolio and monitoring them within your overall asset allocation, you assume they'll then have to charge you for these services. This is grating, primarily because you sourced these ideas and did the analysis that determined it could be a good investment. Moreover, if they do think it's a good investment, there's the risk that they'll try to adopt it for their other clients. Your source could be inundated with inappropriate requests and regret sharing it with you. This doesn't sit well with you.

You are, therefore, quite confident that you don't need to incorporate all of your investments into your wealth plan. Keeping those investments you've independently sourced out of the discussion is the best course of action to follow. It preserves your independence and flexibility and reduces your costs. No one is likely to convince you otherwise. While confidence is important, the type of certainty that prevents you from evaluating alternative arguments can mean you've encountered a blind spot. If you are focused on building and transferring your legacy, it may be worthwhile to re-examine your approach. Incorporating "outside investments" into your wealth planning process may provide new insights into ways to grow and transfer your wealth that reduce risk and/or improve your after-tax estate. As successful as any "outside" investments might be on their own, you may find that by including them in your plan, you'll have made more of them, and opportunities to grow and transfer your legacy may have been enhanced rather than constrained.

FOMO or Fundamentals?

Let's begin by considering the emotional drivers that can underpin independently sourcing outside investments. Fear of missing out (FOMO) and its underlying psychological factors: the potentially blinding wish to identify with the apparently successful person advocating an investment, the willingness to accept the returns as advertised, and what's known as motivated reasoning serve as important reminders that "outside investments" can come with significant risks. These factors are often overlooked—especially because many of us want to believe that we are further evolved than to fall subject to our emotions.

Psychological Factors

Almost everyone today is familiar with FOMO. FOMO is "a pervasive apprehension that others might be having rewarding experiences from which one is absent," according to marketing strategist Dr. Dan Herman, who published the first academic paper on the topic in 2000 in *The Journal of Brand Management*.[1] While the acronym may be twenty-first century, the psychological underpinnings date back at least as far as the Tulipmania that gripped the Netherlands in the 1630s. Perhaps the most famous asset bubble of all time,[2] the Dutch tulip bulb market bubble was followed by the South Sea Company bubble of 1711–1720 and the Mississippi Company bubble of 1719–1720. The same psychological factors that underpin FOMO recur each time. Greed, the desire to accumulate wealth and social status, herd behavior, social influence, peer pressure, anchoring bias (the reliance on past prices), availability bias (reliance on prevalent narratives), overconfidence, and confirmation bias (selective use of information that supports one's beliefs)[3] were all at play. FOMO continues to be present in more recent speculative frenzies and animate today's concerns about a potential AI and/or cryptocurrency bubble. As much as we all may think we've learned our lesson, studies estimate that nearly 70% of adults in developed countries suffer from FOMO.[4]

It's tough to pause and ask yourself whether you're investing based on objective analysis—or just a fear of missing out. In the same way that you can easily ignore your inner voice telling you to pass up the next dessert, cocktail, or cigar, it's not difficult to focus on the potential return of an attractive investment idea without really evaluating the fundamentals that underpin it. The hype surrounding an idea, the excitement of something new, and the fun of talking about it—combined with the fact that others you respect are "in"—can push you to make an investment that, had you done some objective analysis, you might have avoided. If you've bought into a bubble or chased the latest investing fad only to lose your investment, you're certainly not alone. It's human nature to want to get in on what everybody else is doing.

The Desire for Identification

What's more, FOMO is exacerbated when you identify with the person extolling the benefits of the investment. Although it's sometimes natural to think the person advocating the investment is just like you, it's often not the case. Remember, your financial situation is unlikely to be similar to theirs, and what you are hearing may not reflect how the investment actually works.

When you identify with someone, it's particularly challenging to pause and consider how different you actually are and how little you may know about their financial situation. Do you know their risk tolerance, portfolio size, investment skill, or level of financial understanding? You may not know or lose sight of the fact that they are significantly wealthier than you are and easily able to tolerate loss, whereas you are less so. You may not know or ignore the fact that they recently suffered a loss and are actively reaching for additional risk to try to achieve what they hope will be a life-changing return. On one hand, this individual may have invested a tiny percentage of their portfolio, the loss of which would be inconsequential for them, whereas for you, it would matter greatly. On the other hand, they may have invested much more than you would ever consider and are "talking their book"—touting an investment they already own to help increase its value. People tend to talk only about their successful investments and rarely discuss when they lost money. It's challenging to determine how talented an investor they truly are overall.

It's also unlikely that you can evaluate the depth of their investment skill or judgment from one cocktail party discussion. Keep in mind that you can't be certain that they, themselves, fully understand the details surrounding the investment and are correctly explaining them to you. They may be bragging about a successful investment without taking into account the associated fees or taxes, or its performance in prior years, all of which may make it much less profitable over the long term than it appears.

Motivated Reasoning

Perhaps you believe you are immune to emotional drivers and are someone who simply wants the independence and flexibility to make investments "on your own." Your reluctance to share your thoughts with your financial adviser stems from your confidence in the strength of your analytical skills. You are not caught up in FOMO and don't succumb to emotional pressures. You can evaluate investments objectively on your own. You don't want to deal with convincing your adviser, especially if it's a complex investment you don't think they'll understand fully, or have the discussion about paying fees for an investment you sourced.

Keep in mind that even in this case, a subtler form of FOMO can be at play. Even when you've conducted thorough research that suggests an opportunity is a good investment, there is always the risk that your analysis was influenced by "motivated reasoning"—subjective preferences, emotions, or motivations. In her transformational article, "The Case for Motivated Reasoning[5]", Israeli social psychologist and Princeton professor Ziva Kunda explains that "the notion that goals or motives affect reasoning has a long and controversial history in social psychology." Her research settled much of the controversy by proving that "motivation may affect reasoning through reliance on a biased set of cognitive processes: strategies for accessing, constructing, and evaluating beliefs . . . it is now clear that directional goals do affect reasoning. People are more likely to arrive at those conclusions that they want to arrive at." In other words, how you conduct your research can be influenced by your desired outcome, providing you with compelling yet possibly flawed confidence to act based on an analysis subtly molded by your desires or subjective perspective. While this may be difficult to accept for those of us analytical types, we need to consider that we may have unacknowledged emotional or cognitive biases that create the illusion of objectivity in our analysis. Or we may be rationalizing our desire to invest by using seemingly logical reasoning to justify what is really an emotionally driven desire.

Excluding Your Adviser

Whether emotionally driven or the result of your analytical skills, you've decided to make investments on your own without bringing your adviser into the conversation or making them aware of the assets. Given that the adviser is managing what you believe to be your core capital, you don't think that omitting one or two additional investments can really affect your overall future. You believe that you can afford to extend yourself a little further.

The key issues to address are whether, by omitting these investments, you are inadvertently increasing risks to your legacy or missing opportunities to enhance it. Concerning increasing risks to your legacy, the first question to answer is whether what you've identified as your core capital is really sufficient to meet your spending goals or whether you might actually need the funds allocated to outside investments to meet your lifestyle needs. The second question is whether your outside investments are increasing your overall risk to an unanticipated degree. It may seem unlikely, but sometimes, even one more investment may put you in a situation where, for example, your concentration risk becomes potentially damaging to your lifestyle and/or your liquidity is severely constrained. A third important question is whether the outside investments unduly constrain your liquidity (access to cash). As opposed to increasing risk, when it comes to missing opportunities to enhance your legacy, the question becomes whether you are overlooking ways to help make the most of your outside investments by ignoring planning techniques that might arise if you evaluated them within the context of your overall wealth plan.

Risk: Core Capital Sufficiency

Consider Josh, who loved attending cocktail parties where he knew there would be numerous "finance types" from whom he could learn what investments were popular. Although Josh's wealth plan called for investing the proceeds from the sale of his home back into the portfolio, upon the sale, Josh sent only 90% of the proceeds to Amy, his adviser, explaining that they had actually received less from the sale than the plan called for. He kept the other 10% to invest on his own so that he could act on what he learned at the various cocktail parties he attended. He assumed that adding 90% to his portfolio would be good enough—how bad could it be to hold back 10%? After all, it was easy to believe that he might not have received 100% of his asking price from the sale of the house in the first place. When the proceeds from the home sale were added to his portfolio, Amy updated Josh's wealth plan, noting that his probability of successfully meeting all his goals without running out of money had decreased and was now on the lower border of the confidence zone. Amy became concerned. The plan had called for the entire proceeds to become part of the core capital Josh and his wife would rely on to maintain the growth necessary to have a probability of success within the confidence zone—and now the capital was less than expected. Despite Amy's desire to meet to look for alternative paths, Josh didn't seem worried at all and repeatedly brushed off Amy's concerns. The situation remained the same for several years. Amy and Josh would meet to review the plan. When Amy raised ways that the probability of success could be increased, Josh listened, understood, but did not want to take any action. Finally, at one meeting, Josh focused much more keenly on what Amy was suggesting. What Amy wasn't aware of was the fact that while Josh's outside investments had grown in the first year, they declined substantially in the subsequent four years. He was left with half of the 10% he had initially held back. Without explaining what had happened, he told Amy he had some funds he could add to the portfolio. While the funds helped to slightly increase the portfolio's probability of successfully meeting Josh's goals, the fact that they were half of what had been expected and delayed by five years (therefore having lost the ability to compound in the core portfolio for five years) meant that Josh still had to take additional steps. Although it didn't seem to Josh that holding back the 10% would matter, the outside investment had significantly reduced the core capital needed to meet all his spending goals. At this point, to bring his probability of success back into the confidence zone, Amy could only recommend that he reduce their charitable giving and delay some discretionary spending plans.

Although those actions would improve his situation, it wasn't the way Josh had envisioned the next few years. Had Josh brought Amy into the discussion up front, he might have avoided having to take these steps. He would have known up front how significant the 10% was to the probability of success. He would have been able to make a more informed decision about allocating capital to some outside investments. Amy might have been able to carve out a smaller yet still meaningful amount of capital for Josh to use by testing smaller amounts and/or delaying its use, allowing it to grow inside the portfolio.

One way to make room for outside investments is to establish a "play bucket." Working with Amy before the sale of his house, Josh might have been able to identify a portion of his portfolio that could have been safely excluded from what his core capital (those assets needed to maintain a high likelihood of meeting his wealth management goals). Josh's non-core assets could have been side-pocketed to a separate account that was not part of his discretionary portfolio on which he paid fees. This would have provided a fund from which Josh could have tested his ideas with the assurance that, even if they failed, his legacy would not likely be at risk. Josh could have explored investments knowing that if he lost money from that bucket or if it became tied up longer than he expected, his lifestyle and goals were not likely to have been affected. The size of the "play bucket" could be adjusted, or part of the assets could be transferred to another structure, if Josh achieved substantial success or failure with an investment.

Bringing Amy into the conversation earlier would have made Josh aware of the risks and potential opportunities of making outside investments. He could have made them with greater knowledge of what the outcome might be. By excluding Amy from his thinking rather than enlisting her help, Josh reduced his options and increased his risks.

Risk: Over-Concentration

Edna was considering adding to her position in ABC following the company's strong results in its fiscal second quarter that ended in March 2025 and the announcement of a $100 billion stock buyback program. If the company had such confidence in buying back its stock at that price, she thought it made sense for her to follow suit and make a sizeable investment. Although she had mentioned that she held a few shares of ABC in an outside account, she didn't share the number of shares she owned with Jim, her adviser. Whenever Jim inquired about the holding, she replied that she really owned very little and would never sell her shares because she would have to pay sizable capital gains taxes as she had bought them long ago at a much lower cost than the current market value. No matter how many times Jim tried to get her to open up and include the holding in her wealth plan, Edna didn't budge. She felt she had done pretty well on her own with this investment and wanted to keep adding to it. She didn't realize that ABC was also part of her core portfolio holdings. Jim eventually stopped pressing her and accepted the fact that she didn't hold very much. Edna's largest U.S. equity holding in her overall portfolio was the S&P 500 Index. By April 2025, ABC's market capitalization represented 5.8% of the S&P 500 Index. After Edna more than doubled her outside position, her personal exposure to ABC increased to more than 10% of her overall portfolio—but neither she nor Jim was aware of that concentration level. Had Jim been aware, he might have apprised Edna of the concentration risk she was taking on. If something happened to ABC, her portfolio was at risk of losing as much as 10% of its value. He might have counseled Edna to reduce her ownership to no more than 5% of the overall portfolio. Many advisers apply a 5% maximum rule of thumb to single stock ownership to preserve diversification and manage risk. By capping ownership at that level, one can mitigate potential portfolio loss from a company's poor performance or an unexpected event such as a corporate scandal. As a result of excluding Jim, Edna's risk to her legacy remains elevated.

Risk: Constrained Liquidity

Jeff had more than 30% of his portfolio invested in private investments and sought to increase that allocation. There was nothing Jeff liked better than learning about new investments that weren't widely distributed and being able to invest in them. Jeff relied on the distributions from one set of private investments to meet the capital calls from newer investments. Not wanting to realize any capital gains by selling his low-basis public equities, he used the income from his municipal bonds to cover his living expenses. Everything seemed to work perfectly. Jeff came from the financial services industry and felt confident that he only needed an adviser to manage his bond portfolio. He would oversee his private investments personally and keep his low-basis equities in a separate account as he had no interest in selling them. Jeff's adviser, Jeanne, was aware of his portfolio structure and repeatedly counseled him to consider the potential liquidity risks. She was concerned with how he would raise cash if it became necessary. First, in her view, the overall allocation of 30% to private investments was high and meant that if Jeff needed a large sum unexpectedly (for medical expenses, a significant purchase, or help for one of his children), it might be difficult to convert any of the private investments to cash. Private investments have restrictions on the timing and availability of withdrawal windows, and it can take time to return funds even after the window has been used. He might be forced to sell his low-basis equities and pay significant taxes or reduce his bond holdings. Not only would a sale of his municipal bonds reduce his income, but he might also realize less from the sale of a bond than he had anticipated. There can be a significant price reduction when selling a municipal bond before maturity due to the reduced liquidity in the municipal market compared to Treasuries or major corporate bonds, especially for small sizes or issuers during periods of market stress. Second, Jeanne pointed out that although distributions from certain funds had been able to cover capital calls from others, that might not always hold true. The timing of both can change in times of market stress. Again, without any sort of cash cushion to meet those needs, Jeff would be forced to sell either equities or municipal bonds, and depending on the market stress, those values could be depressed. Third, Jeanne addressed his reliance on bond income to cover living expenses. If interest rates declined (reducing future coupons), any of his bond issuers defaulted (shrinking his holdings), or inflation increased (reducing the purchasing power of his income), he would again be put in the position of selling low-basis equities and/or redeeming from a private investment over time. She acknowledged that his structure worked for the moment but was concerned that it might not hold. She explained that situations that seem manageable in "normal" periods may not be in the face of economic slowdowns, recessions, or another black swan event (an event no one predicted but that significantly impacts your wealth, either globally or in your own life such as September 11, the 2008 Financial Crisis, or COVID-19). Jeff agreed that everything was working, believed it would continue, and decided he didn't need an adviser.

When the pandemic occurred, distributions from Jeff's private investments slowed down and his capital calls increased, putting him in a situation where he had to sell assets that he had preferred to keep. As Jeanne had cautioned, he was now forced to sell some equities at a steep discount since the S&P 500 had declined sharply and still pay capital gains taxes. Had Jeff worked with Jeanne, he might have been able to liquidate some positions at higher levels to create a cash cushion that would have sustained him in times of market stress rather than significantly reducing his overall capital.

Opportunities: Identifying Ways to Enhance Your Legacy

In addition to inadvertently increasing risks to your legacy by omitting investments from discussion with your adviser, you may also be missing opportunities to enhance it by structuring the investment more efficiently. Analyzing the potential sources of funds for the investment as well as its goals (e.g., income for you, growth for you or your heirs) within the context of your overall wealth plan can lead to outcomes that have a better chance of meeting your objectives. Perhaps funding it from an account you hadn't thought of or executing it outside your estate in a trust for your children or grandchildren would enhance your legacy by removing it from a portfolio that would pay estate taxes?

Jason was planning to invest some of his personal funds in one of the new compelling private opportunities he had been shown. Once he understood that his adviser, Susan, wasn't surprised or offended by the fact that others were showing him investment opportunities, Jason shared the details with her. Susan suggested that Jason fund the opportunity from his IRA rather than from his taxable account. She was able to show Jason that she could reallocate his IRA to make room for this investment, incorporate it, and maintain his overall target asset allocation. Not only did Jason not have to sell taxable investments to fund it from his taxable account, but by using the IRA, he had shifted the investment into an account in which he wouldn't have to pay annual income tax. In addition, Jeff's initial hesitation to disclose the origin of his investment idea to his adviser proved to be unfounded. As a discerning and seasoned professional, she had no intention of appropriating the opportunity for other clients. Susan's knowledge and established access to investment products rendered it unnecessary for her even to consider appropriating the idea for other clients. Moreover, she fully understood and respected the exclusivity of Jason's private source.

Ellen wanted to purchase additional life insurance to increase her children's inheritance. She knew that creating an irrevocable life insurance trust (ILIT) and having the ILIT purchase the policy would mean that the death benefits would be excluded from her estate and therefore be available for the kids to use to pay her estate taxes. Confident in her understanding of the transaction, she almost didn't bring it up with her adviser, Peter. Ellen wanted to leave as much as she could to her children and had both charitable intent and a very large Traditional IRA. When she casually mentioned the idea over lunch, Peter, who had a deep knowledge of her resources and legacy goals, was able to suggest a different, far more powerful structure. He proposed she consider converting the IRA to a Roth IRA so that her children would receive a tax-free account with the possibility of continuing to grow it tax-free for 10 years following her death. To offset the income tax that would be due from her conversion, he suggested she create and fund a charitable lead annuity trust (CLAT); the CLAT would use the donated funds to purchase bonds, along with the life insurance policy. His analysis showed that upon her passing, the death benefits would satisfy the donation to the charity, which was entitled to some additional proceeds for the children. Although complex, this transaction would leave the children with tax-free Roth proceeds plus some additional death benefits and provide a meaningful donation to the charity. It also left her estate smaller as a result of converting her IRA from Traditional to Roth, thereby reducing some of her estate tax. By bringing her adviser into what had initially appeared to be an isolated insurance transaction, Ellen was able to expand her legacy significantly.

It takes tremendous self-discipline and introspection to resist temptation and genuinely consider whether FOMO or potential overconfidence might be underlying your behavior. Unfortunately, either can cause you to take actions that don't serve your best interest. In both cases, your adviser can provide valuable assistance. Even if the investment proves to be worthwhile, bringing your adviser into the discussion provides validation and an essential safety net. Ask yourself whether your reluctance to discuss this investment with your adviser is simply because you are letting your emotions take over or you don't want to hear the other perspective. By independently evaluating the risk/return characteristics of the investment and incorporating it into your overall plan, you'll be able to see the effect it has on your probability of success in meeting your objectives.

Each time you want to invest, it is crucial to consider the potential impact on your wealth management plan, liquidity, and lifestyle. That's what your adviser is there for. They are experienced in integrating investments, evaluating the pros and cons, and discussing them with you. Utilizing your wealth management plan to test and integrate a new investment can help you conduct an objective analysis against which to evaluate the investment.

Bringing Your Adviser into the Conversation

Realizing you may not want to exclude your adviser from discussing "outside investments" and may even want to include them in your overall wealth plan, how do you handle what might be an awkward conversation? Let's consider three possible issues. First, the question of paying fees on investments you've sourced. Second, handling potential pushback from the adviser. Third, the possible roots of reluctance to discuss the information.

Your hesitation to address the question of fees on an investment you sourced can be overcome in one of two ways. If you've asked your adviser to help carve out a "play bucket" and that will be from where your outside investments are made, then the issue of paying fees on those outside investments is unlikely to arise. If, on the other hand, you've asked your adviser to review the investment(s) and give you their opinion on its potential soundness as well as how it might be incorporated into your wealth plan, then paying fees on these investments can become more easily accepted. If the investment becomes integrated into your plan, you are likely to recognize the substantial analysis and advice provided by your adviser that enabled her to endorse it and incorporate it into your plan through a structure that adds value to your legacy. In addition, you are likely to appreciate the fact that the investment will contribute to your portfolio not just because it was added but also thanks to the ongoing monitoring, rebalancing, and discussions with your adviser. You understand that you are paying fees for services that go far beyond the sourcing you may have provided.

If your adviser pushes back on the investment, consider that they may be looking out for your best interests rather than objecting to an investment they didn't source. Reflect on the possibility that your adviser's resistance might be a good thing, because your adviser has your best interests at heart. When a client brings an adviser a new investment they're very excited about, it's far easier for the adviser to support their client. It's flattering to the client if the adviser gets on board, agrees that the investment sounds like a great opportunity, and encourages them to invest. Even if the adviser is forsaking some capital addition to the portfolio, agreeing makes the client feel good and can preserve the relationship for the adviser. What's more, it's likely to be a long time before the impact of a poor decision affects the portfolio. Consider how much more challenging it is for the adviser to push back on your idea. In the end, you may not enjoy their critique, but through understanding their objections, you may learn something that may help you in the future. Consider whether, rather than avoiding the pushback, you may want your wealth manager to be highly selective on your behalf.

Finally, if you are truly reluctant to bring your adviser into the conversation and just want them to focus on what you've given them to manage, if deep down, you suspect your adviser may discourage you from making certain investments for their own reasons or you believe your adviser would be unable to understand the complexities of the investment itself, then consider for a moment what this could be telling you about the relationship you have with your adviser. Your discomfort should be trusted. It may indicate that your adviser lacks the level of trust, experience, and communication that your situation warrants. You may be right, and if your goal is to build and transfer your legacy, the answer then would be to consider moving on to a new adviser in whom you have more trust and confidence. (More about this in Blind Spot 10.)

Financial Health Management

As with managing your health, the goal isn't to continually change your diet and exercise regimen to incorporate every new superfood or workout routine but rather to develop the discipline and discernment to be selective in your choices and create a balance of elements that positively affect your well-being.

The same is true of wealth management. It's not just about having access to investment ideas—it's about fitting them into a framework that includes risk management and diversification so that you know whether an idea is right for you. Just as you would consult a doctor before taking a new medicine, working with your adviser can add knowledge you may not have considered. And just as you would find a new doctor if you found yourself uncomfortable sharing your concerns with them, you might consider finding a new adviser if you felt similarly.

Your wealth management plan provides the framework. Since it is customized to your family's particular situation—your asset base, different account types, earning potential, age, tax rate, unique family circumstances, specific risk tolerance, and aspirations, and models of possible scenarios over time—it reveals risks and opportunities to the knowledgeable adviser. Evaluating a new investment within the context of that plan enables you and your adviser to consider all these factors, test the investment's impact on the probability of successfully meeting your goals, and help build the legacy you envision.

Does Every Asset Need to Be in Your Plan?

If you are focused on building and transferring your legacy, then incorporating "outside investments" into your wealth planning process may provide new insights into ways to grow and transfer your wealth that reduce risk and/or improve your after-tax estate. By including them in your plan, you may be able to reduce your risk and enhance your opportunities to grow and transfer your legacy.

Key Takeaways

- Omitting certain investments from your wealth plan may expose you to risks—such as over-concentration, reduced liquidity, or insufficient core capital to meet your long-term goals. It may also mean missing opportunities to structure those investments more efficiently, uncover tax advantages, and enhance your legacy through planning techniques that emerge only when all assets are considered together.
- Emotional biases like FOMO and overconfidence can influence even experienced investors. Working on a wealth plan with an adviser helps you test ideas objectively within a disciplined framework and can help you avoid decisions driven by hype or peer influence.
- Independence and flexibility can still be preserved within a structured plan. Tools like "play buckets" or side accounts may allow you to pursue personal investment ideas without compromising your overall strategy.
- Bringing your adviser into the conversation can unlock strategic advantages. When you share all your investments—including those you've sourced independently—your adviser can help you assess risks, uncover tax efficiencies, and structure opportunities in ways that better support your legacy goals.
- Transparency with your adviser doesn't mean giving up control. It means gaining insight, validation, and the ability to make more informed decisions. Constructive pushback can be a sign of a strong advisory relationship.
- Reluctance to share certain investments might signal a deeper issue of trust or confidence in your adviser. If that's

the case, it may be worth reassessing the relationship to help ensure you're supported by someone who understands and respects your goals.
- A well-designed wealth plan functions like a health plan—it's not about reacting to every new opportunity but about integrating the right ones in a way that supports long-term well-being.

Blind Spot 7

"I Can Focus on My Wealth Planning After I Sell My Business"

There are 36.2 million small businesses[1] in the United States. Small businesses are defined as those independently owned and operated for-profit businesses that have 500 employees or fewer, if they are manufacturing companies, or average annual receipts under $7.5 million[2] if they are nonmanufacturing businesses. Small businesses represent 99.9% of all U.S. businesses and employ more than 59 million people, nearly half (46%[3]) of American workers. Baby Boomers own 41%[4] of small businesses (12 million) and are expected to turn over $10 to $14 trillion of business value in the next eight years.[5]

On average, equity in their business represents 34% of a family's nonfinancial assets, exceeded only by the value of their primary residence at 45%.[6] Yet despite its financial importance, nearly 60% of privately held business owners lack a transition plan.[7] Even among older owners, those age 65 or older, 47%[8] still do not have a transition plan in place. Moreover, among those who have sold their businesses, *the overwhelming majority*, 81%,[9] regretted not preparing earlier.

Small business owners can often find themselves in one of two situations: either postponing wealth planning due to the overwhelming task of juggling daily operations with complex planning or moving ahead too quickly when a purchase offer arises without laying the strategic groundwork for wealth planning that could help them grow and transfer their legacy.

It's understandable that even contemplating the sale of your business while running it can make you want to postpone planning. In a 2025 study by Wilmington Trust, the top reason, cited by 42%[10] of sample respondents for not having a transition plan, was that they were too busy to start planning for a sale. You may feel overwhelmed. You need to keep the business running at full speed and growing, while simultaneously figuring out how to get an appropriate valuation, find the right purchaser, decide whether and how to involve your family, make sure your employees continue to be looked after with the same level of care you provide, and find time to execute the transaction. In addition, deciding whether to sell the business outright or keep it within the family may also be a stumbling block, involving the need to reconcile competing priorities and strong emotions. Undertaking a transition plan for the business appears to be an enormous and time-consuming endeavor. You've delayed deciding what to do and how to do it because the outcomes appear unclear, complex, or unappealing, and you just don't have time. You care deeply about your company's future and the implications of the sale on the well-being of your loved ones, your employees, and your customers. You may even believe you owe more time and attention

"I Can Focus on My Wealth Planning After I Sell My Business"

to your stakeholders and the business than to yourself. You hope to ensure optimal outcomes for all these stakeholders, so for now, you keep deferring wealth planning for yourself, believing you'll address the sale and its implications for your wealth at some point in the future.

If, on the other hand, you are approached with an unsolicited offer by a potential purchaser or their agent or the idea arises organically in a conversation, it's human nature to want to respond and follow through. Once again, thoughts of personal wealth planning are often put to the side because you want to begin immediately analyzing the opportunity. The potential values presented may be more than you anticipated and may be realized far earlier than you may have thought possible. You're flattered by their confidence in your business and what you've accomplished. You may feel validated by their proposals and may be concerned that if you do not move quickly, they may disappear. You may have personal goals or dreams of starting another business that the proceeds from this sale could help make a reality long before you ever expected. You simply don't have time to do wealth planning before the sale. Here, too, you are not alone. Among owners who sold their businesses, 73% spent two years or less preparing for the sale—with 32% spending less than a year and 41% taking one to two years.[11]

In both cases, planning for your personal wealth, beyond simply trying to grow it to increase the valuation of the business, can often take a back seat. Deep down, you may believe that increasing the business valuation will more than offset any costs you may encounter due to a lack of personal planning. You may even suspect that planning won't make that much of a difference to your future. As tempting as it may be to think you'll get to wealth planning "later" or after you sell, this blind spot can be far more costly to your business and your legacy than you might initially appreciate.

Advance Planning

Delaying your personal wealth planning until after a sale can be very costly. Before the sale of a business, you have the opportunity to take steps that can significantly increase your wealth, steps that will disappear if you wait. This is a one-time opportunity that it is advisable to complete well in advance of a sale, ideally 12–36 months, to provide you with the flexibility to take as many steps as practical and not be at risk of the IRS challenging them as transactions designed solely to avoid tax.

Planning early can enhance your legacy across five categories: estate planning, tax efficiency, legal structuring, family governance, and wealth planning. Estate planning sets the overall framework for who receives what assets, when (upon death, second-to-die, while living), and how (type of structure). Through the use and timing of different structures, tax efficiency tries to reduce the taxes paid or due and optimize when they are paid. Legal structuring is the foundation that makes estate planning legally enforceable. It is the bridge between strategy and execution but requires time to draft and redraft documents. With respect to family governance, early planning can create an opportunity to align family goals, avoid conflict, and preserve legacy across generations. Wealth planning can help you estimate the amount you need to net from the sale to meet your retirement, philanthropic, and legacy goals. Each of these five areas requires time and teamwork on the part of your wealth adviser, estate planning attorney, accountant, insurance agent, and philanthropic adviser. These are complex and significant decisions that require time to analyze and put in place.

Estate Planning

As of 2026, Americans have a lifetime gift/estate tax exemption[12] of $15 million per individual or $30 million per couple, increased annually for inflation. This means your estate would be subject to estate taxes if your net worth exceeds that limit upon your death or the second to die in a couple. Federal estate tax rates range from 18 to 40% with the average effective tax rate across all taxable estates typically in the 16–20% range[13] after deductions and credits. In addition, 10 states impose state estate taxes ranging from 12 to 20%. Once you've used up your lifetime gift and estate tax exemption, assets left to your estate would be subject to federal and state estate tax. You can significantly reduce the value of your estate by using your gift/estate tax exemption to gift shares to individuals or structures (trusts) outside your estate while you are alive.

If your current net worth makes it seem like reaching the $15 or $30 million limit is unlikely, it's important to remember the effects of compounding. To reach the $15 million limit, an estate 20 years from now would need to be worth only $5.6 million today at a 5% real (after inflation) growth rate. If you have a time horizon of 30 years, a net worth of $3.5 million today would reach the limit, and if you are a young entrepreneur with a 40-year horizon, a net worth of $2.1 million would reach the limit. Remember too, that your estate includes all your assets, not just your financial assets and your business but also your other nonfinancial assets such as your home.

If, on the other hand, you are approaching or already have a net worth above the limit, then the sale of your business is likely to engender an estate tax bill. Advance planning may help you reduce its size. Gifting assets before a sale to a structure outside of your estate can reduce the value of your estate and, therefore, lower your estate tax obligation. What's more, depending on how they are structured, transfers may allow for valuation discounts due to a lack of control or marketability, enabling you to remove a greater amount from your estate than is used up from your lifetime exemption.

In her thirties, Susan founded and grew a health and beauty business, which is currently valued at $50 million. She hopes to sell it within the next two years for at least $60 million. She and her husband want to pass the proceeds to their children and grandchildren while minimizing estate taxes. Susan's wealth manager, Shelley, advises her to consider using a Dynasty Trust. A Dynasty Trust is a long-term irrevocable trust designed to preserve and transfer wealth across multiple generations while minimizing the impact of estate, gift, and generation-skipping transfer tax (GSTT). The GSTT is a federal tax (at 40%) applied to gifts that "skip" a generation. It is designed to prevent bypassing estate taxes that would otherwise be due if assets were transferred to the next generation. Shelley explains that Susan would transfer shares of the business into the Dynasty Trust using her and her husband's lifetime gift exemption before taking any steps involving a potential sale. This transfer could be structured so the business can qualify for a valuation discount due to lack of marketability, reducing the size of Susan's gift from $50 million to, for example, $37.5 million. As a result, Susan would pay gift taxes of $3 million at 40% of $7.5 million—the amount over the $30 million exemption—even though she transferred $50 million of value into the trust. Had she not received the valuation discount she would have paid $8 million in gift taxes (40% of $20 million, the amount over the $30 million exemption). Moreover, assuming Susan sells the business for $60 million, the proceeds will be received by the trust and will therefore be outside Susan's estate. If she had kept the business in her estate, she would have paid $12 million in gift taxes (40% on $30 million that exceeded the $30 million exemption). The Dynasty Trust reduced her gift tax bill from $12 million to $3 million.

What's more, the primary objective of a Dynasty Trust is long-term wealth preservation, and it is written to last for multiple generations. Most states still enforce the Rule Against Perpetuities, which traditionally limits the life of trusts to 21 years after the death of the last measuring life, typically the youngest beneficiary alive at the trust's creation. While this can still offer decades of protection, Shelley explained that Susan could have the trust drafted in a more favorable state, like Delaware, where it can be perpetual. The longer the trust exists, the longer the assets Susan has gifted can grow estate tax-free for her children and grandchildren. At a 5% return, over

30 years, the $60 million would grow to $259 million. In addition, assets in the trust can be shielded from claims by creditors or divorcing spouses. Since Susan could afford the tax bill from her and her husband's assets, she saw creating the Dynasty Trust as a powerful tool to pass on wealth from the sale of her business. Fortunately, she had discussed this with Shelley in time to put everything in place before starting the sale process. Had Susan waited to implement this strategy close to the start of the sale process, the IRS might have challenged the legitimacy of the transfer.

Tax Efficiency

Estate planning and tax efficiency often overlap and reinforce each other. However, there can be meaningful distinctions between the two. Whereas the goal of estate planning is wealth transfer across generations and, when well executed, can reduce taxes, the goal of tax efficiency is to minimize tax liabilities more immediately. The need for tax-efficient planning is often triggered by a liquidity event, such as the sale of a business, where estate planning is often considered as a result of aging, incapacity, death, or generational wealth transfers. The focus of tax efficiency is on valuation discounts and the timing and structuring of transactions, more than on control, asset protection, and family governance characteristic of estate planning.

Don is the majority owner of ABC LLC, a business valued at $10 million. Don forms the Smith Family Partnership LLC with his wife and children as members. He then transfers 40% ($4 million) of ABC into the Smith Family Partnership. Since Don is transferring his own assets, this is not a gift. It is an exchange of assets for membership interests in Smith. Don typically names himself as the managing member of the newly funded LLC, giving him control over investment decisions, distributions, and admission of new members. This enables him to retain control of Smith even after gifting some of the economic interest in the business. Next, Don will gift 98%

nonvoting membership interests to his wife and children, retaining 2% ownership, voting rights, and managing member status. The nonvoting, minority membership interests are still considered minority interests because Don is the managing member and exercises control. As a result, the minority interests qualify for a valuation discount because there is no public market for ABC, transfers by minority members are restricted, there is limited liquidity, and each owns a minority interest. Assuming 30% valuation discount, Don's gift of $3.92 million (98% of $4 million) is reduced by $1.176 million to $2.74 million. Assuming a 40% federal estate tax rate and no state estate tax, Don has saved his heirs $470,400 in estate taxes ($1,176,000 × 0.40 = $470,400). Don has removed $3.92 million from his estate but has used only $2.74 million of his lifetime gift exemption. Because Don gifted shares at the current business valuation, which is likely to be lower than the eventual sale price valuation, he used up less of his lifetime credit. Don and his wife are still left with $27.26 million in exemptions.

The longer Don waits to implement this strategy, the closer it gets to the sale ABC, and the more likely it is that the applicable valuation discount will be reduced or disallowed. Whereas in the case of Susan creating a Dynasty Trust, the IRS might be focussed on the legitimacy of the transfer, in Don's case, they are likely to be focused on the justification for the valuation discount and whether the transaction was engendered by the sale of ABC and executed purely to avoid taxes. Consider that like Don, you may be able to maximize the use of gifting strategies as long as you implement them well in advance of a sale. The Internal Revenue Service (IRS) has three years to audit the gifting of closely held shares. As a result, it is wise to implement these strategies two to three years in advance of a sale not just to reduce your taxes but also because potential purchasers would not want to take the risk of unstable or disputed ownership structures.

Planning strategies available to you before a sale to reduce the tax bite and enhance your resources become inaccessible once even a letter of intent is in place. A letter of intent (LOI) is a nonbinding agreement that outlines the potential transaction. It includes the proposed purchase price, transaction structure, timing of the transaction, right to exclusivity for a period of time, and nondisclosure agreement to maintain confidentiality during the due diligence process. Once an LOI is in place, your gifting options become reduced. The valuation and illiquidity discounts may disappear or be harder to justify. You will be gifting portions of the business that carry the valuation in the LOI, which is likely to be higher than your current valuation. In addition, after obtaining an LOI, you are no longer able to apply the valuation discount due to lack of marketability since the business is closer to liquidity. This will increase the taxable value of the shares you are gifting and means your lifetime gift credit (the amount you can give away without paying gift taxes) will not go as far.

Legal Structuring

Legal structuring is the foundation that transforms wealth planning from concept to enforceable reality. It involves designing and implementing the legal entities, trusts, agreements, and governance frameworks that support your estate and tax strategies. This includes drafting trust documents, forming LLCs or partnerships, creating buy-sell agreements, and ensuring compliance with federal and state laws. Legal structuring is not just paperwork—it's the architecture that helps ensure your intentions are carried out, your assets are protected, and your legacy is preserved. Because these structures must be tailored to your unique goals, family dynamics, and business complexities, they require time to develop, review, and refine. Rushing this process can lead to costly errors, missed opportunities, or IRS scrutiny. Starting early allows for thoughtful collaboration among advisers, proper sequencing of transactions, and the flexibility to adapt as circumstances evolve—making legal structuring a critical pillar of successful pre-sale planning.

In addition, structures and opportunities to enhance your resources need to be put in place before the sale. Have you evaluated the optimal structure and timing of a sale? Are there significant estate planning documents, such as trusts or LLCs, that need to be drawn up for gifting purposes? Are you sufficiently insured for the unexpected, or might you need to take out key man or other types of insurance? Have you implemented incentives to encourage your employees to stay with the business during a transition? Do you have the optimal corporate structure? Have you formulated a communications plan for your employees and customers?

Family Governance

When a founder prepares to sell a business, family governance becomes especially critical—not just to preserve wealth but to manage the emotional and strategic complexities that arise when children have differing levels of interest or involvement. Some heirs may have worked in the business and feel deeply connected to its legacy, while others may prefer to pursue independent paths. These differences can lead to tension, confusion, or unmet expectations if not addressed proactively.

Family meetings before a sale can provide a structured way to clarify roles, align values, and set expectations for how the proceeds will be managed and distributed. Meetings may involve sharing and discussing the founder's goals and vision, as well as addressing the potential role of children in the business and how to compensate or equalize benefits for those who do or don't wish to work in the business. In the case where a business will be fully sold and the proceeds remain in a shared trust, these meetings can help determine and explain how the assets are going to be managed. Structures like investment committees or a family council may be created to help ensure that all voices are heard and that decisions about shared assets—whether reinvested, donated, or used to fund future ventures—reflect a collective understanding.

Importantly, this process takes time. It requires open dialogue, emotional readiness, and often professional guidance to navigate sensitive topics like fairness, control, and legacy. Rushing these conversations after the sale, when wealth has already changed hands, can lead to conflict, resentment, or fragmentation. However, when done early and thoughtfully, family governance becomes a powerful tool for unity, helping the family transition from operating a business to stewarding a legacy.

Wealth Planning

Wealth planning is typically the bedrock for almost all decisions regarding the sale of a business. Planning for the sale of your business and personal wealth planning go hand in hand and reinforce each other. Wealth planning can help you estimate the amount you need to net from the sale to meet your retirement, philanthropic, and legacy goals. Evaluating whether that is a realistic expectation for the sale proceeds can inform whether you are ready to sell or need additional time to grow the business. The target value for a sale can then feed back into your plan to help you evaluate the usefulness and impact of different estate and tax planning structures on your long-term wealth. Wealth planning can help you evaluate different scenarios for the full or partial sale of the business. The length and iterative nature of the process underscores the importance of allocating enough time in advance of a sale to take all the necessary steps that can help you build the legacy you envision.

Wealth Planning Roadmap

The good news is that your wealth adviser can provide significant help. Moreover, you can continue to focus on operating your business while your adviser leads you through the process of examining the sale of your company and implementing various estate and tax planning structures while taking into account your family's overall wealth and financial goals.

Figure 7.1 presents a typical roadmap for this process. It contains five basic steps: a preliminary valuation of the business to

Figure 7.1 Wealth Planning Roadmap

Understand Resources Available to Meet Needs	Identify Personal Financial Needs	Initial Wealth Modeling	Assess Need or Opportunity To Enhance Resources	Develop Exit Strategies and Timing
Preliminary Valuation	Spending Needs	Asset Allocation	Business Growth Potential	Exit Plan
Nature of Current Asset Base	Longevity Outlook	Probability of Success	Timing and Cost	Estate and Tax Structuring
	Gifting Objectives	Scenario Comparison	Insurance Assessment	Philanthropic Strategy
	Philanthropic Goals	Estate Taxes		Family Gifting
	Current Assets	Estate Flow		

understand the resources that could be at your disposal, a deep dive on the life you imagine post-transition and the legacy you would like to leave, a model of whether your resources will support your lifestyle and legacy goals for the rest of your life, an assessment of whether there is a need or an opportunity to grow the business further before selling, and, finally, the development of an exit plan and wealth transfer strategies customized to maximize your legacy.

Understand the Resources Available: Preliminary Valuation

Your adviser can begin by performing a preliminary valuation on your business using two to three years of financial statements or tax returns. Unless you are a small business, you're likely to eventually need a certified business valuation from an accredited professional to transact the sale of your business, gift shares, and file taxes. However, a preliminary valuation will be sufficient for wealth planning purposes. It will provide you with an estimate of the sale proceeds, evaluate the nature of your assets, and enable you to analyze the critical drivers to increase your valuation. You will be able to see the impact of further growth or efficiency on your valuation and estimate how long it will take to achieve a higher value. A preliminary valuation can also be used to attract or evaluate any interest when exploring a sale and help you better prepare for any unsolicited offers.

Identify Your Financial Needs, Aspirations, and Legacy Goals. Next, you'll begin wealth planning by evaluating your current spending needs, thinking about how those might change, and developing your legacy goals. Many sellers are deterred by the prospect of having to create a budget and involve their spouse in evaluating expenditures. Rather than causing a protracted delay or avoidance, this can be addressed by examining total spending (derived from take-home pay) and then identifying and adding back expenses that will continue and are incurred through your business. All that is needed is a reasonable estimate. As part of estimating your lifestyle post-sale, you'll consider questions such as:

- What are your spending needs likely to be to maintain your current lifestyle?
- What are your aspirations for lifestyle expansion, such as additional homes, travel, or family growth, and family support?
- Are you interested in transferring wealth only to the next generation, or are you interested in subsequent generations as well?
- What is your ideal scenario?
- Have you considered unexpected illness or long-term incapacity?
- How can you protect yourself against other potential (nonmarket) risks?

Initial Wealth Modeling

You and your adviser will then begin work on a comprehensive wealth model for you and your family. Since you now have an estimate of your sale proceeds, your wealth adviser can begin to integrate your financial needs and legacy goals above with the preliminary valuation into your wealth model. Modeling the evolution of your portfolio and the probability of successfully meeting your goals under different scenarios can help you home in on your preferred path. This requires iterative scenario building and testing.

If gifting is part of your goals, wealth planning will also give you a sense of the size of gifts you are able to make to family members and philanthropic interests. Analyzing the impact of receiving less from the sale proceeds now due to transferring ownership with a buy-out structure over time can also be incorporated. You'll be able to consider better the cost/benefits of selling to a family member or someone who needs to pay over time.

You will be able to test the probability of successfully meeting your goals under different asset allocations and retirement ages, business valuations, etc., once you've run the model several times. This will enable you to clarify answers to some fundamental questions:

- What is the probability of successfully meeting your needs, and can your asset base post-sale support you and your spouse or partner, if you are partnered, for the rest of your lives?
- Will the proceeds from the sale be enough to support additional goals, such as financially supporting your loved ones or engaging in meaningful philanthropy during your lifetime?
- Are you able to make gifts to family members and/or philanthropic causes while you are alive or need they be testamentary bequests?
- Do you have the desire to make a large philanthropic gift? Is this a non-negotiable passion, a function of tax efficiency, or both?
- Are there family members already involved in the business who can and would like to take on a larger role?
- Can they afford to purchase their share?
- Can you afford to transfer some of the ownership of the business to family or others over time and receive fewer proceeds upon sale?

Don't let what might feel like the overwhelming nature of having answers ahead of time delay you. You don't need to have all of this figured out before embarking on the roadmap; the ramifications of different choices can be presented to you and tested with you until you find an acceptable path.

Assess Opportunity to Enhance Resources

With this preliminary modeling, you can assess whether the sale proceeds will be life-changing or life-enhancing for you and your family. The preliminary valuation of your business enabled you to identify the critical drivers to increase your valuation. By testing alternative valuations in your wealth model, you'll be able to see the impact of further growth or efficiency on your valuation and determine whether it makes sense to work longer to try to achieve a higher value. This will enable you to consider further whether there are steps you can take to grow or protect the business that would be worth pushing a transaction out into the future. In particular, you would want to consider additional insurance, buy-sell agreements, and employee retention methods.

You need to determine whether you are sufficiently prepared for the unexpected. One or more unforeseen events could set you back if you haven't planned for them. Are you sufficiently insured, and do you have continuity plans in the event of the death or disability of key team members or your own premature death or disability? Protecting against these scenarios now can alleviate concerns. Your adviser can integrate your insurance agent into the discussion and come up with a plan for your review. The amount of time and money required is often minor compared to the value at risk.

Moreover, it may make sense to address these issues in advance by putting in place buy-sell agreements if the business has multiple owners. A buy-sell agreement can clarify how ownership transitions will occur, help ensure business continuity, and reduce uncertainty for the buyer. It is a legally binding contract among current shareholders designed to manage the transfer of ownership among current owners and avoid disputes if or when a triggering event occurs such as death, disability, retirement, divorce, bankruptcy, or voluntary departure. Types of agreements include:

- **Cross-purchase agreements** in which each owner agrees to buy the interest the other owner when a triggering event occurs

- **Redemption agreements** in which the business itself agrees to buy out the interest
- **Hybrid agreements**, which include elements of each of the above

These agreements can be funded through the purchase of life insurance policies so as to provide liquidity for the buyout.

You may also need to implement incentives like stock options or retention bonuses for key employees to assure the purchaser that the business will remain stable during the transition. These all take time to analyze and implement, which is why you need to work with your adviser to marshal the appropriate professionals to help you plan well before any transaction.

Develop Exit Strategies and Timing

Once you have the basic outlines, wealth planning can also help you evaluate how to maximize the assets received from the sale by examining the exit strategies and timing issues. You may consider moving to a lower tax state or a state that does not have estate tax taxes so that you receive the proceeds of the sale as a resident. These states currently include Alabama, Alaska, Arizona, California, Florida, Nevada, Texas, and Wyoming. Changing residency for tax purposes requires time to implement and establish.[14]

Exit Plan: Timing and Type of Sale. Outlining your goals for your personal wealth and business may help you decide when to exit your business, especially if you choose to transfer significant wealth. On one hand, it will help you determine if you want or need to work longer to accomplish your legacy goals. In addition, it will help you evaluate the environment. For example, if interest rates are elevated and markets are stressed so that valuations are down, conditions may be particularly favorable for gifting business interests to your family. Many other variables can factor into the timing of your exit, yet having a plan in place ahead of time may allow you to act more quickly when you are ready and result in considerable tax savings and other benefits.

Your exit plan will include evaluating and selecting the type of sale for the business. There are multiple ways to structure a sale with attendant tax implications depending on whether you are selling a sole proprietorship, a partnership, or a corporation. Beyond tax efficiency, restructuring the business may also increase its appeal to potential buyers. For example, separating real estate and operational assets can streamline the sale process and offer flexibility to the buyer. And sometimes, there are opportunities to change the structure of your business to take advantage of the structure that would be best for you.

- **Stock versus asset sale:** If your business is a corporation, you can choose to sell stock or assets. By selling stock, you can limit your taxes to capital gains rates, which are lower than the likely income tax rates you would pay from selling the assets. Sellers and buyers have different interests and incentives, with sellers preferring a stock sale (so that taxes on the gain will be long-term capital gain) and buyers preferring an asset sale (so that they can begin depreciating the assets, creating a tax deduction).
- **Installment sale:** An installment sale means you will receive payment over several years (or at least more than one), enabling you to defer and potentially lower your taxes. Keep in mind that you take the risk that the buyer may default in the future.
- **1031 exchange** (for real estate): To the extent that your business owns real estate, you may be able to isolate the proceeds from selling it and reinvest them into a qualifying property, thereby deferring taxes on that portion of the sale.
- **Corporate structure:** You may want to change the corporate structure from an "S" to a "C" corporation so that you can exclude up to 100% of capital gains up to $10 million from a sale and avoid capital gains taxes as well as federal and state income taxes on the gains. This is available only if you hold the shares for at least five years and meet other Qualified Small

Business Stock (QSBS) criteria.[15] It is essential to evaluate different strategies for transferring business interests to your family, management team, or employees versus an outright sale well before you plan to exit your business. Doing so allows you to take advantage of tax-efficient transfer techniques.

- **Employee stock ownership plan:** If your business is a C-corporation (or an S-corporation beginning in 2028) and you want to sell to your employees, you may be able to sell to an employee stock ownership plan (ESOP) to reduce or defer taxes.

Your exit plan should also include a well-thought-through communications plan that addresses the potential concerns of employees, customers, and your community. By clarifying the values that made your business unique and communicating them to the buyer, you enhance your chances of ensuring a smooth transition. You may consider documenting your history, creating community involvement events and/or creating a foundation to perpetuate your business's values. By focusing on these strategies, you can help ensure that your business's legacy and reputation remain intact and continue to thrive under new ownership.

Estate and Tax Structuring. Next, your adviser can present a series of estate and tax structures for your consideration. Several different types of trusts can be used to give gifts to family. Different types of trusts have provisions that make them ideal for specific uses. They differ along the following dimensions: ideal use case, purpose (control/ownership of the assets, inclusion or not in your estate), tax benefits (who pays what type of tax, e.g., capital gain versus income tax, generation-skipping transfer tax), duration (i.e., beneficiaries in one or across multiple generations), and structure. Table 7.1 summarizes the ideal use case, purpose, tax benefits, and duration for each structure discussed here:

- **Grantor trusts** are basic trusts that move assets out of your estate but can allow you to retain control by retaining certain rights. These rights can include the ability to determine who receives income and principal, add/delete beneficiaries, substitute trust assets for other assets of equivalent value, borrow trust assets, revoke the trust, veto or approve distributions, and use assets to support a beneficiary. The more control you retain, however, the more likely the assets become includable in your estate. Income is still taxable to you, the grantor, making the gift to the beneficiary larger. These trusts can be revocable or irrevocable.

- **Intentionally defective grantor trusts (IDGTs)** allow you to transfer assets out of your estate, thereby reducing your estate tax burden, and also leave you responsible for paying income taxes for the trust. This allows the trust assets to continue to grow tax-free, increasing your children's inheritance. It is ideal for transferring high-growth assets. The word *defective* refers to intentional provisions in the trust that make it a grantor trust for income tax purposes but an irrevocable trust for estate tax purposes.
- **Descendants' trusts** enable you to give gifts to your lineal descendants (children and grandchildren, born or future) with the oversight of a trustee you select. This trust offers protection from creditors, divorce attachment, and potential tax benefits, such as exemptions from generation-skipping transfer taxes (GSTTs). The IRS imposes a GSTT at the highest estate tax level (currently 40%) to prevent individuals from avoiding estate taxes by skipping over their children and gifting directly to their grandchildren. However, as is the case with the unified credit (gift/estate tax exemption), you can avail yourself of a GSTT exemption (currently set at the same level as the gift/estate tax exclusion). The GSTT exemption is allocated when funding the trust to shield all future growth and distributions from GSTT. Without a descendants trust, assets left to your children would be taxed in their estate once they die, resulting in less going to your grandchildren than would be the case with a descendants trust. The length of time the trust can exist is limited by state law. Many states follow the common law rule against perpetuities

which generally limits a trust's duration to 21 years after the death of the last living beneficiary alive when the trust was created. States follow different rules and they can be quite complex. You would want to consult a competent estate planning attorney to understand the possibilities.[16]

- **Dynasty trusts** are a specialized form of a descendants trust designed to last for multiple generations or in perpetuity. Unless you live in the seven states that currently permit trusts to last in perpetuity (Alaska, Delaware, Nevada, New Hampshire, South Dakota, Tennessee, and Wyoming), you would need to hire counsel and draft your trust in one of those states.
- **Grantor-retained annuity trusts (GRATs)** allow you to transfer assets to a trust at presale levels in exchange for annuity payments for a set period of years. If structured properly, at the end of the term, any appreciation above the IRS-mandated interest rate passes to beneficiaries free of tax and any post-sale appreciation passes to your heirs free of estate taxes.
- **Electing small business trusts (ESBTs)** allow S Corporation stock to be held in trust while maintaining the tax benefits of an S corporation and can be structured to exclude the shares from your estate.
- **Irrevocable life insurance trusts (ILITs)** hold life insurance policies. The proceeds upon death are payable by the insurance company to the trust, thereby keeping them out of your estate. This type of trust is often used to segregate funds with which to pay any estate taxes so that other accounts do not need to be depleted.
- **Charitable remainder trusts (CRTs)** combine charitable giving with income generation, providing you with income, an income tax deduction, and reduced estate taxes. The trust is irrevocable, and the remainder goes to the charity.
- **Spousal lifetime access trusts (SLATs)** transfer assets out of your estate into a trust for your spouse.

Table 7.1 Comparison of Trusts

Trust Type	Ideal Use Case	Purpose	Tax Benefits	Duration	Structure
Grantor Trust	Retaining control while transferring assets	Possible estate tax reduction and income tax flexibility	Income taxed to the grantor, reducing estate size, but assets may remain in grantor's estate	Depends on trust terms, often shorter	Irrevocable or revocable trust
Intentionally Defective Grantor Trust (IDGT)	High-growth/value asset transfer. Desire to increase heir's inheritance	Tax-efficient wealth transfer and asset appreciation outside of estate	Estate tax reduction, Grantor pays income taxes, shielding trust assets	Usually lasts for several decades	Irrevocable with "intentional defect" for tax purposes
Descendants Trust	Multigenerational asset protection—bloodline preservation	Protection from in-laws, creditors, divorce	Removes assets from child's taxable estate	Lifetime of direct descendants, i.e., children, grandchildren	Typically irrevocable, tailored to heirs

(continued)

Table 7.1 (Continued)

Trust Type	Ideal Use Case	Purpose	Tax Benefits	Duration	Structure
Dynasty Trust	Perpetual wealth preservation. Preserve wealth indefinitely across generations	Multigenerational wealth transfer and tax efficiency	Exempt from estate, and GST taxes across generations using GST exemptions to avoid federal estate taxes at each generational transfer	Can continue for centuries or perpetuity	Irrevocable, with rules set by the grantor
Grantor Retained Annuity Trust (GRAT)	Transferring appreciating assets	Freeze asset values for tax purposes	Reduces gift taxes and taxable estate by transferring future appreciation	Fixed term, often short (e.g., 2 to 10 years)	Irrevocable, with retained annuity payments

Trust Type	Ideal Use Case	Purpose	Tax Benefits	Duration	Structure
Electing Small Business Trust (ESBT)	Holding S Corporation stock	Enable Trust ownership of S corporation	Allows S Corporation stock to be held in trust while maintaining pass-through income tax benefits	Depending on trust terms, often shorter	Irrevocable, with specific S Corporation provisions
Irrevocable Life Insurance Trust (ILIT)	Estate tax reduction	Provide liquidity for estate taxes or business succession	Tax-free Death benefits. 3-year window for estate exclusion	Until the insured's death	Irrevocable, holding life insurance policies
Charitable Remainder Trust (CRT)	Philanthropy with income stream	Combine charitable giving with income generation	Income tax deduction and reduced estate taxes	Fixed term or lifetime	Irrevocable, with remainder going to charity
Spousal Lifetime Access Trust (SLAT)	Spousal access while reducing estate	Provide financial benefits to spouse while removing assets from estate	Gift tax exclusion, estate tax exclusion	Until the spouse's death	Irrevocable, benefiting the spouse and possibly descendants

In addition to gifting to a trust, you may want to consider forming a family limited partnership or LLC, like Don did in the previous example. LLCs can offer benefits that shield your personal assets from potential liabilities associated with the sale. They can provide flexibility in how income and gains are allocated among partners. This can allow you to structure the distribution of proceeds differently among beneficiaries (now shareholders) as well as tax-efficiently, potentially reducing your overall tax liability. Limited partnerships offer flexibility in how profits and losses are allocated among partners, which can be advantageous when you have multiple stakeholders with varying interests and investment levels. They can be useful for transferring ownership interests in the partnership to heirs or beneficiaries while potentially reducing estate taxes. Transfers can often be made after discounting the valuation due to lack of marketability. In addition, pre-sale, you can convert shares into voting and nonvoting classes and thereby retain control by gifting nonvoting shares at discounted valuations. Limited partnerships carry administrative and compliance requirements, potential conflicts among partners, and specific tax and legal issues based on your jurisdiction, so it is important to consult with professionals.

Philanthropic Strategy. Wealth planning will also help you evaluate how to use charitable giving after selling your business to maximize your wealth and legacy. Your preliminary valuation will provide an initial estimate of the taxes due upon sale. These can be mitigated through a collection of philanthropic and family gifting before and concurrent with the sale.

You can examine the impact of donating appreciated assets to a charity or donor-advised fund to offset your tax liability. You may consider steps such as:

- Creating a foundation or donor-advised fund enables you to gift assets, which then can grow tax-free, providing an immediate tax deduction for you today as well as the potential to make a larger philanthropic impact in future years.

- Gifting assets to a charitable trust such as a charitable remainder trust (CRT), which can potentially provide you with income for a set number of years or for the rest of your life, after which the assets transfer to a charity of your choice. Several types of charitable trusts provide different types and timing of benefits.

Wealth planning before you sell your business can help you carefully structure both your estate and the sale of the business, reducing the chance of overpaying in taxes or missing opportunities to make the most of what you have. The right wealth planner will help you model different scenarios; collaborate with your tax adviser, estate-planning attorney, and insurance agent; and maintain the forward momentum to help you truly build the legacy you envision. They should be able to structure conversations and options for you such that your decision-making becomes simplified rather than overwhelming.

The opportunities described are complex and time-consuming. They can significantly impact your wealth, taxes, and legacy for generations to come. As busy as you are operating the business or as tempted as you may be to respond to an unsolicited purchase offer, the costs of postponing wealth planning can be substantial. Consider initiating discussions with your wealth adviser early—ideally when your business's intentions begin to take shape and well ahead of any potential sale. Your wealth adviser can work closely with you to smooth the path, simplify the process, and help you build the legacy you envision.

Can You Focus on Wealth Planning After You Sell Your Business?

Of course, you can wait to focus on wealth planning until after you sell your business, but it may cost you and your heirs significantly. Whether it's through enhancing control, protecting assets, enhancing family relationships, improving outcomes for your employees, reducing capital gains, estate and/or gift taxes, accessing valuation discounts, avoiding IRS challenges or obtaining a higher sale value by leaving the business in better governance shape, pre-sale planning can enhance and protect your legacy. Bringing an experienced wealth adviser into the conversation as early as possible can enable you to continue running your business and/or be prepared for an unsolicited offer while building the legacy you envision.

Key Takeaways

- Delaying wealth planning until after a business sale can be costly—many owners miss critical opportunities and later regret not preparing earlier.
- Advance planning unlocks five essential areas that shape your financial future and legacy:
  1. Estate Planning: Defines who receives what, when, and how—and helps reduce estate taxes.
  2. Tax Efficiency: Minimizes taxes through timing, valuation discounts, and strategic structuring.
  3. Legal Structuring: Turns strategy into enforceable action through trusts, entities, and agreements.
  4. Family Governance: Aligns family roles and expectations, especially when heirs have differing interests in the business.
  5. Wealth Modeling: Projects future needs and helps determine how much you need from the sale to meet your goals.
- Following a wealth planning roadmap can provide a structured process to evaluate your financial needs, model sale scenarios, assess the usefulness of different estate planning and tax efficient structures to grow or protect resources, and develop a customized exit strategy.

- Evaluating and implementing these strategies requires time, coordination, and experienced guidance—ideally starting 12–36 months before a sale.
- Working with a wealth adviser and acting early can help protect your legacy, enhance outcomes, and give you flexibility that disappears once a sale is underway.

Part III

Transferring Wealth

Part 1 of this book invited you to consider whether you hold any blind spots that might interfere with getting the full benefit of working with an adviser. We reviewed the ins and outs of adviser compensation, standards, and incentives, the characteristics of a holistic wealth manager, the benefits of having them as your quarterback, the risks of not fully collaborating with your adviser, and, finally, the trade-offs in working with multiple advisers rather than consolidating the supervision of your portfolio with a single wealth management adviser.

Part 2 addressed blind spots that arise when developing your wealth plan. We explored the nuances of performance evaluation, the trade-offs when considering how or whether to incorporate noncore assets into your plan, and the potential costs of postponing wealth planning until after the sale of your business.

Part 3 focuses on issues that arise when transferring wealth to future generations and/or philanthropic causes, as well as how to evaluate whether your current adviser is well-suited for this journey. In thinking about the transfer of your wealth, it's important to:

Blind Spot 8: I Don't Need to Share My Intentions with My Kids; It's All in My Will.
Evaluate the pros and cons of sharing your intentions with your heirs while you are alive.

Many investors are reluctant to discuss their intentions with their heirs before they die. They view the concept as fraught with potential pitfalls that could constrain their actions or disrupt family harmony. This chapter will discuss the potential benefits of having "the talk" while you are alive, lay out a roadmap for holding one or more family meetings, and suggest some ways to overcome obstacles hindering you from having the discussion.

Blind Spot 9: We're Very Charitable; We Don't Need a Philanthropic Strategy.
Reflect on whether developing a philanthropic strategy may serve your interests more effectively than continued ad hoc giving.

Many people and families give generously when moved by personal ties or urgent causes. This kind of ad hoc giving can be emotionally rewarding, socially meaningful, and convenient. However, such ad hoc contributions may lack long-term effectiveness and alignment with broader financial or legacy planning goals. This chapter will explain how, by leveraging a philanthropic strategy, donors can take advantage of potential tax efficiencies, enhance the long-term impact of their giving, create purpose and direction, and offer educational and engagement opportunities for their heirs.

Blind Spot 10: I Could Never Leave My Current Adviser.
Consider whether your current adviser is serving your long-term needs.

Many investors have formed very close relationships with their advisers over time. Chapter 1 of this book showed you how to evaluate the landscape of financial advisers and determine whether you are working with an adviser whose incentives are aligned with yours. This chapter will help you understand how to assess whether your adviser is meeting your legacy building needs, and, if you decide to move on, how to overcome any apprehension, guilt, or discomfort you may have in changing advisers.

By helping you reflect on whether you may have encountered blind spots in connection with wealth transfer, these chapters will enable you to consider ways to address them so as to grow and transfer your legacy more effectively.

Blind Spot 8

"I Don't Need to Share My Intentions with My Kids; It's All in My Will"

Very few people want to talk to their children about what they may inherit. More than a third of Americans (35%)[1] and nearly half of Baby Boomers (47%)[2] do not plan to discuss their wealth transfer with their families, despite the fact that 48%[3] of all Americans and 97%[4] of wealthy Americans intend to leave an inheritance.

Reluctance to discuss inheritance with children is natural. It often stems from the combination of personal and/or financial considerations, fear of upending family dynamics, and hesitation over upsetting heirs.

On the personal level, reluctance to confront your own mortality is often at work or you and your spouse/partner may feel that your financial situation is a topic that should be kept between the two of you. These are sensitive matters, and the desire for privacy surrounding wealth, investments, and estate plans is understandable. You may also have been brought up believing that discussing financial matters openly is unseemly or taboo. In addition, concerns about unforeseen changes in circumstances, such as financial downturns, health issues, or changes in family dynamics, cause you to fear making "promises" you may want or need to change over time. After all, you don't know how long you will live, and you don't know, in advance, how markets or the economy are going to perform. You may be worried about your ability to meet your retirement needs and how those needs may change over time, especially if you or your spouse becomes ill. You want to maintain the flexibility to spend more than you planned if something attractive comes up. You don't want to make promises to your children that you might have to renege on. You believe it's therefore important to preserve the flexibility to change your mind about distributions in your will without having to explain those changes to your kids—and so, your plans will remain private.

In addition to your personal considerations, reluctance to discuss wealth is often also caused by the potential impact on your family dynamics. Fear of exacerbating existing tensions or triggering disagreements can lead to a desire to avoid conversations altogether. You may worry that already complicated family relationships will make discussions about asset distribution even more challenging. You may anticipate disagreements or conflicts among family members and fear that revealing your plans could lead to tension, disputes, or strained relationships. How will you answer questions about the financial implications of your spouse remarrying? How do you address the implications for your children if there are children from a previous marriage? There may also be issues surrounding the education, wealth, or career path differentials among your children.

You may feel guilty or hesitate to justify financially favoring a less financially successful child over one who has done very well or splitting assets equally when one child has a greater need. You may be aware that one child is likely to understand and handle a financially sophisticated conversation, while another is likely to feel overwhelmed. What if the conversation reveals that your children's values are more different from your own than you might have expected? How will you handle that newfound knowledge? You may also be concerned about the impact of wealth on your children's ambition. Perhaps you fear that your beneficiaries will become reliant on their expected inheritance at the expense of developing their financial independence. In addition, you may be uneasy about opening up conversations about why you haven't already given them more, especially if they believe it could be used to make their lives easier now. Children often believe they are likely to inherit everything you have, and you don't want to defend a decision to spend more now and/or make a large bequest to charity, rather than leaving more to them.

As a final consideration, your inclination to avoid the conversation may be because you want to protect your children from a potentially upsetting subject for *them*, a conversation in which *they* might not want to engage. Discussing inheritance and end-of-life matters can be emotionally challenging for your heirs, too. It may be that *you* want to talk, but your children are the ones who are a bit reluctant to have the conversation. *They* might not want to face your mortality. They may not wish to seem greedy or interested in their inheritance over their love for you. And they might fear taking on the level of responsibility required to fulfill your wishes around your legacy. You don't want to stir up all these emotions.

These potential landmines make postponing discussions or avoiding them altogether easier than sharing your intentions with your heirs. What's more, you fear that, if you do have the conversation, you might not be equipped to answer the questions that arise. That uncertainty is disconcerting. Deep down, something tells you that sidestepping the conversation isn't a good idea, but you just don't see any way of avoiding the many potential pitfalls. As a result, while you may have an estate plan, you have decided not to share it with your family anytime soon. You believe that there's no point in even exploring the potential benefits of so doing. The door is shut. Unwillingness to even consider this option could be a sign that you've encountered another blind spot. It may be worth opening that door. Whenever you find yourself sidestepping a conversation you think you should have, it can be useful to explore alternative ways to address the issues. Perhaps there are benefits to sharing all, or portions of your plan, that might give you greater peace of mind or improve family harmony even without disclosing all the details? Perhaps there are ways of overcoming obstacles that you may want to consider.

You Are Not Alone

You are not alone in your hesitation to share your intentions. Nearly 60%[5] of adult children are unaware of the contents of their parents' wills. More than half (52%) of adult children don't even know where their parents keep their estate documents, and only 36% know or have access to their parents' online accounts and passwords.[6] (Note that 64% of American adults who work with financial advisers have never even discussed their estate plans with their adviser.[7]) Yet more than half of adult children (51%) will be responsible for executing their parents' wills.[8]

This stands in direct contrast with the goals stated by investors for creating an estate plan in the first place. As Figure 8.1 illustrates, the top two motivations for creating an estate plan are achieving peace of mind in the event of the unexpected (49.8%) and protecting loved ones (49.6%).[9] These two goals exceed all financial considerations, such as providing financial security for heirs (34%), avoiding probate (29%), or minimizing tax liability (14%).

Figure 8.1 Motives for Creating an Estate Plan

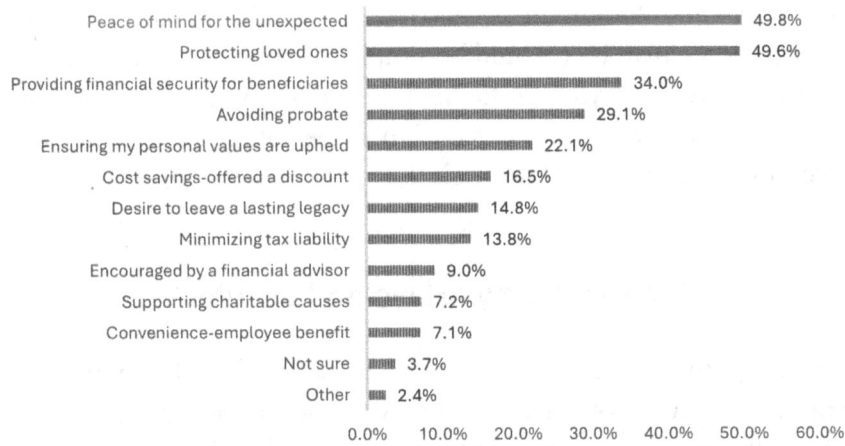

Source: Adapted from Trust & Will 2025

If peace of mind usually connotes freedom from worry and stress, consider for a moment whether you are providing it for yourself and your loved ones if you don't discuss your plans with them. By avoiding "the talk," you may be avoiding short-term stress, but you may continue to live with a nagging, long-term fear that tensions and misunderstandings may erupt after you are gone. This is why part of the rationale for having the discussion may be to look out for *your* priorities and *your* peace of mind, while you are alive.

It may also be beneficial for your children. Consider whether you may be short-changing your loved ones by not discussing your plans and enabling them to express their thoughts while you can consider them. Not discussing your plans means you've missed a critical opportunity to help them understand and accept what you've set up. Having the discussion will allow you to learn about their preferences, biases, and/or needs that can lead to misinterpreting your intentions, and potentially fix them. Might that not give you greater peace of mind? You may find it very satisfying to be aware of any potential misunderstandings while you can still potentially resolve them. Wouldn't it be valuable to be able to make a change to your estate plan that would be simple for you and make an enormous difference to your children? Reconciling yourself to thinking "They'll just have to work it out" may be much less freeing than knowing you've worked through the challenges together.

Isn't This Why I Have an Executor?

You may think that there's no need to have "the talk" with your children because you have an executor. You or your spouse's executor will handle your will and take charge of distributing the assets. While this may be the case, your executor is unlikely to be able to tell your loved ones why you made the decisions you made or give them a chance to ask questions and discuss your rationale. They may be unable to—and most likely will not want to—address misunderstandings or console an heir who feels slighted.

Thinking that your children are just going to "get it"—that they will understand your values and your legacy because you've brought them up—is often not borne out in practice. Experience has taught me that most children are unaware of their parents' true wishes or the reasons behind certain decisions. Without a conversation, amid the pain and loss, the realities of your estate decisions and their implications flood in, leaving no opportunity for your loved ones to understand the reasoning behind them.

As a result, children may find themselves struggling to reconcile their emotional responses to their parents' decisions—especially after the death of the second parent—with the notion that "it was their money to do with as they pleased." This internal conflict, paired with a sincere desire to do the right thing (even when they're unsure what that is), can lead to confusion that not only complicates the grieving process but also becomes part of the emotional legacy you leave behind.

The Value of Speaking Openly

Notably, even Warren Buffett, one of the most experienced and respected investors in the world, took the time in a recent letter to shareholders to urge people to share their intentions with their children: "Be sure each child understands both the logic for your decisions and the responsibilities they will encounter upon your death.... You don't want your children asking 'Why?' in respect to testamentary decisions when you are no longer able to respond.[10]"

Let's take the case of David and Jeanne, who have two children. Stephanie excels academically, secures a prestigious job, prioritizes career over family, and ascends to the top of the corporate ladder, having chosen not to marry or have children. She earns an excellent living. Meanwhile, her younger brother, Steven, is married, has three kids, and holds a steady job, but his career never takes off enough to provide him with excess income.

David and Jeanne are contemplating how to divide their legacy. Should the inheritance be split 50/50 between their two children? Should all or more of the funds go to Steve, where they are most needed? After all, he has the grandchildren, whose futures they can help provide for. Won't Steve wonder why his parents didn't understand that he needed the funds more than Stephanie? Might he ask "why" his parents did not understand his needs? On the other hand, would leaving more for Steve be unfairly penalizing Stephanie because she has made a lot of money, will she ask "why" after they die, or will she understand their thinking? People I've asked have vastly different thoughts on what should be done in situations like this.

Dave and Jeanne decided to split their inheritance, giving half to each of their children. Fairness was an important value for them. They held a family meeting and had "the talk." To their surprise, they learned that Stephanie didn't want the inheritance; she even suggested creating 529 accounts with some of what would have been her portion of a 50/50 inheritance to support the grandchildren. Stephanie explained that instead of receiving a direct inheritance, she would prefer to be made president of the foundation David and Jeanne are creating in their will. Dave and Jeanne were creating the testamentary foundation to utilize the resulting tax-deductible contribution to offset their estate taxes. It hadn't occurred to them that Stephanie might like to oversee it. They were ecstatic at the outcome. Explaining your rationale to your family and being open to their responses can be very informative. Ideas that you had never thought of may be uncovered in a conversation that benefits everyone.

During the conversation, Stephanie also raised the question of what would happen if Jeanne were to remarry. Given the significant age difference between David and Jeanne, there was no chance of the new couple having more children together, but how would it work, Stephanie wondered, if Jeanne's new husband had children? What if the new spouse and/or his children needed financial support? Would the assets be spent down before they had a chance to reach Steve (and his family) and the foundation Stephanie wants to manage? How might underlying concerns about inheritance affect the relationships among the children from both marriages? Might these concerns create resentment on the part of Stephanie and Steven toward the new spouse? Airing these concerns during "the talk" enabled David and Jeanne to explain how they had considered and addressed the issues using a dual trust strategy (discussed below) to provide for Jeanne but also protect Stephanie and Steven's inheritance. This gave both Stephanie and Steven tremendous comfort.

Benefits of Having "the Talk"

Far from being your worst nightmare, discussing your plans with your children can allow you to guide them, answer their questions, and potentially see the pride they experience as they understand their role in continuing your legacy. It may be by simply continuing their own lives and raising your grandchildren to be productive members of society or, like Stephanie, by participating in family philanthropy to promote your family's values. When planned and done thoughtfully, sharing can have many long-lasting benefits for you and your family.

Let's consider five potential benefits of having "the talk." The conversations—and there are usually more than one—can (1) promote clarity, (2) enhance family harmony, (3) help educate your children, (4) provide transparency, and (5) prepare your children so that they can mourn your death (and celebrate your life) rather than focus on their inheritance. These benefits can significantly contribute to achieving your ultimate goal of enhanced peace of mind.

Promoting Clarity

First, discussing your plans can provide clarity to your heirs and prevent misunderstandings. Explaining what assets you have, how they are titled, and how they will be distributed in your will can help your children understand the structures you have put in place and the rationale behind your decisions. Estate planning tools are complex. They differ in terms of control, taxation, beneficiaries, and duration. You may even have forgotten the nuances surrounding why you put specific structures in place—imagine how challenging it is likely to be for your beneficiaries to understand the rationale without explanation.

Consider how potentially unclear or confusing even a basic trust you may have established for the benefit of one or more children could be to them. Many beneficiaries do not understand that money held in trust for them is not actually "owned" by them. It's "owned" by the trustees, who can only distribute it according to the provisions of the trust document. The fact that the trust must pay annual income taxes, potentially depleting the principal, may also not be evident to them. In addition, if the amount in the trust is shared with them, they may "bank" on "having" that amount and not realize the distributions will incur capital gain taxes that will reduce the principal they may eventually receive. Providing clarity with respect to control, taxes, duration, and distributions can prevent misunderstandings, conflicts, court challenges, or surprises after your death and, if you have a spouse, after theirs. It can also reduce extra legal costs that arise when estate administrators need to spend time explaining provisions or take on tasks that could be accomplished by others.

Sharing whom you've selected to act as executor, the person who administers your estate, and how they will be compensated, can be a double-edged sword that benefits from explanation. The choice may cause relief or resentment. If your children feel ill-equipped to handle the role, they may appreciate the selection of a third party. If, on the other hand, one or more feel capable, they may resent your decision to assign a third party, whereas you thought you were doing them a favor by not burdening them. Uncovering any resentment at least gives you a chance to address it. Providing clarity by explaining your rationale can go a long way toward building trust and reducing feelings of being overlooked, especially if one of your children is experienced in finance or planning. It also clears the path for your executor to implement the plan with less drama. Let's say you choose one of your children over the other(s) because they are experienced in finance or wealth planning or, in your view, have the personality type to accomplish all the steps required to administer the estate. Explaining the limitations on their actions and the burden of the time-consuming role to other children may reduce their resentment and create support for their sibling. Similarly, choosing a third party over all or one of your children may engender resentment that can evolve into relief, given the complexity and time commitment required to fulfill the role. In either case, sharing who the executor is early can enable them to gain a thorough understanding of both your wishes and your assets, such that the estate can be administered smoothly.

In addition to your will, any discussion about estate planning is likely to bring up the topic of your end-of-life preferences. Your heirs are likely to be concerned about how to handle your care, how to meet your wishes, and how to manage the costs. Having a conversation about your end-of-life preferences may feel awkward at first, but, typically, as you review the plans, clarity provides comfort for your children. Your advanced healthcare directive (AHCD), which usually includes a living will and a healthcare proxy, typically summarizes your decisions. (Table 8.2, toward the close of this chapter, provides additional details.) Sharing your advanced healthcare directive allows you to discuss your decisions regarding roles and wishes for your medical care. The living will helps you inform them of the type of medical treatment you do or do not want if you are unable to communicate. The healthcare proxy (durable power of attorney for health care) will let them know whom you have appointed to make decisions if you are unable to communicate. This is an opportunity to designate one or more of your children or a third party to carry out your wishes. If you've selected one of your children to act as executor, this may provide an opportunity to give another child a vital role. By having "the talk," you may be surprised to learn that one or more of your children would not be able to carry out your wishes, providing you with an opportunity to adjust your plans accordingly, rather than create a potentially agonizing stalemate when decisions are required.

Enhancing Family Harmony

Second, discussing your plans can sometimes promote family harmony rather than creating conflict. Open communication fosters a sense of unity and reduces the likelihood of disputes among family members. It helps prevent potential rifts due to unclear or contested estate plans. Providing the second generation with the opportunity to discuss your plans with you can also provide a chance to accommodate reasonable requests and reduce the likelihood of unresolvable disputes arising from differing expectations, variations in inheritances, or perceptions. Sharing your plans helps prevent the emergence of hidden agendas or secret dealings among family members. Open discussions allow you to address concerns and provide context, minimizing the potential for resentment or jealousy. These can be addressed directly, thereby leaving less room for misunderstanding or misinterpretation. Openness can promote a culture of trust, reducing the chances of family members feeling excluded or suspicious of each other's motives.

Unlike David and Jeanne's situation, in which they had "the talk" with Stephanie and Steven, Ken chose *not* to share his estate plans with his three daughters. Like David and Jeanne, he had also established a marital trust for his second wife, Kandy, intended to provide her with income from the trust to support her lifestyle while preserving the principal for his three daughters upon her death. The trust included provisions for distributing some principal if necessary to maintain Kandy's lifestyle. Since he appointed his eldest daughter, Susan, as co-trustee along with Kandy, he felt that they would be able to agree on appropriate distributions that would strike a balance between Kandy's interests and those of his daughters. Had Ken had "the talk," he might have uncovered a crucial fact. Although Susan had always acted with respect toward Kandy out of deep love and respect for her father, she resented Kandy and never really trusted her. Kandy also disliked Susan and believed that a marital trust was intended for her use, with only any residual assets, if any, to be passed down to the girls. Once Ken died, there was tremendous conflict among the beneficiaries, with Susan prioritizing the daughters' inheritance and Kandy prioritizing her own needs. The animosity that developed gave rise to deadlocks that stalled decision-making. Each co-trustee accused the other of acting in their own self-interest and breaching their fiduciary duties, resulting in litigation and substantial legal and accounting fees. This also led to a lack of appropriate asset management and poor investment decisions, which compromised the trust's growth and income. Missed tax deadlines also caused costly penalties. Ultimately, the trust's assets were depleted, family harmony was destroyed, issues became public, and the plan failed to fulfill Ken's intentions. Had Ken engaged his daughters in a conversation about his plans, he might have discovered the tension between Susan and Kandy. At that point, he could have considered appointing a neutral, third-party trustee, such as a corporate fiduciary or incorporated mediation or trust protector provisions to resolve disputes.

Clear explanations help family members understand the reasons for specific choices, promoting a sense of fairness and equitable, if not equal, treatment. Involving family members in the conversation fosters a collaborative approach to estate planning. Giving them a chance to object or discuss issues directly with you can reduce the likelihood of potential lawsuits down the road. The family can become a more cohesive unit, working together toward shared goals. This unity can extend beyond the distribution of assets to other aspects of family life.

Of course, not every aspect of your conversations around legacy may be pleasant. There may be difficult topics to cover, such as a decision to leave your children unequal inheritances. However, just because certain aspects of the conversation may be challenging doesn't mean they are less important to discuss. It may well be one of the most important discussions you can have because it allows your children to understand your thinking better. Family members are more likely to accept and support your decisions when they understand the reasoning behind them, reducing negative emotions that can strain relationships. Working together to understand and respect each other's perspectives can reinforce family bonds, possibly leading to a more supportive and cohesive family unit. Even if they don't accept or support your decisions at the moment, perhaps they will be able to do so over time. Having had the opportunity to explain your reasoning may, at the very least, give you greater peace of mind.

Offering Education

Third, involving your children in the discussion also allows them to understand and prepare for their own financial futures as well as any responsibilities they may have associated with managing the estate. The knowledge that an inheritance is likely (and perhaps some indication of timing and size) can spur your children to seek guidance on their own financial matters and begin or expand work with a financial adviser. Discussing your wealth-transfer plans can be an educational experience, imparting valuable financial lessons and fostering responsibility. It enables you to share your values and principles, contributing to their financial literacy and decision-making skills. The good news is that children want to learn from you. Nine out of ten children in families with an estimated net worth of at least $1 million state that the most important thing they will inherit from their parents is their values, and 84% indicate they want to carry on their families' legacies. They are most interested in learning more about basic financial literacy and protecting themselves and family assets.[11] While younger generations may be more comfortable with technology than their parents, their lack of traditional financial experience and open family discussions can lead to an overreliance on digital tools. This dependence may expose them to scams, high-risk investments, and financial blind spots. Having learned to navigate these obstacles through offline experience and interpersonal guidance,[12] older generations are able to impart a good deal of wisdom. Note, however, that education goes both ways, and you may also learn from having "the talk." Be prepared to learn what's important to your children and that your values may differ somewhat.

Providing Transparency

Fourth, transparency in asset distribution establishes a legacy of openness and honesty within the family that can be passed down through generations. Grandchildren appreciate the fact that it was the forethoughtfulness of their grandparents that enabled them to attend college or buy a home. Multigenerational planning can foster a culture where family members are comfortable discussing essential matters and making joint decisions. Open communication about asset distribution promotes family harmony by addressing potential points of contention, fostering understanding, and creating an environment of trust and collaboration. When family members are involved in the process and clearly understand the decisions made, it contributes to a more harmonious and supportive family dynamic.

Strengthening Preparedness

Finally, sharing your estate plan with your children allows them the space to mourn without uncertainty over your plans. They know what is likely to come their way, over what period, who the executor is, and, most importantly, why you've structured your estate and made the decisions you have. They may have benefited from the time they've had to adjust to certain decisions you've made. They have the peace of mind knowing that all the documents are in place and accessible to promote a straightforward implementation of the estate plan.

While sharing your estate planning intentions with your children can offer many benefits, it's important to acknowledge that not every family is well-suited to benefit from such transparency. In some cases, longstanding tensions, unresolved conflicts, disabilities, or differing values may make open conversations of limited value, or more harmful than helpful. If one child has a history of financial irresponsibility or substance abuse, sharing details about inheritances or roles may exacerbate the situation. Similarly, if your children are at vastly different stages of maturity or emotional readiness, the conversation may lead to confusion or resentment rather than understanding. Cultural norms, or past experiences, may also make it difficult for some parents and children to engage in these discussions comfortably. Ultimately, the decision to share should be guided by your unique family dynamics, your goals, and your sense of what will help preserve peace and protect your legacy.

Overcoming Obstacles to "the Talk"

In the face of all these benefits, why then don't more people have "the talk"? The top reasons cited for not having "the talk" are:

1. **Perfectionism:** The desire to be sure the plan is right before sharing it (49%)[13]
2. **Preparation:** Feeling unprepared to answer questions likely to come up in discussions (36%)[14]
3. **Procrastination and Paralysis:** Never feeling like it's the right time to discuss (30%)[15] and feeling unsure how to initiate such a conversation (29%)[16]
4. **Parental Prudence:** Not wanting to demotivate their family (23%)[17]

Working with a skilled wealth adviser can help you address each of these concerns.

Perfectionism

The desire to ensure the plan is "correct" before sharing it is the most frequently cited reason for not having the discussion. Yet no matter how much time you invest, it's unlikely that your plan will ever be perfect for more than a moment in time. The very nature of families, markets, and regulations is that they are constantly evolving. External changes may therefore alter your thinking, latitude, or priorities over time. Accepting this and communicating to your family from the outset that plans can change over time should enable you to overcome your hesitation about sharing the plan, even if you feel it isn't perfect.

The very conversations with your children, combined with the planning process itself, will give rise to "Plan B" thinking. What happens if something changes in your, your partner's, or your children's lives? For instance, let's say you decide to leave money for your grandchildren's education so they can attend college, but then one of them decides to pursue a career on the stage. Does that child not get the same benefits as the rest of the grandchildren? Or what happens if one of your children decides not to have children? Do they then get the funding that would have been provided to their offspring? What if one of your children dies? Do their children get their parents' share (the legal term is per stirpes), or does that share go to the surviving siblings? Your wealth adviser can help you evolve your plan as life happens. It is typically far less time-consuming and expensive to amend documents as needed compared with drafting them in the first place. It may be better to have something in place and amend it over time than risk not having documents when they are needed.

As a result of working with many clients over the years, a holistic wealth manager will not only have experience with the many tools and techniques available to both minimize estate taxes and involve your spouse or children, but they are also accustomed to revisiting and amending plans as your objectives evolve. They can bring together your estate planning attorney and/or accountant in evaluating the impact, cost, and advisability of ideas that merit consideration.

Preparation

Before any estate planning conversations with your children, it is essential to have worked with your wealth adviser to develop a wealth plan that addresses significant estate planning questions. With a wealth management plan that shows your probability of successfully meeting your goals under a broad range of market scenarios, you will know whether there will be enough money for everything that matters to you. Sophisticated wealth planning models enable you to test the impact of establishing different estate planning tools on your financial future while making sure the probability of successfully meeting your needs over your lifetime is kept high. You can "pre-experience" the future and have a greater sense of what the possibilities are for you and your funds when you die. This will give you a good idea of the size and nature (trust, charitable, etc.) of gifts you are likely to be able to make at different points during your lifetime, as well as after you and/or your spouse dies.

Once you've completed your wealth plan, you'll have much more clarity about what is and isn't possible. This sets the stage for more robust and productive conversations with your children. While it is unlikely you'll be able to anticipate every possible question or objection, with the help of your wealth adviser and estate planner, you'll be able to explain the rationale for what you've done and entertain clarification questions and/or suggestions. Recognize that conveying your plans and providing enough time for your children to absorb and react to what you've said is likely to require multiple sessions. Your wealth adviser can suggest an appropriate order within this roadmap to address topics and help you customize an agenda for each discussion. You can also invite them to take the lead on explaining certain portions.

It is normal to feel that you may be unable to answer all the questions from your children in your initial conversation, but solid wealth planning is likely to help you feel prepared to handle most issues. Alerting your children that there will be subsequent discussions in which you can further address questions can dissipate the concern you may have about having all the answers.

Procrastination and Paralysis

After developing your wealth and estate plan, drafting your mission statement, and preparing a meeting agenda, your reluctance to schedule your first meeting will likely evaporate. Rather than procrastinate, I've seen couples become impatient to start. Moreover, the idea of beginning by sharing their family mission statement and following an agenda such as the one described eliminates uncertainty over how to initiate the conversation. No longer perplexed about how to conduct the meeting, the urge to procrastinate becomes neutralized. Paralysis about how to initiate the meeting has dissipated. Parents often become eager to see how the discussion unfolds. If they don't feel ready to address the most challenging aspects of the plan in detail, then the discussion can be handled by communicating the direction rather than the specifics of how the estate will unfold. Even if there are some hard truths to convey, the parents' mood frequently shifts to "getting it communicated" so that they can help address any fallout.

Parental Prudence

Many parents worry about the effect wealth will have on their children, with 50%[18] concerned that disclosing family wealth, especially the size of an eventual inheritance, will demotivate their children or sap their ambition.

Figure 8.2 illustrates what worries affluent parents the most about the effect of wealth on their children.

Figure 8.2 Inheritance Concerns of Affluent Parents

WHAT WORRIES AFFLUENT PARENTS MOST ABOUT THE EFFECT OF WEALTH ON THEIR CHILDREN[12]	PERCENT WHO ARE WORRIED
Too much emphasis on material things	60%
Naive about the value of money	55%
Spend beyond their means	52%
Have their initiative ruined by affluence	50%
Not do as well financially as parent would like	49%
Not do as well financially as parent did	44%
Hard time taking financial responsibility	42%
Resented because of their affluence	36%
Suffer from parent not being around	35%
Date or marry someone who wants affluence	34%
Limited exposure to non-affluent people	33%
Feel they have big shoes to fill and will fail	18%

Source: U.S. Trust survey of Affluent Americans XIX, December 2000

Their concern is warranted. Many of us have heard the adage "shirtsleeves to shirtsleeves in three generations." In the United States it's estimated that 70% of affluent families will lose their wealth by the second generation and 90% by the third.[19] While we may think of the Vanderbilts or the Astors, this phenomenon is not just American folklore; it exists in almost every culture. In the Netherlands, the proverb is "clogs to clogs in three generations."[20] While often cited as a country that defies the "three-generation curse," even Japan proffers the cultural proverb "from rice paddy to rice paddy in three generations," reflecting the same concern: that wealth built by one generation is often lost by the third.

The first generation, often starting from extremely modest beginnings, works hard to build wealth based on a strong work ethic and extreme financial discipline. Their children (the second generation) grow up accustomed to the benefits that the first generation has provided them. While they may have observed the hard work put in by their parents, they may not have the same focus, discipline, or frugality. Their children, the third generation, are born into wealth and may even take it for granted. As a result, they typically haven't developed the same work ethic or financial self-discipline and eventually spend away the family fortune, returning the family to "shirtsleeves."

What appears to underlie the persistence of this phenomenon is the fact that there was *limited* family discussion of wealth and its transfer. Research shows that 60% of the transition failures were caused by a *breakdown of communication* and trust within the family unit.[21] It's not that the second and third generations were unaware of the family's wealth; access to credit cards, nice cars, multiple homes, and club memberships were all a natural part of life. They knew wealth was there; the problem was that it wasn't talked about. The absence of honest conversations, clarity, and shared values left room for entitlement and poor decision-making. It was lost *because* it was unspoken and therefore easily taken for granted.

Younger generations *want* to engage in these conversations and seek to do so at an earlier age than their parents did. Whereas Baby Boomers felt that it was appropriate to begin conversations about family wealth with their parents when they were 55 years old, Millennials want to engage a full 10 years earlier, at age 45.[22] Despite this growing interest, most young people say their families rarely discuss financial matters. More than 90% report not having regular conversations about family finances, and only one in three recall ever having a formal family meeting on the topic.[23] Among those who don't meet regularly, six in ten believe such discussions would be beneficial.[24]

There is no assurance that sharing their inheritance won't sap your children's ambition, but if handled well, the opposite can be true. It's not enough just to rectify the breakdown of communication and trust that caused 60% of the transmission failures; it's crucial to educate the inadequately prepared heirs who were responsible for an additional 25% of the failures.[25] Open conversation explaining roles and responsibilities, paired with clear values, financial education, and expectations, can often inspire greater purpose and drive. Nonetheless, be prepared to encounter differences in perspectives about what's important. If you feel they may not value hard work and achievement as much as you did, you may be right. Compared to their parents, Generation Z and Millennial children are generally less focused on the importance of formal education (−18% in generational value differential) and hard work (−13%) and more focused on the importance of family (+11%), enjoying life (+30%), making a difference in the world (+24%), and charitable giving (+18%).[26] When children, even adult children, are thoughtfully brought into the conversation, they can learn, as well as develop confidence, direction, and a sense of stewardship for the next generation. Avoiding the conversation often backfires, creating entitlement, overconfidence, or complacency.

Consider how you might want to adapt any education you are providing based on the ages of the children you are preparing to assume new roles. For example, as new parents, we all thought about when and how much to give our children for an allowance. Some of us may have introduced the concept of the "three buckets" and the requirement to allocate part of the allowance for spending, saving, and charitable contributions. We often begin with firm intentions to monitor the execution of chores, but, buffeted by the demands of everyday life, we eventually find ourselves handing out the allowance, whether the tasks were completed, or letting the allowance idea slip by the wayside. If you have young children and this feels like one more task you don't have time to pursue perfectly, know that merely repeated attempts and the ensuing discussions can meaningfully set the stage for future responsibility. Discussing effort (chores), responsibility (saving for the future), and helping others (through charitable contributions) helps children associate money with a purpose. These messages form the emotional blueprint,[27] the subconscious beliefs and attitudes about money, that will shape their financial behaviors and how they will relate to money as they grow up.

The need to engage in conversation is greatest during the teen and young adult years because this is when the impact is likely to be most profound. It's also the most challenging time to discuss money. Peer pressure and the desire to participate in costly aspects of social life become acute for children. Their wealth can enable them to feel special and part of the "in" group. As clinical psychologist, Dennis Jaffe, PhD, explains, "wealthy children grow up with a sense of specialness that sometimes translates to feeling that wealth makes them better than other people. This is called entitlement; its opposite, a sense of service and responsibility to sustain the wealth and add to it, is called stewardship."[28] At the same time, the urge to hover increases for helicopter parents. "For parents, anxiety and desire for the best for their children can lead to rescuing them from any nascent difficulty, setting up a cycle of codependency where the child knows parents will always be there to take care of them."[29]

It's tough, as parents, to balance financial restraint with social pressures. Add to that the idea of sharing that there will be a future inheritance, and the fear that ambition will be stunted becomes all too real. The most productive approach for teens and young adults is to involve them in substantive decision-making. Engage them in real-life decisions whenever possible. If you prefer not to share details of the child's accounts with them, the conversation can focus on a specific charitable contribution or a foundation's grant-making or investment strategy. Position the conversation around trust, values, and responsibility, not entitlement. By engaging them in decisions about philanthropy, investing, and income, you can demonstrate that access to wealth comes with responsibilities. If they see your confidence in their ability to make wise choices (even if there are mistakes along the way), it can deepen their drive to impress you. Ambition is often strengthened when young people feel seen, trusted, and challenged. Helping them to adopt a "growth mindset" can enable them to embrace learning about money[30] rather than simply expecting it to be there.

For adult children, withholding financial information may do more harm than good. If you want them to conduct their lives as if there were no additional resources to help them, then it may make sense to avoid sharing their potential inheritances with them. However, if you want to support them as they make major financial decisions concerning type of career, purchasing a home, growing a family, and then providing them with a clearer understanding of what you may be willing to fund along the way and after you pass not only can provide clarity for them but also serve as a way to engage them in financial conversations. You will be able to demonstrate and explain that wealth is not a reward but rather a resource to support family values; however, it does not replace effort. By involving them in your vision, you tap into a deeper ambition—one rooted in purpose, legacy, and impact.[31]

Working with you and your estate attorney, your wealth adviser can adapt to the situation you are facing and help you identify what and how to communicate, as well as provide various tools to help you balance your need for control with the goals of greater involvement.

How to Have "the Talk"

Family situations can be complicated, but you can make significant progress by having conversations with your wealth adviser and estate planning lawyer, who can guide you through the legacy process, before eventually discussing your plans with your children. Once you've completed your wealth management plan, you should have a good sense of how and which accounts will be spent down or grown over time, and the size and types of inheritances you are likely to leave. Your first step before calling for a family meeting might be to draft a family mission statement with your spouse or partner that details what's important to you, what you wish for your children and grandchildren, and what causes are important to you and why. Every time I've helped clients create one of these statements, it has been extraordinarily positive and productive for them as individuals and as a couple. Drafting such a statement enables you to pause and reflect on what you want to convey to your children and others, thereby helping you envision your potential legacy. This exercise alone—even if you never share it with your children—can create a meaningful guide path for your future. But having the chance to share it with your children, instead of having it communicated in a will by an executor after your death, takes your legacy from "Here's money for this and that" to "As your parents, we want to share our values, hopes and wishes with you—and, as a consequence, explain to you how we will contribute to your lives during our remaining lifetimes and after our deaths."

As parents and/or donors, having a family mission statement allows you to articulate your core values and take pride in your achievements. It offers children, and/or the charitable institution receiving your gift, the opportunity to absorb and discuss what is being done. It allows recipients to ask questions about your decisions, creating a dialogue that enables them to become clear about what matters to you and why. Sharing your thoughts and plans opens the opportunity for you to build the legacy you envision.

Sharing your mission statement becomes the anchor from which your family meeting unfolds. Often, discussing your family mission statement becomes the entire content of your first meeting. Providing space and time to consider what you've presented enables your family to think over what they've heard and absorb the implications.

Roadmap

A wealth adviser with experience in holding these sessions will be able to help you prepare, conduct, and follow up on them, bringing in other advisers, such as your estate planning attorney, where helpful. Whether accomplished in one or more meetings, Figure 8.3 shows a sample roadmap for a family meeting(s) that you may want to review and adapt to your personal situation with the help of your wealth adviser.

Figure 8.3 Roadmap for Family Meeting(s)

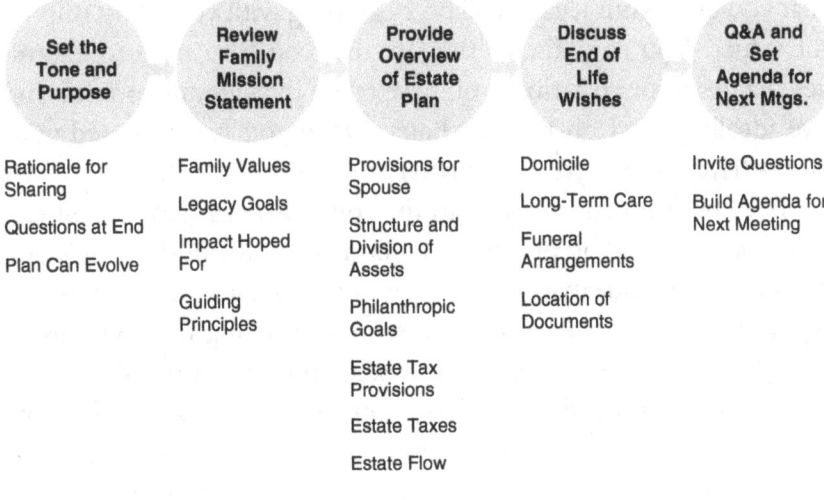

Set the Tone and Purpose. There is no substitute for being in person for this type of meeting, so, if at all possible, it's important to consider how and when you can assemble the family. Once gathered, you may want to begin by setting the overall tone and purpose for the meeting by explaining why you want to discuss your estate plan. Emphasize your desire for transparency, family harmony, and clarity about your wishes. While you can invite questions and concerns, it's often more effective to request that they be held until the end of the presentation so that you have an opportunity to cover everything once. You can acknowledge that emotions may arise and explain that you hope this is the first of periodic meetings, that the plan can and will evolve, and that you are willing to revisit the conversation as circumstances or wishes change.

Review Family Mission Statement. Next, you may want to share the family mission statement that you have drafted before the meeting, outlining your values and goals for the legacy you want to create. Here, you can explain that you want to share and discuss the statement before jumping into your financial details, and note that discussion of the statement may take up the remainder of the meeting. You can read or even hand out the mission statement, which will describe what you hope your legacy will be, beginning with your most important values. You may discuss the fact that you have tried to express these values through actions you have taken throughout your life and have ideally passed on to your heirs. Once you have covered your values-driven legacy, you can further comment on the financial assets you have built up and your goals for your financial legacy. You can then share the guiding principles behind your distribution decisions, such as areas or endeavors you want to support (education, for example), and whether you are seeking equitable sibling distributions or not. There is no need to mention dollar amounts in this discussion, unless you feel compelled to do so. There is a lot to absorb, reflect on, and review in a discussion of a family mission statement. It may be appropriate to take a break or even end the conversation at this point so that your heirs have some time to absorb what they've heard.

Provide Estate Plan Overview. Third, provide a high-level overview of your estate plan. It can be very useful to include your estate planning attorney and wealth advisor in this part of the meeting so that they can address any questions and learn about any issues that may arise. At a summary level, you may want to cover provisions for each of you and for the remaining spouse, division of remaining assets, charitable contributions, and provisions for estate tax obligations. Simply sharing a simple estate planning flow chart that outlines how your assets will pass, such as the following one, can be very helpful at this point.

Let's return to David and Jeanne and review their flow chart, as illustrated in Figure 8.4.

Revocable Trusts

Both David and Jeanne have each created a revocable (living) trust with the other named as successor trustee. Working with their wealth adviser, they have been careful to retitle every financial account and property into the name of the trust so that the trust's provisions will govern them. While each will also have a "pour over"

Figure 8.4 Estate Flow Chart

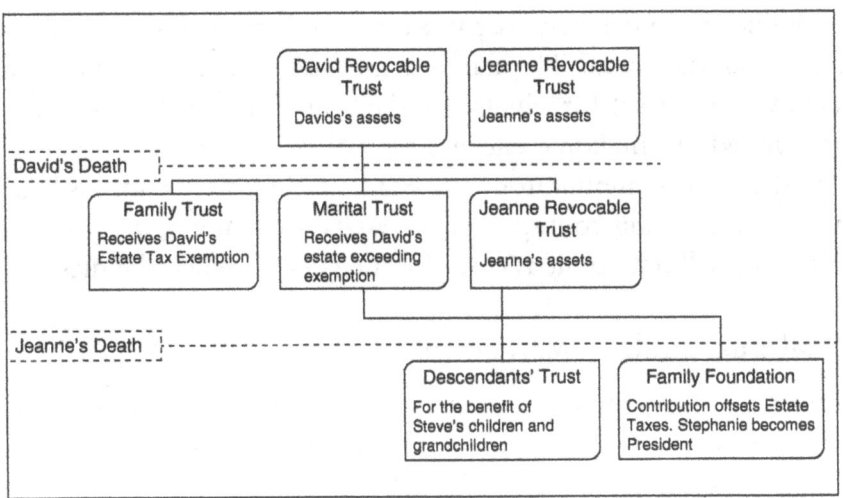

will to capture their wish to have any undiscovered or un-retitled assets poured over into the revocable trust, the revocable trust will be the primary document that governs their wishes. A revocable trust offers them three major benefits: privacy, probate avoidance, and protection in the event of incapacitation. Whereas wills are public documents that can be discovered by anyone who looks, revocable trusts are private. In addition, they avoid the potentially lengthy and costly process of probate. The wills will still have to be probated and letters testamentary issued, giving the executors eventual power to act; however, upon the death of David, Jeanne, as trustee of his revocable trust, is empowered to act immediately in accordance with the terms of the trust. This also becomes the case if David were to become incapacitated or no longer want to administer the trust. Jeanne, as successor trustee, would be able to take over the responsibilities immediately, protecting her ability to access any of David's accounts to pay bills or make distributions or access any assets held in the name of the trust.

Dual Trust Strategy: Family Trust

Since David is several years older than Jeanne and is likely to pass away first, he has created a two-trust strategy using both a family trust and a marital trust. This dual trust setup offers strategic benefits, including tax efficiency, asset protection, control maintenance, and legacy advancement. The family trust (also known as a bypass or credit shelter trust), for which he is the trustee, was created to receive his unused $15 million estate and gift tax exemption. As a result, he can shelter that amount from estate taxes and preserve it for his heirs while maintaining control over the assets. In addition, the assets in this trust will not count as part of Jeanne's estate when she dies.

Dual Trust Strategy: Marital Trust

David also establishes a marital ("A") or unified credit ("portability") trust upon his death with his remaining assets to support Jeanne during her lifetime. Marital trusts enable couples to defer estate taxes, ultimately benefiting their children or other beneficiaries. As of January 1, 2026, the federal gift and estate tax exemption will be set at $15 million per individual ($30 million per married couple) as a result of the One Big Beautiful Bill Act (P.L. 119-21). This amount is indexed to inflation and, therefore, likely to increase slightly each year. The $15 million applies to the combined total of gifts made during one's lifetime as well as estate distributions at death, which is why it is referred to as "unified gift and estate tax exemption." Transfers exceeding this amount are taxed at a flat 40% federal estate tax rate plus any applicable state estate tax rate. Importantly, a surviving spouse can inherit any unused exemption from their deceased spouse. This is known as portability.

Even though portability allows a surviving spouse to use any unused estate tax exemption from the deceased spouse, marital trusts still serve important purposes such as control, protection, and flexibility. A marital trust allows the first spouse to ensure that assets go to their children or heirs rather than to a potential new spouse of the surviving spouse or other beneficiaries. Assets inside the trust are also generally protected from potential creditors or lawsuits. The marital trust also enables growth to occur outside the surviving spouse's estate, potentially reducing the surviving spouse's estate tax bill. Some states (like New York) have lower estate tax exemptions than the federal level and don't allow portability. A marital trust can help preserve the state-level exemption. Marital trusts can also provide structured income to the surviving spouse while preserving principal for heirs.

The assets transferred by David to the marital trust qualify for the marital deduction and, therefore, pass to Jeanne without estate tax. Any marital trust assets remaining after Jeanne's death will be included in her estate and may be taxed, but they will pass to Steven and the family foundation, the beneficiaries David has designated. The marital trust postpones the estate tax until after Jeanne's death, thereby taking advantage of the unlimited tax exemption for transfers to a spouse, qualifying the estate for both members of the couple's lifetime estate tax deduction, and ensuring children/beneficiaries receive an inheritance even if Jeanne remarries. The trust document governs distributions to Jeanne, who cannot unilaterally deplete the trust or change the beneficiaries (unless the trust gives her that power).

Once they understood how the marital trust works, Stephanie and Steve were no longer concerned about the risk of Jeanne remarrying and their father's assets going to her new spouse or his children. Knowing that they will remain the beneficiaries of their father's estate, especially in the case of a second marriage, helped reduce their anxiety over a second marriage and ideally will help build harmony in a possible blended family in the future.

Upon Jeanne's death, the assets in both the family and marital trusts will pass to a descendant's trust for Steve and his heirs, as well as to the foundation, of which Stephanie will be president. The contribution to the foundation was expected to be large enough to offset any remaining estate taxes incurred by Jeanne's estate.

After reviewing the flow chart, Stephanie and Steve felt informed, reassured, and ready to be of help in implementing any required steps. David and Jeanne emerged from this part of the conversation feeling renewed peace of mind.

David and Jeanne implemented some of the most common estate planning structures. There are myriad possibilities for implementing these and other structures,[32] each of which needs to be tailored to your individual situation. There is no substitute for working closely with your wealth advisor and estate planning attorney to model the potential growth trajectory of different accounts and the implications of estate planning structures on achieving your legacy objectives. Table 8.1 provides a brief overview and use case for some additional structures.

Once the broad outlines of the estate plan have been discussed and the specific structures that have been created or will be established after death have been outlined, you, like David and Jeanne, may want to follow up with an even greater level of specificity with regard to which assets will be transferred into each structure. This could be when you choose to let your family see the list of your

Table 8.1   Estate Planning and Asset Retention Tools

Tool	Key Features	Tax Efficiency	Use Case
Durable Power of Attorney (POA)	Appoints someone to manage financial and legal affairs if incapacitated; ends at death	Not tax-related	Essential for incapacity planning
Last Will and Testament	Directs asset distribution after death; names guardians and executors; subject to probate and public record	No tax benefits; subject to probate	Basic estate planning; ensures legal documentation of wishes
Revocable Living Trust	Avoids probate; can be amended or revoked during lifetime; provides continuity in incapacity	No immediate tax benefit	Privacy, incapacity planning, and control over asset distribution
Pour-Over Will	Transfers any remaining assets into a revocable trust at death	No direct tax benefit	Complements a revocable trust to ensure all assets are captured

(continued)

Table 8.1 (Continued)

Tool	Key Features	Tax Efficiency	Use Case
Bypass (Credit Shelter) Trust	Uses the estate tax exemption of the first spouse to die; assets bypass surviving spouse's estate	Reduces estate tax liability	Estate tax efficiency for married couples
Marital QTIP Trust	Provides income to surviving spouse; principal passes to other beneficiaries at second death	Defers estate tax until surviving spouse's death	Protects assets for children from prior marriages or blended families
Qualified Personal Residence Trust (QPRT)	Transfers a home at a reduced gift tax value	Reduces estate tax on personal residence	Useful for passing down a family home
Charitable Remainder Trust (CRT)	Provides income to donor or beneficiaries, remainder goes to charity	Income tax deduction; capital gains deferral	Philanthropy with income stream and tax benefits
Grantor Retained Annuity Trust (GRAT)	Transfers asset appreciation to heirs with minimal gift tax	Reduces gift/estate tax on appreciating assets	Ideal for transferring high-growth assets

Table 8.1 (Continued)

Tool	Key Features	Tax Efficiency	Use Case
Dynasty Trust	Designed to last for multiple generations; avoids repeated estate taxation	Avoids estate and generation-skipping transfer (GST) taxes	Long-term family wealth preservation
Descendants' Trust	Assets pass directly to descendants, often in trust	Can be structured for tax efficiency and asset protection	Protects inheritance from creditors, divorce, or mismanagement
Spousal Lifetime Access Trust (SLAT)	Irrevocable trust benefiting spouse while removing assets from estate	Removes assets from estate; indirect access through spouse	Estate tax reduction with retained family benefit
Irrevocable Life Insurance Trust (ILIT)	Owns life insurance policy outside of estate	Excludes death benefit from taxable estate	Tax-efficient transfer of life insurance proceeds
Special Needs Trust (SNT)	Provides for a disabled beneficiary without affecting government benefits	Preserves eligibility for Medicaid/SSI	Supports loved ones with special needs

(continued)

Table 8.1 (Continued)

Tool	Key Features	Tax Efficiency	Use Case
Disclaimer Trust	Allows surviving spouse to disclaim assets into a trust post-death	Provides post-mortem estate tax flexibility	Flexible estate planning based on future tax laws or needs
Intentionally Defective Grantor Trust (IDGT)	Irrevocable trust where grantor pays income tax but assets are outside estate	Removes appreciating assets from estate; income tax paid by grantor boosts trust value	Ideal for transferring appreciating assets to heirs while minimizing estate and gift taxes
Beneficiary Defective Inheritor's Trust (BDIT)	Created by a third party for the benefit of the beneficiary, who is treated as owner for income tax; not for estate tax	Income taxed to beneficiary; assets excluded from estate	Asset protection and estate planning for beneficiaries who want IDGT-like benefits but cannot create the trust themselves
Nevada/ Delaware Incomplete Gift Non-Grantor Trust (NING/DING Trust)	Incomplete gift, non-grantor trust in Nevada or Delaware	Potential state income tax savings	High-income earners in high-tax states seeking tax mitigation

"I Don't Need to Share My Intentions with My Kids; It's All in My Will"

Table 8.1 (Continued)

Tool	Key Features	Tax Efficiency	Use Case
678 Trust	Beneficiary-deemed owner trust under IRC §678; beneficiary has the power to withdraw income or principal, which causes them to be treated as the owner of the trust for income tax purposes	Income taxed to beneficiary (who may be at a lower bracket); estate exclusion possible	Income shifting and asset protection; keeps assets out of the beneficiary's estate while giving them tax ownership
Spousal Lifetime Access Non-Grantor Trust (SLAT)	Non-grantor version of SLAT; provides income tax benefits	Income taxed outside grantor's estate; estate tax benefits	Combines SLAT benefits with non-grantor tax treatment
Qualified Subchapter S Trust (QSST)/ Electing Small Business Trust (ESBT)	Trusts eligible to hold S-Corp stock without disqualifying S-Corp status	Maintains S-Corp election; special tax rules apply	Business succession and continuity planning
Family Bank Trust	Trust lends or gifts funds to family members for investment or business	Can reduce estate; enables income shifting	Intergenerational wealth building and family enterprise funding

assets (choosing to share or not to share the specific values). This is also when you may choose to provide further details about the roles and responsibilities within each vehicle and explain which documents govern transfers or distributions. In addition to your trusts, you would want to ensure that you include discussion of your real assets (homes, property, cars, personal effects, etc.), financial assets (investment and bank accounts), and insurance policies.

Discuss End-of-Life Wishes. Next, you might choose to review your advanced healthcare directives and end-of-life wishes in more detail. Table 8.2 provides a comparison of these documents.

In addition to reviewing these documents, you might also want to outline where and how you'd like to live out your life under different circumstances, provisions you may have made for long-term care and what preference you may have for your funeral. It's also helpful to provide a list of contacts and offer suggestions on whom to call and in what order. This part of the conversation can often be the hardest. In fact, many individuals neglect even having advanced healthcare directives or durable powers of attorney executed. While 55% of Americans over the age of 55 have a will, only 18% have all three documents in place.[33] By keeping in mind the potential stress that can arise from a lack of direction in end-of-life situations, you may be encouraged to tackle the topic with resolution.

Provide for Q and A and Schedule Next Meeting. The pace at which you move through the steps outlined in the roadmap will naturally vary, shaped by the unique dynamics of your family—your heirs' ages, emotional readiness, financial literacy, and capacity to engage with complex topics. Some conversations may require multiple meetings just to establish a shared understanding of the purpose, or to thoughtfully craft and revise your family mission statement. Other topics may take even longer to explain or reach consensus on than you may have initially expected.

Table 8.2 End-of-Life Documents Comparison

Document	Purpose	Who It Involves	When It Takes Effect	Key Features	Other Notes
Advance Healthcare Directive	Broad document outlining medical care preferences and appointing a proxy	Individual, healthcare proxy	When individual is incapacitated	May include living will + health care proxy; varies by state	Often used as umbrella term for other documents
Living Will	Specifies medical treatments to accept or refuse (e.g., life support)	Individual, medical providers	When individual is terminally ill or unconscious	Focuses on end-of-life care decisions (e.g., resuscitation, feeding tubes)	Does not appoint a decision-maker
Healthcare Proxy	Appoints someone to make medical decisions on your behalf	Individual, proxy (agent), medical providers	When individual is unable to communicate	Proxy can make decisions not covered in living will	Also called medical power of attorney

(continued)

Table 8.2 (Continued)

Document	Purpose	Who It Involves	When It Takes Effect	Key Features	Other Notes
Durable Power of Attorney (POA)	Appoints someone to manage financial/legal affairs *prior to* death	Individual, agent	Immediately or upon incapacity	Covers banking, property, taxes, contracts, etc.	"Durable" means it remains in effect if incapacitated
Do Not Resuscitate (DNR)	Directs medical staff not to perform CPR or advanced cardiac life support	Individual, medical providers	Immediately upon cardiac or respiratory arrest	Must be signed by physician; often part of hospital or hospice care	May need to be renewed or reissued in different settings
POLST/ MOLST	Physician/Medical Orders for Life-Sustaining Treatment	Individual, physician, medical providers	Immediately, especially in emergencies	Medical order that complements advance directives; portable across settings	Varies by state (e.g., POLST in CA, MOLST in NY)
HIPAA Authorization	Allows designated individuals to access medical records	Individual, authorized persons	Immediately upon signing	Ensures proxy or POA can access health info to make informed decisions	Often overlooked but essential for full access

To foster a productive and inclusive process, it's essential to allow generous time for questions, reflection, and open dialogue before progressing to the next topic. Consider creating a "penalty-free" environment—one where no question is off-limits and no concern is left unspoken due to discomfort, fear of judgment, or misplaced deference. This kind of space encourages honesty, builds trust, and helps prevent misunderstandings that could otherwise linger.

Equally important is setting clear boundaries around time. Establishing a defined duration for each meeting helps prevent fatigue and keeps the process focused and respectful of everyone's schedules. If a topic isn't fully explored, it can be revisited in a future session. Whenever possible, create a meeting schedule in advance—or at the very least, agree on the next meeting date before concluding the current one. This structure supports continuity and ensures that important conversations aren't left unfinished.

Do I Really Need to Share My Intentions While I Am Alive?

Successful wealth transfer is challenging. While you don't "need" to share your intentions while you are alive, doing so can help further your legacy for generations to come. Helping your heirs understand your decisions and reasoning can provide the peace of mind underlying at least part of your motivation for wealth and estate planning. Enlisting an experienced wealth adviser well in advance of any discussions can help you develop and follow a roadmap tailored to your situation. Rather than cause disagreement, discussion can promote family harmony and be well worth pursuing. Success isn't assured, but it can be worth the effort.

Key Takeaways

- Many people avoid discussing their estate plans with their children due to emotional and practical concerns such as discomfort confronting their mortality or fear that sharing financial details could create tension or entitlement. Concerns about the potential for circumstances to evolve, unequal treatment among children, or the impact on family dynamics often lead to procrastination or complete avoidance of the topic.
- While avoiding "the talk" is common, the lack of communication can lead to confusion, stress, and conflict—especially during emotionally vulnerable times, standing in direct contrast to the goal of providing peace of mind that may have motivated your estate planning in the first place.
- Sharing your estate plan with your children has the potential to promote clarity, enhance family harmony, offer education, provide transparency, and strengthen the preparedness of your heirs. It can help prevent misunderstandings and resentment, educate heirs, foster trust, and help ensure that your children are emotionally and practically prepared to carry out your wishes.
- The urge for perfectionism, the need to feel fully prepared, the ease of procrastination, paralysis regarding how to initiate the talk, and concern about demotivating children are concerns that can be managed by working with professionals skilled at helping you prepare for and structure the conversation.
- A structured family meeting, guided by five key steps, can make "the talk" productive and meaningful.
- Having "the talk" may not guarantee family harmony but it is worth undertaking.

Blind Spot 9

"We're Very Charitable; We Don't Need a Philanthropic Strategy"

You and your family respond generously when asked by friends and/or organizations to support causes that are meaningful to you. You make periodic and annual donations to the schools you and/or your children have attended, as well as religious and cultural institutions. You actively support issues that are important to you. Additionally, you constantly find yourself meeting unforeseen ad hoc requests that arise throughout the year. You respond when a friend asks or a need is urgent, and you seek to advance causes that matter to you. Even if there are cases in which you feel obligated to contribute, the ability to make these donations is extremely satisfying. Recognizing the impact that these groups or individuals have had or have the potential to have on your life, you want to give back. Contributing is a responsibility you are pleased to take on.

You are not alone in your generosity. According to a survey by The Associated Press-NORC Center for Public Affairs Research, 75% of U.S. adults say their household contributed money to a charitable organization in 2024—although only 37.7% of American filers reported charitable contributions in 2021 (the latest available data[1]). Americans donated $557.16 billion to charity in 2023, representing a 1.9% increase over 2022 but a 2.1% decline when adjusted for inflation. Individuals accounted for the vast majority of donations (67%), followed by foundations (19%), bequests (8%), and corporations (7%). The top five destinations receiving donations (75% of the dollars) were religion (24%), human services (14%), education (14%), foundations (13%), and public-society benefit (10%).[2]

Whether you're happy to help or feel duty-bound to contribute, you continue to give, perhaps spurred on by the tax-deductibility of your donations. Although you have occasionally supported something in a substantial manner, in most cases, the donations you've made have been small to medium gifts that, without analyzing, you "know" you can afford. You may even have established a donor-advised fund (DAF) and are confident that you've therefore optimized your giving through a relatively inexpensive structure. You've contributed to the fund when you had liquidity and/or needed to offset a tax bill, but you've never discussed a philanthropic strategy with your wealth adviser. Once again, you are not alone: 39% of pre-retirees and 49% of retirees report never having had a conversation with a professional adviser about charitable planning or giving.[3] Doing something more than ad hoc giving, such as creating a foundation or a charitable remainder trust, you fear would require too much time and effort. Moreover, you are concerned about the expense, and ongoing management responsibilities associated with creating a vehicle, such as a foundation, to implement a philanthropic strategy.

Nonetheless, when you tally your donations for your tax returns or review your DAF, you begin to wonder whether your giving is optimized. Have you been haphazard in what you've done? Could you have a greater impact if you rationalized your donations? Could you and your family be remembered for supporting a cause that is important to you? Could you be building a legacy?

As year-end approaches, and you are inundated with requests for charitable donations, you resolve that next year you will think through a strategy to ensure your charitable donations are accomplishing your philanthropic and financial goals effectively. However, as vacations and holidays unfold, finding the time and energy to address your philanthropy becomes less of a priority, and evaluating your charitable giving gets put on the back burner. Then, suddenly, another year has gone by, and you find yourself once again in the same position.

Continually postponing what you know might be a valuable endeavor could be a sign you've bumped into a blind spot. Perhaps there is more to consider than just what you see before you. Rather than tackling this on your own, you may want to examine how your wealth adviser can make it easier for you to evaluate different possibilities.

What Is a Philanthropic Strategy?

A philanthropic strategy is a structured, intentional approach to giving that is guided by clear goals, long-term planning, and a focus on creating a sustainable impact. At its heart, a philanthropic strategy is a way to align your values with your actions—transforming generosity into a legacy of meaning, connection, and lasting change. It can be an enormously satisfying endeavor. It can also offer four significant benefits: a tax-efficient opportunity to gain satisfaction from supporting causes that are meaningful to you; a means to have a more significant impact in an area than might be possible with ad hoc giving; an opportunity to provide a sense of purpose and direction, helping you to be more discerning in your response to ad hoc charitable requests and enabling you to explain clearly to those asking for support why, as worthy as their cause may be, it does or doesn't fit with your mission; and, finally, a powerful learning and engagement tool for you and your family.

Tax Efficiencies

There are as many as three potential tax savings from donating to any IRS-approved charitable organization: income tax, capital gains tax, and estate tax. With respect to income tax, the IRS permits charitable contributions to be deductible when they are made to qualified 501(c)(3) organizations, including many charities, religious groups, and educational institutions. For taxpayers who itemize deductions, charitable contributions generally reduce taxable income, subject to applicable limitations. Cash donations to public charities are generally deductible up to 60% of adjusted gross income (AGI), while donations of appreciated property—such as stocks, artwork, vehicles, or real estate—are typically deductible up to 30% of AGI. Beginning in 2026, itemized charitable deductions are allowed only for the portion of contributions exceeding 0.5% of AGI, and the tax benefit of such deductions may be capped for higher-income taxpayers. Unused charitable deductions may generally be carried forward for up to five years.[4] Donating appreciated securities can also provide capital gains tax savings by avoiding tax on unrealized appreciation. If transferred directly to the organization, those securities receive a step-up in cost basis, which eliminates any capital gain. This benefit is in addition to the income tax savings. Finally, any assets you contribute to a 501(c)(3) are no longer part of your estate, saving you potential federal and state estate taxes on those assets.

Impact

In addition to tax efficiencies, planned giving may enable you to have a greater impact than might otherwise be achieved using an ad hoc approach. More than just a financial strategy, it is a way to express your values and create a lasting legacy that reflects what matters most to you. It becomes a living expression of your values—an enduring way to shape the world not just through generosity but through thoughtful, heartfelt commitment to what matters most to you and your family. First, as a result of thinking through your philanthropic goals, you may naturally decide to concentrate your donations in a specific area, thereby increasing the impact you are likely to have. Second, several structures enable assets you transfer into them to grow in a tax-advantaged manner. For example, when you contribute to a DAF or a private foundation, those assets grow tax-deferred, enabling the benefit of compounding to take effect. Although possibly apocryphal, Einstein is reputed to have called compounding the "greatest invention of the twentieth century." Compounding is the process whereby returns are earned on prior returns, thereby growing the investment exponentially. In the case of a tax-deferred investment, because the investment's size is not reduced by taxes, subsequent returns are earned on an increasingly larger base, thereby increasing the return in and of itself.

Purpose and Direction

By providing a sense of purpose and direction, a philanthropic strategy can serve as a guiding framework for your giving decisions. It helps you articulate your values, priorities, and the specific impact you aim to achieve. This clarity empowers you to be more discerning when responding to ad hoc charitable requests, which often come from well-meaning individuals or organizations with compelling causes. Rather than feeling pressured to say yes out of guilt or social obligation, you can evaluate each request against your established mission. If a request falls outside your strategic focus, you can decline with confidence and grace—explaining that while you recognize the importance of their work, your resources are committed to initiatives that align with your defined goals. This not only preserves the integrity of your philanthropic vision but also fosters transparency and mutual respect in your interactions with others. Over time, this approach can help build a reputation for thoughtful, mission-driven giving, encouraging others to engage with you in ways that are more aligned and impactful.

Engagement and Learning Opportunity

Involving children in your philanthropy can be an enormous opportunity to educate them. From helping to define the areas you want to support to evaluating requests for support, identifying and monitoring metrics by which to measure success, understanding governance and administrative responsibilities, and learning about investment management, philanthropy can be a powerful way to expose and involve your heirs. It's also a wonderful opportunity to learn from them—seeing the world through their eyes can challenge assumptions, spark new ideas, and infuse your giving with fresh energy and relevance. In this way, philanthropy becomes not just a legacy you pass on but a shared journey of growth, empathy, and impact across generations. What's more, involving your children is likely to receive a warm reception: 51% of children in families with an estimated net worth of at least $1 million list charitable giving among their most important personal values, and 40% want a stronger voice in their family's giving.[5]

As an example, let's take the case of Joan, who was able to avail herself of all four of the benefits of developing a philanthropic strategy. Joan had been contemplating the sale of the very successful family business she had run for 10 years since her husband's death. After thorough wealth planning to efficiently transfer the proceeds to her and her two sons, who would be well taken care of, and incorporating her spending needs and ad hoc charitable donation goals for her life expectancy, she faced an estate tax bill of more than $4 million.

Rather than putting her sons in a position where they would have to sell assets to cover the bill, she decided to develop a strategic philanthropy plan. While she could have contributed to a DAF, she wanted more control and the opportunity to pursue philanthropy with her sons. She therefore decided to create a foundation and put them on the board alongside her. Joan had four underlying goals. First, she knew that establishing a foundation would be tax-efficient. The contribution to the foundation would remove those assets from her estate in advance of her death, reducing her federal and state estate tax. Since she was transferring appreciated stock she had held for a long time, she would also avoid paying capital gains tax on the sale of those shares once inside the foundation. As a result of contributing highly appreciated shares, the contribution would also provide an income tax deduction from her adjusted gross income, with any excess contributions carried over for five years. Additionally, she knew the foundation would benefit from the tax-deferred growth of the assets she transferred, allowing for compounding growth. Second, she thought working together on the foundation could rally her and her sons around a cause or several causes on which they could have a significant impact, especially funding cancer research to fight the disease that had taken her husband and the boys' father. With the potential to make sizable grants, she thought the family could become recognized as a force for cancer research and have a significant impact. Third, she felt the foundation would create purpose and direction for the family's philanthropy, enhancing their ability to rationalize and consolidate their donations. Finally, she hoped working together on the foundation would be an excellent opportunity to educate her sons about financial and investment management as well as philanthropy. As the mother of young adults, she was acutely aware of their limited financial literacy and the lack of educational opportunities to learn about personal finance. Creating and sustaining a foundation would necessarily involve discussions around governance, investment management, grant-making, and impact evaluation.

If all went well with the foundation, she knew from working with her wealth adviser that she would be able to either add to the foundation over time or leave a substantial bequest without affecting the wealth transferred to her boys. After modeling different scenarios with her adviser, they decided she could seed the foundation with $3 million. A 5% distribution rate would provide them with $150,000 to allocate annually, leaving room for the assets to appreciate as well. She began by "allocating" $50,000 to each of them to grant as they saw fit in keeping with the foundation's broad mission. However, over time, the boys realized that they could have a more significant impact if they and their mother pooled their resources and made a few larger gifts. As a family, they refined the foundation's mission and goals, developed processes and metrics for making and evaluating grants, worked with their wealth adviser on an investment plan, and met regularly with investment managers to evaluate performance. Working on the foundation together proved to offer tax efficiencies while providing a force for meaningful impact, purpose and direction, and a powerful learning opportunity for her family.

Following through on your strategy does not require committing a substantial amount of funds or using a specific vehicle. By going through the exercise of thinking through the nature of the legacy you want to leave and the amounts your wealth management plan can support, you will uncover the structures, timing, and size that make the most sense for your family and develop your philanthropic strategy.

Developing a Strategy

Developing your strategy will involve making trade-offs across the four benefits: tax efficiencies, impact, purpose, and engagement. By working with your wealth manager to iteratively test and size the elements in each step, you can analyze the probability of successfully giving life to your values both while you are still alive and/or after you pass away. As a result, you can home in on the philanthropic strategy and apply the appropriate planned giving tools that make the most sense for you and your family. As Figure 9.1 illustrates, there are four steps to building a philanthropic strategy:

Figure 9.1 Philanthropic Strategy Development

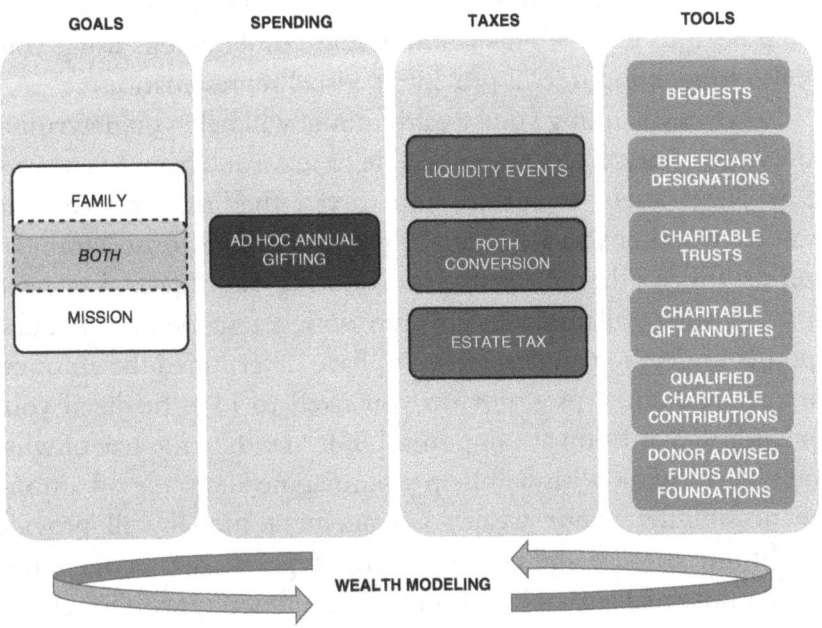

defining your goals, incorporating an ad hoc spending component, anticipating the impact of taxable events, and selecting the appropriate philanthropic tools.

Goal Setting

Developing your strategy begins with considering the overall goals for your financial legacy. Is your objective to maximize the inheritance for your heirs, to fulfill a philanthropic mission, or to do some of both? Is your desire to provide support for either or both while you are alive or after you pass? Where you are heading will determine the approach you and your adviser use to achieve your goals. For example, if your goal is to maximize the assets you leave to your heirs, you and your adviser will focus on philanthropic strategies and structures that minimize taxes both during your lifetime and at the time of your estate's distribution. If you don't have heirs and/or they are already well-provided for, your focus may be more on having a philanthropic impact during your lifetime and/or leaving a bequest from your estate. If you want to do both, you'll need to test the effect of different combinations using your wealth model. Figure 9.2 provides a visual representation.

Iteratively running your wealth model will help you determine how large a legacy you might be able to leave and from what types of accounts/assets. It enables you to test the "runway." You can evaluate whether you are financially positioned to create a foundation or utilize other charitable tools during your lifetime or need to fulfill your philanthropic mission with a testamentary bequest upon your death. You don't need to have determined the amounts for these potential uses, nor do you need to have finalized your philanthropic mission at this point. Understanding the size of what you have to work with will help you imagine and trade off among the possibilities. Your wealth management model will provide insight into the size and nature (i.e., the type of assets or accounts) of your potential legacy, based on testing different portfolio returns over your lifetime.

Figure 9.2 Philanthropic Strategy Development: Step 1

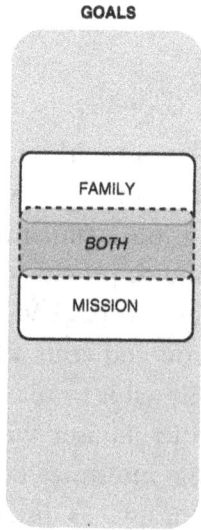

Furthermore, sophisticated wealth models provide an estate flow chart that enables you to visualize the types of accounts and assets that will exist once you and/or your spouse pass away. Figure 9.3 illustrates how different accounts may have grown or shrunk by the time the first of you dies, how they flow down to the second to die, what estate administration and probate costs might be, what inflows from irrevocable insurance trusts may be available outside your estate, how much estate tax is likely to be due, and what your heirs are likely to inherit.

The model's output is typically based on receiving the average historical return for your asset allocation over your lifetime, adjusted for taxes, inflation, spending, required minimum distributions, Social Security, and other inflows. As you run and rerun the model, you will be able to make adjustments across all of these factors and explore several different scenarios. This will enable you to gauge whether your heirs will be sufficiently taken care of after you pass (which may lead you to consider gifting more to them during your lifetime). It will also enable you to gauge whether you can create a philanthropic strategy that benefits both you during your lifetime and your heirs upon your passing.

Ad Hoc Gifting

As part of your initial review of the model, you will need to identify how much money you are willing to set aside to respond to annual ad hoc requests outside of your strategy. See Figure 9.4.

Ad hoc charitable requests are those nonrecurring requests from friends to attend an event or support a cause they are championing. Ad hoc charitable giving is typically unpredictable because it is spontaneous, reactive, and driven by immediate needs, rather than a broader plan. However, working with your wealth adviser, you can analyze your past gifts and develop an initial estimate of the amount you need to set aside to respond to these requests. You'll then incorporate that amount into your wealth management

Figure 9.3 Estate Analysis Flowchart

Using What If Scenario 1 - Both Die today - Sarah predeceases Mike

Current Estate - Will without Bypass Trust

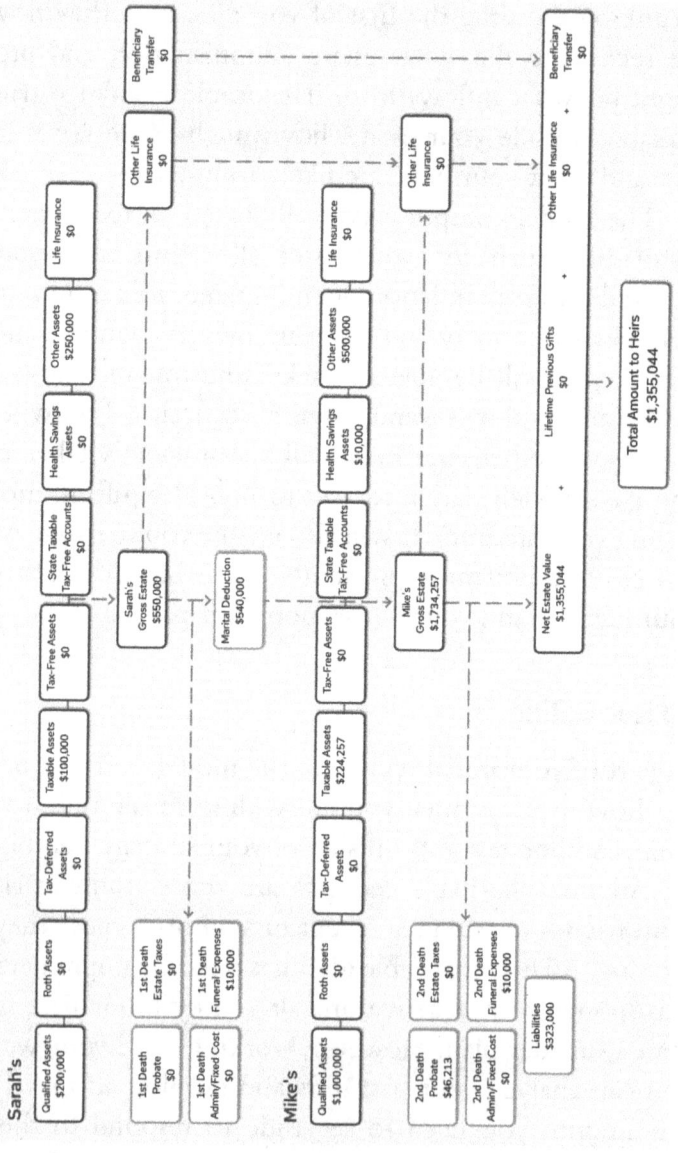

For Illustrative Purposes Only

Figure 9.4 Philanthropic Strategy Development: Step 2

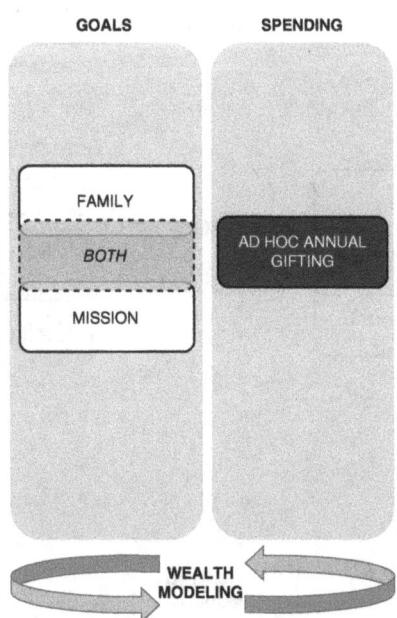

model as a tax-deductible goal and plan on "spending" that every year, making sure it doesn't significantly harm your probability of successfully meeting all your spending goals over your and your partner's lifetimes.

Taxable Events

Next, as Figure 9.5 illustrates, you will want to consider potential events that might result in a future tax liability.

For example, if you face an upcoming liquidity event (such as the sale of a business), plan to raise significant liquidity in the future (such as for the purchase of a home), and/or may wish to do a Roth IRA conversion, then you are likely to realize capital gains (from the sale of the business or securities) or may incur an income tax liability (in the case of a Roth conversion). In any or all of

Figure 9.5 Philanthropic Strategy Development: Step 3

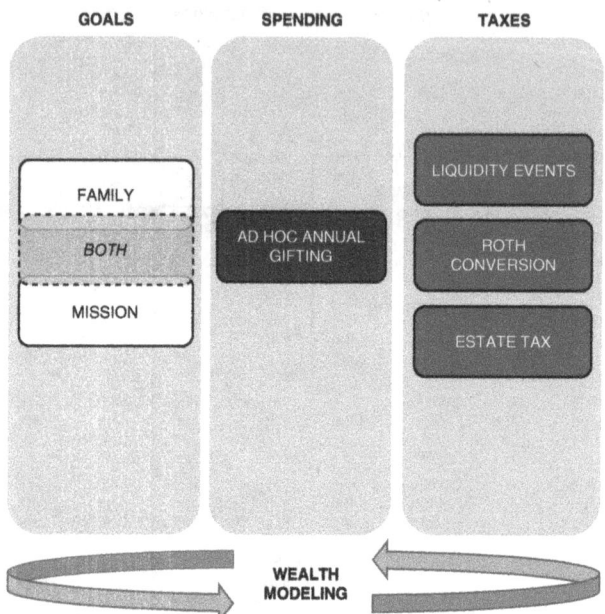

these cases, you and your adviser will be able to analyze the impacts of the amount and timing to optimize its execution. Your adviser will then be able to suggest philanthropic structures that could help offset the taxes and help you evaluate them through your wealth management model.

The second of you to die (if you are/were part of a couple) will be a taxable event as well. Using your wealth model, you and your adviser will need to evaluate the potential size of your estate tax liability. If your estate tax liability is significant, then working with your adviser, you can test the impact of gifting a substantial amount of your wealth today or over time to a nonprofit organization or to a new foundation that you could establish versus leaving a bequest when you die. By testing different strategies, you will be able to find the amount and timing that maximizes your probability of successfully meeting all your goals. You may choose to do one or more of these. It depends on your financial wherewithal, your passion, and your time.

Tools

Once you have incorporated your ad hoc gifting and sized the impact of your taxable events and estate tax, you can turn to the question of how to build the legacy you envision. What are the trade-offs you face in seeking to provide support for your heirs and/or fulfill a philanthropic mission? Working with your wealth model, your adviser will help you analyze the trade-offs by iteratively testing the size, timing, and structures available to you. You've now moved into the world of planned giving.

Planned Giving Implementation

Philanthropic strategies are implemented using a variety of planned giving tools, as illustrated in Figure 9.6. A planned gift is any significant gift, made in a lifetime or at death, from your assets as part

Figure 9.6 Philanthropic Strategy Development: Step 4

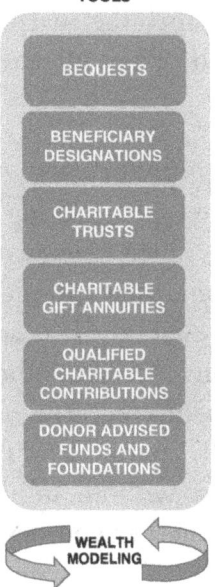

of your overall financial and estate planning. There are many ways to accomplish the charitable goals you want to achieve that also work to your advantage. By working with a wealth manager who is experienced in these different strategies, you can consider and evaluate numerous opportunities to build both your financial and reputational legacy. These may include bequests, beneficiary designations, charitable lead trusts, charitable remainder trusts, charitable gift annuities, qualified charitable donations (QCDs), donor-advised funds (DAF), and contributions to public and private foundations.

If you are not familiar with these structures, you are not alone. While larger percentages of Americans have heard of different types of charitable entities, when asked about familiarity with them, less than 30% indicated familiarity with any vehicle.[6] Each has its own limits, restrictions, and possibilities. Table 9.1 compares some of the most popular planned giving structures grouped into three categories: Deferred Gifts, Income Gifts, Asset Retention Gifts.

Deferred Gifts

Deferred gifts are those in which the charity receives the donation only after the donor's death. They include bequests and beneficiary designations.

Bequests: Simple and Straightforward. Bequests account for more than 90% of all planned gifts, making them the most widely used legacy giving vehicle.[7] Since bequests require no immediate commitment from the donor, they are often easier for donors to consider. Bequests can be established in any size and by donors across the wealth spectrum. Unlike other tools, bequests are relatively easy to implement, requiring little to no legal or accounting knowledge. Still, careful planning is essential to ensure your intentions are fulfilled without unintended consequences. One key consideration is whether you designate a specific dollar

Table 9.1 Planned Giving Tools

Tool	Key Features	Tax Efficiency	Use Case
Deferred Gifts			
Bequests	Gift made via a will or trust; can be a specific amount, asset, or percentage.	May reduce estate taxes; no income tax deduction during lifetime.	Simple legacy gift; ideal for donors of all ages planning their estate.
Beneficiary Designation	Charity named as beneficiary of retirement plans, life insurance, etc.	Avoids income and estate taxes on retirement assets; no lifetime deduction.	Easy to implement; avoids probate; flexible for donors with financial accounts.
Income-Related Gifts			
Charitable Lead Trust (CLT)	Charity receives income for a term; remainder goes to heirs	Reduces estate and gift taxes; limited or no income tax deduction	Estate planning tool to reduce gift/estate taxes while supporting charity
Charitable Remainder Trust (CRT)	Donor or beneficiary receives income; remainder goes to charity	Immediate income tax deduction; avoids capital gains tax; reduces estate taxes	Income stream for donor; tax benefits; ideal for appreciated assets

(continued)

Table 9.1 (Continued)

Tool	Key Features	Tax Efficiency	Use Case
Charitable Gift Annuity (CGA)	Fixed lifetime payments to donor; remainder to charity	Partial income tax deduction; portion of payments may be tax-free; capital gains spread	Simple contract; popular with older donors seeking income and tax deduction
Asset Retention Gifts			
Qualified Charitable Distribution (QCD)	Direct IRA transfer to charity (age 70½+); tax-free	Excluded from taxable income; satisfies RMD; no charitable deduction	Tax-efficient giving for retirees; satisfies RMD without increasing income
Donor-Advised Fund (DAF)	Donor contributes to fund, recommends grants over time	Immediate income tax deduction; avoids capital gains tax; grows tax-free	Flexible giving vehicle; immediate tax deduction; strategic philanthropy
Private Foundation	Donor-controlled entity for charitable giving; subject to regulations	Income tax deduction (limited %); capital gains avoidance; subject to excise tax	Long-term philanthropic strategy; suited for high-net-worth individuals

amount or a percentage of your estate or a particular account. Specific amounts can be straightforward but may inadvertently reduce the funds available for other beneficiaries if the value of your estate decreases over time. Percentage-based bequests tend to be more flexible, adjusting with the size of your estate, which can help preserve balance among multiple gifts. Additionally, the priority or order of bequests matters. If your charitable gift is listed after other fixed obligations (like debts or family bequests), it may be reduced or eliminated if the estate's assets are insufficient. Conversely, placing a charitable bequest too high in priority could unintentionally constrain gifts to loved ones. To avoid these issues, it's wise to consult with your wealth adviser and estate planning attorney to review your wealth plan and coordinate your intentions with the evolution of your estate.

Beneficiary Designations: Pay Attention to Forms. Designating a charity as a beneficiary or partial beneficiary of your IRA, or retirement plan, on your account beneficiary form enables you to continue to take regular withdrawals during your lifetime and leave funds upon your death to the charity. While it doesn't require you to leave a specific amount to the charity, you can specify an amount or a percentage of what is left in the account when you die. You can also easily change the beneficiary designation at any time, should you desire. Charities are increasingly being named beneficiaries of IRAs because the value of the IRA left to a charity qualifies for an unlimited estate tax charitable deduction, reducing the taxable estate. In addition, since charities are tax-exempt, unlike individuals, they do not have to pay taxes on the distribution, resulting in a greater amount being received.[8] Note that if the charity is the only beneficiary of the IRA, it receives a lump-sum distribution upon the owner's death. However, if the charity is a beneficiary alongside other heirs, it may trigger accelerated distribution.[9]

Income-Related Gifts

Several planned giving tools can provide income to you or to a charity during your lifetime, as well as continue through the lifetime of your spouse. These structures include charitable trusts and charitable gift annuities. They are more costly and complex to establish.

Charitable Trusts—Support Charity with Added Benefits.

Charitable lead trusts (CLTs) and charitable remainder trusts (CRTs), depending on how they are structured, enable you to potentially remove assets and their growth from your estate while receiving a tax deduction, retaining investment control, and receiving either income during your lifetime or the remaining principal upon your death. The remaining principal or ongoing income is allocated to the charity.

Charitable Lead Trusts.

When you establish and transfer assets into a CLT, the charity receives payments for a period of time, either the donor's lifetime or a fixed number of years, and the remainder is distributed to the beneficiaries. CLTs are used to support a charity now and transfer wealth to heirs later. Figure 9.7 provides an illustration of how payments flow.

CLTs are typically managed by a trustee chosen by the donor, not the donor themselves. The trustee can be a financial institution, individual, or charity. CLT's come in two types: grantor and nongrantor. Table 9.2 presents the key features of a grantor charitable lead trust alongside those of a nongrantor one. If you choose to retain ownership of the trust assets, the trust is referred to as a *grantor trust* and is treated as part of your assets. As a result, you receive an immediate income tax deduction, but you continue to pay taxes on income. You do not, however, receive an estate tax deduction, making this structure less useful for wealth transfer purposes. If, on the other hand, you do not retain control of the assets, the trust becomes a

Figure 9.7 Charitable Lead Trust

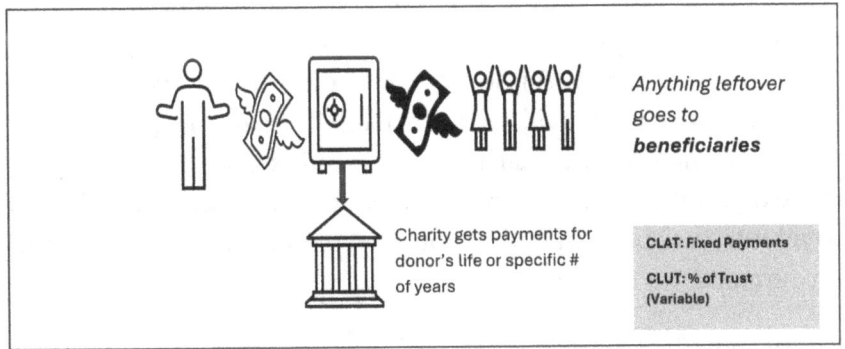

Table 9.2 Comparison of Grantor and Nongrantor CLTs

Feature	Grantor CLT	Non-Grantor CLT
Income Tax Deduction	Yes	No
Trust Taxation	Donor pays tax on income	Trust pays tax on income
Capital Gains Tax	Gains taxed to donor	Gains taxed to Trust
Estate/Gift Tax Deduction	No	Yes
Wealth Transfer	Not typical	Useful

non-grantor CLT. In this case, you don't receive an immediate income tax deduction; instead, the trust pays tax on income. In a *non*-grantor CLT, you do receive an estate tax deduction, making this a more useful strategy for wealth transfer.

Both grantor and non-grantor trusts can choose among two different payment structures: annuity payments or unitrust payments. In a charitable lead *annuity* trust (CLAT), the charity receives a fixed annual payment calculated based on the total amount of assets transferred into the trust, the number of years the charity will receive payments, the monthly interest rate published by the IRS (IRS Section 7520 rate) used to calculate the present value of the future payments, and the desired charitable deduction. Donors often structure the CLAT so as to zero out the gift tax that would have otherwise been paid. In a charitable lead *unitrust* (CLUT), the annual payment to the charity is calculated as a fixed percentage of the trust's value, which is revalued each year. This makes CLUT payments variable, depending on the performance of the trust's investments.

Charitable Remainder Trust. In contrast to CLTs, when you establish and transfer assets into a charitable remainder trust (CRT), the *donor* or beneficiaries receive payments for a specified period, either the donor's lifetime or for a specific number of years, and the remainder is distributed to the charity. CRTs are used to generate income now and support charity later. Figure 9.8 provides an illustration of how payments flow.

This structure is popular because it enables a donor to retain an income stream for their lifetime. CRTs can be managed by the donor, a financial advisor, or a trustee (including a charity if designated). Like CLTs, taxation depends on whether the trust is a grantor or non-grantor trust (distinguished by whether the

Figure 9.8 Charitable Remainder Trust

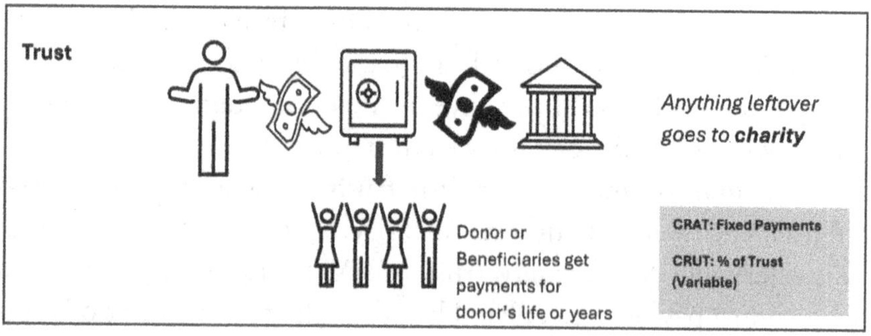

donor retains control over the assets. Table 9.3 presents the key features of a grantor CRT alongside those of a non-grantor one.[10]

Like CLTs, CRT payments to the donor or beneficiaries can also be made on an annuity or unitrust basis. In a charitable remainder annuity trust (CRAT), the income beneficiary receives a fixed annual payment, calculated at the time the trust is created. This payment is based on the total value of assets transferred into the trust, the term of the trust (either a set number of years or the beneficiary's lifetime), and the IRS Section 7520 rate, which is used to determine the present value of the remainder interest

Table 9.3 Comparison of Grantor and Nongrantor CRTs

Feature	Grantor CRT	Nongrantor CRT
Income Tax Deduction	Yes—donor gets an immediate deduction for the present value of the remainder interest going to charity.	Yes—same deduction, but donor does not report trust income.
Trust Taxation	Not tax-exempt—donor pays tax on trust income annually.	Tax-exempt—trust pays no tax; beneficiaries pay tax on distributions.
Capital Gains Tax Deferral	No—donor pays tax on gains realized by the trust.	Yes—gains are deferred and taxed to beneficiaries as distributed.
Estate/Gift Tax Deduction	Yes—assets transferred to the CRT are removed from the donor's estate.	Yes—same benefit; CRT reduces taxable estate.
Use Case	Rare—used when donor wants deduction but is willing to pay ongoing taxes.	Common—used for income stream and tax deferral.

going to charity. CRAT payments do not change, regardless of investment performance. In a CRUT, the annual payment to the income beneficiary is a fixed percentage of the trust's value, which is revalued each year. This makes CRUT payments variable, depending on the performance of the trust's investments. CRUTs are often preferred when donors want the potential for increasing income over time, while CRATs offer predictable, stable payments.

In summary, CLTs are used to support charity now and transfer wealth later, whereas CRTs are used to generate income now and support charity later. Both serve important estate planning functions. CRTs offer stronger capital gains tax benefits, while CLTs are more focused on estate and gift tax planning. Table 9.4 identifies similarities and differences.

Charitable Gift Annuities—Purchase an Annuity and Support Charity

Charitable gift annuities (CGAs) are similar to charitable trusts insofar as they can also provide an income stream alongside a tax deduction for a charitable donation. CGAs are much easier to set up than a trust and are managed entirely by the charity. They are backed by the charity's assets, so, rather than the donor relying on their own or their hired investment management skill to grow the principal, the donor depends on the charity's abilities. However, CGAs are not something a donor can create on their own. They are available only if the charity itself has undertaken the work to set up and offer the product.

In the case of a CGA, the donor makes a gift to a charity, and, in return, the charity agrees to pay a fixed annuity to the donor (or another beneficiary) for life. The donor receives a partial income tax deduction based on the present value of the charitable remainder. Annuity payments are determined by a formula based on the donor's age (or ages, if it is a joint annuity), the type of annuity (single-life or joint-life), the amount of the gift, the annuity rate

Table 9.4 Comparison of Charitable Lead and Remainder Trusts

Feature	Charitable Lead Trust (CLT) *Income goes to charity first, then remainder to heirs*	Charitable Remainder Trust (CRT) *Income goes to donor or beneficiary first, then remainder to charity*
Income Tax Deduction	Yes (only for grantor CLT)	Yes (based on remainder value)
Trust Taxation	Depends on grantor status	Trust is tax-exempt
Capital Gains Tax Deferral	No (unless structured carefully)	Yes (assets sold inside CRT avoid immediate capital gains tax)
Estate/Gift Tax Deduction	Yes (especially for nongrantor CLT)	Yes (assets removed from estate)
Investment Management	Typically managed by a trustee chosen by the donor (can be a financial institution, individual, or charity)	Can be managed by the donor, a financial advisor, or a trustee (including a charity if designated)
Use Case	Used to support charity now and transfer wealth to heirs later	Used to generate income now and support charity later

(which is based on rates recommended by the American Council on Gift Annuities (ACGA), and the timing of payments (immediate or deferred). Importantly, part of the annuity payments you receive may be tax-free for a period. This is because when you fund a CGA, you're making a charitable donation, but you're also receiving something in return: a stream of income.[11]

CGAs are ideal for donors seeking a simple way to support a charity and receive lifetime income. However, note that the actual amount eventually received by the charity depends on whether you live longer than they expected. It is your gift that funds the annuity payments. If you live a lot longer than estimated and therefore receive more payments, the remainder received by the charity may be less than either of you expected. CGAs are most often used by retirees who need an immediate and reliable source of income. The annuity rate may be lower in these cases because payments begin immediately. Younger donors who don't need income now but would prefer higher payments later are often able to defer the receipt of the annuity payments. The annuity rate is higher because the charity holds the funds for a longer period before making payments. This can become a powerful giving tool for younger charitable donors.

Asset Retention Gifts

Asset retention tools enable the donor to retain some measure of control over some or most of the assets while still benefiting the charity. They include qualified charitable distributions from an IRA, donor-advised funds, and private foundations. Charitable lead trusts, as described in the Income-Related Gifts category, can also fall in this category.

Qualified Charitable Distributions: Direct IRA Contributions to Charity

Although introduced in 2006 by the Pension Protection Act, the use of qualified charitable distributions (QCDs) didn't increase significantly until the Tax Cut and Jobs Act of 2017, which raised the standard deduction and capped SALT deductions, making QCDs more attractive. Still in 2024, three out of four retirees said they did not know what a QCD is.[12] A QCD enables people 70½ or older to satisfy their IRA required minimum distribution

(RMD) by donating up to $108,000 ($216,000 per couple) in 2025 from their IRA directly to a charity without incurring income taxes otherwise attached to an RMD. The Secure 2.0 Act further indexed the contribution limits to inflation. While donations can be made from a traditional IRA, inherited IRA, or inactive SEP or SIMPLE IRA, they cannot be made from an active SEP/SIMPLE IRA, 401(k), 403(b), or other employer plans. Additionally, donations cannot be made to donor-advised funds, private foundations, or supporting organizations that exist exclusively to support one or more other public charities.

Donor-Advised Funds: Grow Charitable Funds Outside Your Estate

A donor-advised fund (DAF) is an investment structure administered by a public charity that allows donors to receive an immediate tax deduction for asset contributions (such as cash, stocks, bonds) and recommend to the public charity where the funds should be distributed to other public charities over time. Note that the donor does not have control over the donation but can only recommend where a donation should be made. In practice, public charities follow the donor's recommendation as long as the receiving charity is on their list of vetted 501(c)(3)s. Although the first DAF was established in 1931 by the New York Community Trust,[13] DAFs remained relatively niche until the 1990s, when major financial firms entered the space. Fidelity, Vanguard, and Schwab revolutionized the field by offering low-cost, flexible vehicles to a wider market. However, it wasn't until 2010, after receiving greater clarity from the Pension Protection Act of 2006, that DAFs began to experience explosive growth. As of year-end 2023, DAFs held $252.5 billion of assets, with contributions totaling $59.4 billion. Grants made from those funds reached $54.8 billion. Most DAFs are relatively small, with 49% having assets under $50,000. Unlike private foundations, DAFs have no minimum annual payout requirement, leading to concerns about warehousing wealth and claiming immediate tax benefits while delaying contributions to charities.

Private Foundations: Flexibility with Greater Accessibility Than You Might Anticipate

Establishing a public or private foundation requires obtaining 501(c)(3) status and adhering to the associated regulations, including required financial and tax filings. Public charities typically receive funding from the general public and government, while private foundations usually receive funding from one or just a few individuals, a family, or a corporation. While donor-advised funds have become popular tools for making charitable contributions, private foundations can provide more flexibility and be more accessible than you might realize. You may be surprised at how a private foundation can be established and grow significantly over time with funds you are already donating to charity.

Let's look at Dana and Rick, who would never have thought about establishing a private foundation, assuming it would be out of reach for people of their means. When they met with Kevin, their financial adviser 10 years ago, they had incorporated $50,000 of annual charitable giving into their wealth management plan. In addition, they took advantage of the annual gift tax exclusion and were giving $14,000 annually to each of their three daughters, who were in their early twenties and needed help with their living expenses. Fast-forward five years to a meeting with Kevin in which they mentioned that the girls no longer really needed their help. Well aware of the family's commitment to addressing food insecurity, Kevin suggested establishing a private foundation. Dana and Rick thought that private foundations were suitable only for people far wealthier than they were. Kevin explained, however, that by bundling together their charitable donations plus the amounts set aside for the girls, they would essentially be able to contribute $92,000 a year to the foundation and deduct part of that from their income taxes. Yes, there would be some legal setup costs and an annual accountant's fee for preparing the Form 990 tax return; however, these would be includable in the 5% minimum distribution requirement for the foundation. Private foundations must distribute at least 5% of the average fair market value of their

"We're Very Charitable; We Don't Need a Philanthropic Strategy" 259

non-charitable-use assets annually. This includes grants and certain administrative expenses directly related to charitable activities. (It does not include the 1.39% excise tax on net investment income.) The first year is typically exempt from a distribution requirement because the 5% is based on the ending value of the prior year's assets, which were zero before the foundation was founded. Fast-forward another five years with average annual investment returns of 6%. Even after making charitable donations each year, the foundation now had $485,000[14]—more than the total contributions of $460,000—even after the required minimum distributions. Table 9.5 demonstrates the potential growth of contributions to Dana and Rick's private foundation.

Had Dana and Rick distributed the full 5% (excluding the allowable legal and accounting fees) to increase the amount going to charity, the foundation would have approximately $476,000, still more than the total of the original contributions. Table 9.6 illustrates how much the foundation might grow if Dana and Rick choose to have the entire required distribution go to the charity and have the foundation fund the accounting and legal expenses over and above the required distribution.

Five years into their philanthropic plan, the foundation had grown to close to half a million dollars. At this point, Kevin suggested that Dana and Rick consider converting a portion of Dana's $1 million Traditional IRA to a Roth IRA to leave the girls and their families an income tax-free inheritance, which they could maintain and continue to grow tax-free during the surviving spouse's lifetime and for 10 years beyond the second to die of Dana and Rick. This would provide a nice nest egg for their daughters. Since they continued to have a combined adjusted gross income over $320,000 and lived in New York, Dana and Rick's combined tax rate was 47.9% (they reached the top federal marginal rate of 37% and the top New York bracket of 10.9%). Converting the traditional IRA would leave a Roth IRA with $521,000 and produce a tax bill of approximately $479,000.

Table 9.5 Sample Foundation Growth

Year	Annual Contribution	Investment Income	Excise Tax	Minimum Distribution Required	Qualifying Expenses	Remaining Distribution	Total Distribution	Ending Balance
0	$0	$0	$0	$0	$0	$0	$0	$0
1	$92,000	$5,520	$76	$0	$10,200	$0	$10,200	$87,243
2	$92,000	$10,754	$149	$4,362	$2,200	$2,162	$4,362	$185,486
3	$92,000	$16,649	$231	$9,274	$2,200	$7,074	$9,274	$284,629
4	$92,000	$22,597	$314	$14,231	$2,200	$12,031	$14,231	$384,681
5	$92,000	$28,600	$397	$19,234	$2,200	$17,034	$19,234	$485,651

For Illustrative Purposes Only

Table 9.6 Sample Foundation Growth—Funding of Expenses Additional

Year	Annual Contribution	Investment Income	Excise Tax	Minimum Distribution Required	Qualifying Expenses	Remaining Distribution	Total Distribution	Ending Balance
0	$0	$0	$0	$0	$0	$0	$0	$0
1	$92,000	$5,520	$76	$0	$10,200	$0	$10,200	$87,243
2	$92,000	$10,754	$149	$4,362	$2,200	$4,362	$6,562	$183,286
3	$92,000	$16,517	$229	$9,164	$2,200	$9,164	$11,364	$280,209
4	$92,000	$22,332	$310	$14,010	$2,200	$14,010	$16,210	$378,021
5	$92,000	$28,201	$392	$18,901	$2,200	$18,901	$21,101	$476,729

For Illustrative Purposes Only

Here's where Kevin suggested that the foundation could be useful from a tax efficiency perspective as well as extend the impact of their charitable giving. As Table 9.7 illustrates, contributing $479,000 in cash to the foundation, Dana and Rick would be able to save approximately $229,000 in taxes over the next five years, assuming they continued to earn at the current level and used the five-year carryforward to fully deduct the amount.

Dana and Rick were thrilled that this would bring the size of the foundation to almost $1 million only six years after its founding. As Table 9.8 shows, having essentially front-loaded five years of donations, by year 6, they were able to distribute nearly $50,000 in annual grants to charity without making any additional contributions to the foundation.

With their daughters now in their late thirties/early forties, it was a perfect time for Dana and Rick to tell them about the foundation and bring them onto the board. They viewed this as a wonderful opportunity to further the girls' philanthropic education and keep them engaged and involved in matters of substance with purpose and direction. Together, the family was able to make an impact while strengthening their bonds through shared purpose and meaningful dialogue. Dana and Rick found deep satisfaction in watching their daughters grow not only in knowledge but in confidence—grappling with complex decisions, voicing their perspectives, and shaping a legacy that reflected both generations' values.

Table 9.7 Estimated Five-Year Tax Savings

Item	Value
Minimum AGI per year	$319,333
Annual deduction limit (30% of AGI)	$95,800
Total deduction over 5 years	$479,000
Estimated tax savings (47.9%)	$229,441

For Illustrative Purposes Only

Table 9.8 Sample Foundation Growth Including Roth Conversion Offset

Year	Annual Contribution	Investment Income	Excise Tax	Minimum Distribution Required	Qualifying Expenses	Remaining Distribution	Total Distribution	Ending Balance
0	$0	$0	$0	$0	$0	$0	$0	$0
1	$92,000	$5,520	$76	$0	$10,200	$0	**$10,200**	$87,243
2	$92,000	$10,754	$149	$4,362	$2,200	$2,162	**$4,362**	$185,486
3	$92,000	$16,649	$231	$9,274	$2,200	$7,074	**$9,274**	$284,629
4	$92,000	$22,597	$314	$14,231	$2,200	$12,031	**$14,231**	$384,681
5	$92,000	$28,600	$397	$19,234	$2,200	$17,034	**$19,234**	$485,651
6	$479,000	$57,879	$804	$48,232	$2,200	$46,032	**$48,232**	**$973,493**
7	$0	$58,409	$811	$48,674	$2,200	$46,474	**$48,674**	$982,416
8	$0	$58,944	$819	$49,120	$2,200	$46,920	**$49,120**	$991,420
9	$0	$59,485	$826	$49,571	$2,200	$47,371	**$49,571**	$1,000,508
10	$0	$60,030	$834	$50,025	$2,200	$47,825	**$50,025**	$1,009,678

For Illustrative Purposes Only

Private foundations can be among the most powerful tools for implementing a philanthropic strategy. Bringing it to life requires thoughtful coordination across the full spectrum of planned giving tools based on a deep understanding of their ideal use case. Identifying which options are most appropriate—and experimenting with different amounts and timing to assess their impact—is a nuanced process. Fortunately, it's one that your wealth manager, in conjunction with your other advisers, can help guide you through, step-by-step.

Do You Need a Philanthropic Strategy?

You don't *need* a philanthropic strategy to make charitable contributions. The question is whether developing a strategy can offer you benefits beyond those associated with ad hoc giving. Working with a skilled wealth adviser can help you answer this question and explore planned giving tools and possibilities you may not have known existed. A philanthropic strategy can provide significant benefits to you, your family, and causes that are important to you through tax efficiencies, the opportunity to have a greater impact on a cause that is important to you, the purpose and direction that can galvanize your commitments, and a powerful tool to engage and teach your heirs. Developing a philanthropic strategy that has meaning to you can be quite powerful. By moving beyond ad hoc donations to create a deliberate, meaningful strategy, you can build and transfer the legacy you envision.

Key Takeaways

- Ad hoc giving, in response to personal connections or urgent needs, is easy and rewarding—but it might reduce opportunities to build your legacy. Without a guiding framework, ad hoc giving often lacks coherence, long-term impact, and alignment with broader financial or legacy goals.
- A philanthropic strategy is a structured, intentional approach to giving. When thoughtfully designed, it can elevate giving from reactive generosity to intentional legacy-building by offering tax efficiencies, creating greater impact, providing purpose and direction, and encouraging family engagement and education.
- Developing a philanthropic strategy involves incorporating goals and legacy intentions into wealth modeling to test strategies, adding ad hoc giving thoughtfully by budgeting for spontaneous giving, anticipating taxable events and deploying structures to offset tax costs, and applying planned giving tools more broadly to address your legacy goals.
- Planned giving tools include deferred gifts (e.g., bequests, beneficiary designations), income-related gifts (e.g., charitable trusts, gift annuities), and asset retention gifts (e.g., QCDs, DAFs, private foundations), which offer different levels of control, timing, and tax efficiency can be tailored to fit your goals.
- Implementing a philanthropic strategy is a dynamic process. Working with a wealth adviser can help you: coordinate across financial, estate, and philanthropic goals, experiment with timing, amounts, and structures, engage family members meaningfully, and build a legacy that reflects your values and aspirations.

Blind Spot 10

"I Could Never Leave My Current Adviser"

Despite a growing awareness that you might need more from a wealth adviser than your current adviser can offer, you can't even consider making a move. After all, you and your adviser have been working with each other for years. It's not just wealth management services that bring you together. Your social lives and family lives have become intertwined. Your spouses are friends. Perhaps your children have gone to school or camp together. You've gone through similar financial or familial milestones together and shared deeply personal conversations. You respect them as a person and are impressed by and happy about their successes. You fear that ending your professional relationship would be hugely disruptive to your life more broadly.

Good news: you might not need to leave your current adviser.

You may be working with the right adviser if:

1. You understand the standards they are held to, are comfortable with their compensation, and believe your interests are aligned.
2. Your adviser is more than just an investment adviser. They are a holistic wealth adviser effectively quarterbacking your investment managers, estate planning attorney, accountant, insurance agent, and philanthropic advisers as necessary. Perhaps, in the past, you weren't aware of or hadn't availed yourself of their services, but you will now.
3. As sophisticated as you may be financially, you've recognized the value of a wealth adviser and are comfortable sharing your thinking and collaborating with them instead of going it on your own.
4. You understand the potential risks and missed opportunities of working with multiple, uncoordinated financial advisers. While different investment managers may manage your assets, you've consolidated oversight with your adviser, who is now monitoring and advising on your overall portfolio.
5. You see the risks of short-term performance-chasing behavior to your overall financial success, and although you monitor performance relative to benchmarks, you are much more focused on building your legacy by meeting your plan's target return over time.
6. You want the freedom to make investments on your own and have worked with your adviser to create that flexibility while not endangering the core capital in your wealth plan.
7. You are aware of the opportunities that exist to transfer wealth more tax-efficiently before selling your business, and you and your adviser have engaged in extensive wealth planning well in advance.
8. You've come to appreciate the benefits of sharing some, if not all, of your intentions with your heirs while you are alive, and together with your adviser, you have developed a plan for communicating with the next generation.

9. You've examined the costs and benefits of ad hoc charitable gifting and have moved beyond it to develop a philanthropic strategy that will enable you to build the legacy you envision.

If you are in this position or actively moving toward it, you have addressed the blind spots that can hinder building and transferring your wealth. You are making the most of your relationship with your adviser and should have no reason to consider changing.

On the other hand, if, after considering these blind spots, you find that you are not able to address them with your current adviser, it may be time to consider whether your conviction that there is no possibility that you could switch advisers might be standing in your way. Holding onto an absolute conviction without examining its validity can often be the sign of a blind spot. Perhaps there are ways to enhance the scope of your professional advice while maintaining your personal relationship.

Identify the Gaps

You may want to begin by considering exactly where you feel there may be gaps between what you need and the advice you are receiving.

1. If you aren't able to understand and/or aren't comfortable with the standards to which your adviser is held, how they are compensated, and whether your interests are aligned, consider whether this adviser is serving your interests.
2. If your adviser offers only investment advice and isn't actively engaging in ongoing, holistic wealth planning with you and your other advisers (tax, estate, insurance, philanthropic), ask yourself whether they are the appropriate adviser to help you build and transfer your legacy.
3. If you still feel reluctant to collaborate with your adviser and share all your investment thoughts and intentions, instead of

going it on your own, evaluate whether this may be due to a lack of confidence in the sophistication and understanding on the part of your adviser.

4. If your adviser is unable or unwilling to consolidate investments across multiple investment managers to monitor and advise on your overall portfolio cost-effectively, assess whether they have the research capabilities, technology, and flexibility to serve your interests.

5. If your meetings with your adviser primarily focus on portfolio performance relative to benchmarks, rather than continually reviewing your wealth management plan and evaluating your performance relative to the plan's target, consider whether they may be more focused on investment performance than on building your legacy over the long term.

6. If you find yourself "chafing at the bit" or reluctant to disclose investments to your adviser, evaluate whether your adviser has the flexibility and experience to identify funds for a "play bucket" while not endangering the core capital in your wealth plan.

7. If you own a business and your adviser hasn't asked about or been persuasive enough for you to discuss your future plans together, examine whether this adviser is sophisticated enough to guide you through the wealth planning implications of transferring your ownership.

8. If your adviser shies away from urging you to address the estate planning issues that emerge from your wealth plan and sharing how your estate is organized, along with some of your thinking with your heirs, reflect on the level of their experience in wealth transfer and whether they have the skills to help you.

9. If your adviser merely incorporates your ad hoc charitable gifting into your wealth plan without discussing the benefits of a philanthropic strategy and the range of philanthropic tools available to implement your wishes, consider whether the adviser has sufficient experience to help you build the legacy you envision.

If you find that you cannot address one or more of these gaps with your adviser and your ultimate goal is to build the legacy you envision, then you may need to consider moving on.

That may not feel easy to do. Very few clients ever want to change advisers. Client retention rates typically range from 90% to 92%, which means "in any given year, 9 in 10 households (or more) remain with their financial adviser.[1]" It's hard to break up. Seventy-five percent of the time, clients are keeping their advisers for emotional reasons.[2] You've built a relationship over the years. You've shared a great deal of sensitive information. You have a great deal of trust in them, and your lives may even have become connected in ways that extend beyond a purely professional relationship. Moving on from them seems unimaginable. You would feel guilty—as though you were betraying them.

So, how can you work your way through this?

Overcoming Guilt

Consider whether your adviser could have been serving your interests up to this point without knowing about your entire financial situation. If they haven't reviewed your financial situation with you in detail and don't have a complete and accurate picture of your income, expenses, and balance sheet—all your assets, including investment accounts not held with them, retirement plans, homes, and partnerships—and your liabilities, could they be guiding your investing in a way that increases the probability of successfully meeting your goals? Simply selecting a target asset allocation for your investments based on risk tolerance doesn't necessarily accomplish that.

If they haven't reviewed your estate-planning documents and how the provisions therein affect the transfer of your wealth, don't know whether you're sufficiently insured, or haven't talked with you about how your children will pay the estate taxes likely to be due, then you may want to reflect on how they can intelligently allocate your investments especially when it comes to making decisions across your accounts within a target asset allocation? Would they be able to help ensure that growth is intelligently positioned in accounts that have the longest horizon and that income-producing investments are placed where they are likely to be most needed?

Ask yourself whether you now believe that investment management should have taken place within the context of all aspects of your financial life, not simply your risk tolerance. Perhaps your adviser offered you wealth management services earlier on in your relationship, but you didn't respond positively. Wouldn't it have been essential for your adviser to periodically remind you of the importance of wealth management so that if your thinking evolved, you wouldn't forget it was part of their service?

It may be worth asking yourself why they haven't pressed you about your entire financial life or asked repeatedly over time to make an overall plan, even if they thought it might have annoyed you. Perhaps they didn't want to risk losing you as a client by repeatedly recommending that you address your financial situation holistically. Consider whether that suggests a far less robust view of your relationship than what you may have thought. Perhaps building a comprehensive plan that integrates investments, taxes, estate planning, and philanthropy is either outside their professional scope or is work for which they would not be compensated. Having removed some blinders, you may find out that your adviser isn't focused on wealth management, which is why it hasn't been part of your work together.

On the other hand, perhaps it was you who resisted engaging on a deeper level. If so, take a moment to reflect on what that might say about your comfort level with your adviser. They may have attempted to initiate comprehensive wealth planning, but you hesitated or declined their overtures. If you now recognize the value of holistic planning, this could be the right time to revisit the conversation.

However, if your reluctance stemmed from concerns about their skills, discretion, or experience, then trust your instincts—those concerns may have been valid. Not every adviser is the right fit, and acknowledging that is an important step toward finding someone who truly aligns with your needs and values.

Ultimately, you need to consider whether you are better served by moving on. The more you evaluate what you need and determine either that it hasn't been provided or that there were good reasons you were reluctant to engage, the more confident you are likely to become in taking action. You may view the decision to stay with your current adviser as satisficing—pursuing the minimum outcome—rather than optimizing for your specific situation. While you don't want to offend someone with whom you have built a good relationship and you don't want to hurt their career advancement by leaving, you also know you don't want to settle for acceptable but not optimal advice.

Focus on Your Objectives

To cut the cord, keep in mind that you want to optimize the advice you're receiving and focus on the reasons you want to move on.

1. You want to work with a fiduciary whose interests are aligned with your own.
2. You want a holistic wealth manager whose experience and knowledge base are broader than just investments, who has the interdisciplinary knowledge and personality to work with your tax, insurance, philanthropic, and estate planning advisers, marshaling your team's resources to identify opportunities to increase your wealth and mitigate risks that threaten it.
3. You want a person with whom you truly feel comfortable collaborating. The idea of acting as your own wealth adviser now seems shortsighted and inadvisable.

4. While different investment managers may manage your assets, you want an adviser who will coordinate and oversee your investments so that they conform to an overall strategic asset allocation derived from your wealth plan.
5. You want an adviser who will keep you focused on building your legacy rather than chasing performance.
6. You expect them to find ways to incorporate some flexibility for you to invest outside your core capital.
7. You expect them to be able to evaluate tax-saving and legacy-building strategies before you sell your business.
8. You believe it is essential for them to provide guidance in communicating your plans to the next generation while you are still alive.
9. You want them to coach you toward a proactive philanthropic strategy rather than just responding to charitable giving requests.

When you keep the skills and qualities you need in mind, it becomes easier to act. Try to remain keenly aware of the fact that it is critical to work with someone who has the specific skills to help you actualize your wealth management plan and build the legacy you envision.

Partially Incorporating Your Current Adviser

If you are emotionally tied to your current adviser or believe that they have provided superb investment advice while falling short on wealth management, then there can be a possibility of keeping them involved in your investment management. While most people want to sever ties completely once they decide to move on, maintaining ties can be helpful in special circumstances. Depending on the size of your portfolio and the number of accounts you have, some of the investments currently held with them can remain with them and still be incorporated into a holistic wealth management plan with your new adviser. Many wealth planners are structured to receive a data feed from assets held away from their primary custodian. This is how wealth managers pull in information about the 401(k)s or 403(b)s, alternative, and other private investments you included in your holistic wealth plan that are held at custodians other than the wealth planner's main custodial bank. You may be able to leave a portion of assets with this adviser, establish a data feed into the overall plan, and work with a new, holistic wealth planner.

Moving On

It may be, however, that you'll choose to commit to a new relationship completely. This means saying goodbye. Losing a client is not a happy moment for the current adviser, but you can take small comfort in the fact that all advisers recognize that it is part of the business. When you choose to leave your current adviser, set aside any guilt, remember the importance of what you have at stake, and act as soon as possible.

Consider Michael's case. After years of working with his financial adviser, Michael found himself at a crossroads. His life had grown more complex—his business was expanding, his children were nearing college age, and he had begun thinking seriously about his legacy. While his adviser had done a solid job managing his investments, Michael realized he needed a more comprehensive wealth planning approach.

Michael spent weeks researching firms that offered integrated services—investment management, insurance, tax strategy, and estate planning. When he found the right fit, he knew it was time to make a change.

Michael chose to call his adviser rather than send an impersonal notice. "I want to thank you for everything you've done," he began. "You've helped me grow my portfolio and navigate some tough markets. But I've decided to move on—not because of any dissatisfaction but because my financial needs have evolved."

He explained that his decision was driven by a desire for a more holistic approach to wealth management. He emphasized that it was a business decision made after careful thought, and he hoped they could maintain their personal relationship. Though the conversation was difficult, it ended respectfully. Michael's adviser appreciated the honesty and offered guidance on the transition. In the months that followed, they occasionally crossed paths socially. While there was some initial awkwardness, their friendship endured.

If you don't want to speak with the adviser you are leaving, it is possible to move assets to another firm without contacting them. Your new adviser can use what are known as account transfer forms (ACATS) to pull assets from the old firm without a conversation. Samantha chose that route. She had been with her adviser for nearly a decade. Their relationship was cordial, but over time, she began to feel that her financial strategy lacked depth. Her growing estate, charitable interests, and complex tax situation required more than just investment advice.

After consulting with a new firm that offered a robust wealth planning platform, Samantha decided to make the switch. She appreciated her adviser's past efforts but felt it was time to take full ownership of her family's financial future.

Rather than initiate a potentially uncomfortable conversation, Samantha opted for a quiet transition. Her new adviser used ACATS forms to transfer her accounts, eliminating the need for direct contact with the former adviser. It was a clean break.

Still, Samantha took the time to write a short, heartfelt email expressing gratitude for the years of service. She explained that her decision was based on evolving financial needs and a desire for a more integrated approach—not a reflection of any shortcomings.

Though she didn't expect to maintain a personal relationship, she hoped the message would be received with understanding. Ultimately, Samantha felt empowered by her decision. She had taken a decisive step toward building the legacy she envisioned for her family.

In many cases, if you've built a relationship with your adviser over time, you may want to have a conversation rather than sending an email. Breaking the news by phone is often more desirable than meeting in person, as it allows both parties to move on after the call and have some space to adjust to the new situation. When you call, begin by expressing gratitude for the investment management services the adviser has provided and state up front that you have decided to move on. Make it clear that your decision has already been made and was driven by a desire for a more extensive wealth planning approach rather than dissatisfaction with their current services. Be direct and honest about your need for a more comprehensive wealth management approach, including investment management, insurance, tax, and estate planning. If necessary, emphasize that your decision is driven by the complexity of your financial situation and a desire for a more integrated approach to building your legacy. You may want to add that the decision is based on your evolving financial needs and not a reflection of any shortcomings on their part. Show respect for their experience and seek guidance on the transition process by acknowledging that you would value their input during the transition period. By emphasizing that this is a business decision made after careful consideration, you can help preserve any friendship that may extend beyond your professional relationship.

Conclude the conversation by expressing gratitude again for the services provided thus far and the positive relationship you've built and, if applicable, hope to continue. Reiterate that your decision is motivated by a commitment to enhancing your overall financial well-being. There may be a period of awkwardness the next few times you see each other socially, but if you persevere, the friendship, if it is indeed genuine, should be able to overcome this setback and move forward.

Newly armed with an understanding of the importance of building a legacy for yourself and your family and aware of what you've been missing, you will fully own the decision to move on and be able to find the right words. Ultimately, it is up to you to take the steps necessary to build and transfer the legacy you envision.

Can You Leave Your Current Adviser?

Even if you have a close personal and family relationship with your current adviser, there are ways to part company professionally and maintain your friendship. First, you may want to take inventory of the gaps between what you now know you need to build the legacy you envision and what you believe your adviser is capable of offering. Next, consider discussing these gaps directly with your adviser to make sure that they are, in fact, real and not the result of miscommunication. If the gaps do not appear to be addressable, stay focused on the objectives that underlie your desire to move forward. Equipped with a clear sense of what you are looking for, you'll be able to identify and evaluate new advisers who can meet your needs. Once you've made your decision, inform your current adviser with care and gratitude, expressing the strong desire to remain friends if that is your goal. While it may be challenging in the short term, take the action that serves your long-term objectives. Keep in mind that ultimately, it's your legacy on the line.

Key Takeaways

- Staying with your adviser may be the right choice if they act as a holistic wealth adviser, coordinating across tax, estate, insurance, and philanthropic planning, align their compensation and standards with your best interests, consolidate oversight of your portfolio across multiple managers, help you focus on long-term legacy goals rather than short-term performance, offer flexibility for personal investment decisions without compromising your core wealth plan, engage in proactive planning for business transitions and tax-efficient wealth transfer, and support communication with heirs and development of a philanthropic strategy.

- It may be time to move on if your adviser lacks transparency in compensation or alignment with your goals; focuses solely on investment advice without engaging in holistic planning; doesn't inspire confidence or collaboration or you feel reluctant to share your full financial picture; is unable to consolidate or oversee your full portfolio effectively across multiple custodians and/or platforms; prioritizes performance relative to benchmarks over the performance target in your wealth plan; avoids deeper engagement in estate, tax, or philanthropic planning; or hasn't initiated conversations about your business succession, legacy communication or wealth transfer strategies.
- If you are ready to make a change, then overcoming any guilt you may feel is essential. Recognize that "satisficing" is not the same as optimizing your financial future, and stay focused on your objectives and valid, strategic reasons for seeking a change.
- When ready to communicate your decision, consider calling rather than meeting in person or sending an email. Express gratitude and explain your evolving needs. Frame the decision as a strategic shift based on complexity and future goals, not a personal critique, and maintain professionalism to preserve any personal relationship.
- Ultimately, remember that your legacy is on the line. Your financial future and family legacy deserve the right partner. With clarity, confidence, and a focus on long-term goals, you can make the decision that helps to build the legacy you envision.

Conclusion

The purpose of this book was to offer you a private opportunity to reconsider convictions you may hold with respect to growing and transferring your wealth so that you might better build the legacy you envision. It invited you to reflect on whether your legacy may be obstructed by one or more of the most common blind spots I've encountered in working with families over the past 30 years and to consider whether you might find it beneficial to discard or alter them. These blind spots are broadly held and completely natural. Many are rooted in apparent logic and/or human nature. They can be difficult to dislodge. I hope you have acquired some new perspectives, tools, and knowledge that empower you to reflect on whether they may be applicable to you and consider ways to move forward.

My wish is that you join the group of clients who are more effective than others at building and transferring their wealth—those clients who work collaboratively with their financial advisers on comprehensive, holistic wealth planning that encompasses investment management, estate planning, tax efficiency, and philanthropic strategies, and whose relationship with their advisers is built on mutual respect and trust, where nothing is left unsaid.

If, as a result of reading this book, you realize that you have encountered blind spots you need to address, now is the time to take action. Consider and enumerate what you've been missing and what type of action you believe is required to fill in the gaps. Then, give yourself some time to embark on an information quest to confirm and/or expand your thinking. First, discuss your goals as a couple and as a family with your spouse or partner, and consider how you can adjust your joint level of engagement in wealth and legacy planning. Together, reflect on whether and how to involve your children or other heirs. If you own a business, discuss your plans with your partner(s) and make sure you have your future thoroughly thought through.

Next, talk to your adviser to determine whether your interests and incentives are aligned. Try to gauge whether they are equipped to fill in the gaps you've identified. Consider whether they have the experience to conduct holistic wealth planning and implement a team approach that incorporates advice from your estate planning attorney, tax professional, insurance agent, and philanthropic adviser. Finally, talk to and, if necessary, increase the involvement of these other advisers to get their input on what you've assessed as your potential gaps.

Once you've finished your information quest, you'll have a better sense of how to address your gaps, who the players will be, and what steps need to be taken. You'll be able to formulate a plan of action with your current adviser or move to a new one to overcome any obstacles and effectively build and transfer your legacy. If you don't take action, you may leave barriers in place that will undermine your ability to make the most of your financial situation.

Legacy isn't just about assets—it's about meaning, values, and the imprint you leave on the lives of those you care about. It's about the stories that will be told, the lessons that will be remembered, and the opportunities you create for future generations.

It's about what you shape forward. Like Ḥoni did, you too are planting seeds for trees whose fruit you may never eat. Taking action now isn't just a financial decision; it's a declaration of intention to shape your legacy with clarity, purpose, and heart. Remember that, ultimately, it's your legacy on the line. It's up to you to protect and advance it.

Thank you for the honor of spending your time reading this book. If you'd like to discuss any of the ideas, please reach out to me by scanning this QR code.

Notes

Introduction

1. *Babylonian Talmud*. Tractate Ta'anit 23a. Translated by William Davidson, Sefaria, www.sefaria.org/Taanit.23a.
2. The Money & Family study was created by Ameriprise Financial Inc. and conducted online by Artemis Strategy Group in January and February 2022. For further information and details about the study, including verification of data that may not be published as part of this report, please contact Ameriprise Financial or go to www.ameriprise.com/family. Ameriprise Financial Services, LLC, Member FINRA and SIPC. © 2022 Ameriprise Financial, Inc. All rights reserved.
3. Goodbout, Ted, "Wealth Transfers Expected to Hit $124 Trillion Through 2048," December 30, 2024, https://www.napa-net.org/news/2024/12/wealth-transfers-expected-to-hit-$124-trillion-through-2048/
4. How Large is Each Generation in the US? From Gen Z and Millennials to Gen X, Boomers, and Traditionalists, https://genhq.com/large-generation-us/
5. Goodbout, Ted "Wealth Transfers Expected to Hit $124 Trillion Through 2048," December 30, 2024, https://www.napa-net.org/news/2024/12/wealth-transfers-expected-to-hit-$124-trillion-through-2048/

6. Goodbout, Ted, "Wealth Transfers Expected to Hit $124 Trillion Through 2048," December 30, 2024, https://www.napa-net.org/news/2024/12/wealth-transfers-expected-to-hit-$124-trillion-through-2048/
7. The PNC Financial Services Group, Inc. "Many Wealthy Americans Have Done Nothing to Protect Assets and Are Worried About Financial Security, Family Values, According to Largest Study of Its Kind Released Today," PR Newswire, Pittsburgh, 1-10-2025. According to this survey by PNC Advisers, "fewer than half (46%) say that they have become happier as they have accumulated more money, nearly one third (29%) of respondents with more than $10 million in investable assets agree that having a lot of money brings more problems than it solves, and 33% agree that having enough money is a constant worry in their life."
8. Cerulli Associates, Affluent Investors Are More Reliant on Advisers Than Ever Before October 17, 2023—Boston, According to Cerulli, "the Adviser-Reliant category of investors has exhibited notable growth, increasing from 36% to 41% of affluent investors as Self-Directed investors and Advice Seekers seek to connect with trusted advisers."
9. Investment News Shut up and take our money, investors say about financial advice, December 01, 2023, By Emile Hallez.
10. Bialik, Kristen, Fry, Richard, Millennial life: How young adulthood today compares with prior generations, February 14, 2019, https://www.pewresearch.org/social-trends/2019/02/14/millennial-life-how-young-adulthood-today-compares-with-prior-generations-2/
11. Schwab.com, 2023 401(k) Participant Study - Gen Z Focus October 2023.
12. Financial Planning, Salinger, Tobias 6 ways independent wealth management firms are consolidating, December 6, 2024, https://www.financial-planning.com/list/how-wealth-management-firms-are-consolidating-in-2024

Blind Spot 1: "I Am Working with the Right Adviser"

1. Note that Financial Planners are not typically registered in the securities industry unless they advise on or sell securities, in which case they must register as Investment Adviser Representatives or become Registered Representatives. While many hold the Certified Financial Planner (CFP®) designation, the CFP® itself does not require securities registration.

2. https://www.jdpower.com/business/press-releases/2024-us-full-service-investor-satisfaction-study
3. Pagliaro, Cynthia A. and Utkus, Stephen P., September 2019, p. 1, Vanguard, https://institutional.vanguard.com/content/dam/inst/iig-transformation/insights/pdf/assessing-the-value-of-advice.pdf
4. CFAI_TrustReport2020_FINAL **Earning Investors' Trust** TRUST .CFAINSTITUTE.ORG, p. 27.
5. Investor and industry perspectives on investment advisers and broker-dealers / Angela K. Hung . . . [et al.]. INSTITUTE FOR CIVIL JUSTICE; LRN-RAND Center for Corporate Ethics, Law, and Governance; Page 117. Copyright 2008 RAND Corporation Permission is required from RAND to reproduce, or reuse in another form, any of our researchdocuments for commercial use. For information on reprint and linking permissions, please see RAND Permissions.
6. Source: FINRA 2024 Industry Snapshot pg. 5 Owners of investment adviser firms may be exempt from registering as Investment Adviser Representatives. Accordingly, these Investment Adviser Representatives are not included in the table. "Broker Dealer Representatives Only" refers to FINRA-registered representatives. "Dual Representatives" refers to FINRA-registered representatives who are also registered as investment adviser representatives. "Investment Adviser Representatives Only" refers to individuals who are registered only as investment adviser representatives and are overseen by the SEC or state regulators. "Securities Industry Registered Persons" represents the totality of registered individuals. Individuals are counted only once regardless of how many firms they represent. FINRA captures requirements on all Securities Registered Persons, including those that are not "FINRA-registered representatives."
7. https://www.investor.gov/introduction-investing/investing-basics/role-sec/laws-govern-securities-industry
8. ia-4889PDF(www.sec.gov)./www.sec.gov/files/rules/proposed/2018/ia-4889.pdf
9. https://www.comply.com/resource/the-secs-view-on-an-rias-fiduciary-duty/?__hstc=171294975.4f0cf12abac72ad2da55aaab83b2d2fa.1741985484068.1741985484068.1741985484068.1&__hssc=171294975.3.1741985484068&__hsfp=2850574025%2F
10. SECURITIES AND EXCHANGE COMMISSION 17 CFR Part 275 Release No. IA-4889; File No. S7-09-18 RIN: 3235-AM36 Proposed Commission Interpretation Regarding Standard of Conduct

for Investment Advisers; Request for Comment on Enhancing Investment Adviser Regulation, pp. 6–9.

11. The Looming Advisor Shortage In US Wealth Management, Zucker, Jill, Zhao, Jimmy, Euart, John, Godsall, and VladGolyk, Jonathan, February 2025, p. 2.

12. RIA Channel Growth Prompts Asset Managers to Increase Menu of Resources, August 6, 2024, https://www.cerulli.com/press-releases/ria-channel-growth-prompts-asset-managers-to-increase-menu-of-resources

13. RIAs Grow Headcount and Assets Faster Than Competitors, November 2, 2023, Holly Deaton, https://www.institutionalinvestor.com/article/2cehebsu1sihrynpvetj4/ria-intel/rias-grow-headcount-and-assets-faster-than-competitors

Blind Spot 2: "I Have All the Advisers I Need"

1. US Wealth Management: Amid Market Turbulence, An Industry Converges, January 2024, McKinsey & Company, *John Euart, Jonathan Godsall, Vlad Golyk, and Jill Zucker*, p. 12.
2. Ibid page 13.
3. Ibid page 13.

Blind Spot 3: "I Can Implement My Plan on My Own"

1. Sachek, Richard, Why The 'Age In Bonds' Rule Can Set Yourself Up For Retirement Success, MoneyDigest, November 17, 2024, https://www.moneydigest.com/1715570/age-in-bonds-rule-successful-finances-for-retirement/
2. Ibbotson, Roger G., and Kaplan, Paul D. "Does Asset Allocation Policy Explain 40, 90, or 100 Percent of Performance?" *Financial Analysts Journal*, vol. 56, no. 1, 2000, pp. 26–33. *JSTOR*, http://www.jstor.org/stable/4480220. Accessed 19 Mar. 2025.
3. Lo, Andrew W., Foerster, Stephen R., In Pursuit of the Perfect Portfolio, pp. 18–50.
4. Ibid. page 32.
5. Asset location strategy isn't static—it shifts with market conditions. For example, in the 1980s, when bonds were yielding around 10%, it made

sense to keep those high-interest Treasury bonds in a retirement account (where ordinary income is deferred) and hold equities in a taxable account. Today, the situation is reversed: municipal bonds provide more tax-efficient income in taxable accounts compared to ordinary taxable bonds in an IRA, so you'd generally prefer munis in taxable and equities in an IRA. But this can always change as interest rates and tax dynamics evolve. That's why constant monitoring and adjustments are critical—capital market conditions play a major role in determining the optimal asset location.

6. Portfolio Rebalancing: Trade-offs and Decisions, Xing Hong, Dimensional Fund Advisers LP, June 2021, ssrn_id4552359_code3887796.
7. The Future of Wealth Is Female, Transamerica 2021, 272669_0121_women-and-investing-white-paper_final_021021-update_digital.pdf, p. 9.
8. Ibid. p. 2.

Blind Spot 4: "It's Smart to Work with Multiple Advisers"

1. https://www.callan.com/blog-archive/custodian-primer/ A Primer on the Role of Custodians, Bo Abesamis, May 20, 2019, p. 1.
2. For a discussion of the differences between banks and custodian see: https://www.sensiblefinancial.com/what-are-the-differences-between-banks-and-custodians/ What Are the Differences Between Banks and Custodians?, Frank Napolitano, J.D., CFP®, CFA® Charter holder—Senior Financial Adviser, April 28, 2023.
3. RIA custodian comparison: which one is right for you?, Investment News, MAR 07, 2024, Ramon Vicente Berenguer, RIA custodian comparison: which one is right for you? - Investment News.
4. https://www.sec.gov/spotlight/secpostmadoffreforms.htm The Securities and Exchange Commission Post-Madoff Reforms.
5. https://www.nytimes.com/live/2023/11/02/business/sam-bankman-fried-trial, Sam Bankman-Fried Trial Fallen Crypto Mogul Convicted in Collapse That Cost Users Billions, David Yaffe-Bellany Matthew Goldstein and J. Edward Moreno.
6. Press Release SEC Charges Samuel Bankman-Fried with Defrauding Investors in Crypto Asset Trading Platform FTX, https://www.sec.gov/newsroom/press-releases/2022-219, December 13, 2022.

7. Ibbotson, Roger G., and Kaplan, Paul D. "Does Asset Allocation Policy Explain 40, 90, or 100 Percent of Performance?" *Financial Analysts Journal*, vol. 56, no. 1, 2000, pp. 26–33. *JSTOR*, http://www.jstor.org/stable/4480220. Accessed 19 March 2025.

8. https://www.schwab.com/learn/story/how-asset-location-can-help-save-on-taxes How Asset Location Can Help Save on Taxes, October 11, 2024, Hayden Adams.

Blind Spot 5: "Success Is All About Getting the Best Returns"

1. And, perhaps more importantly, whether they have done so on a risk-adjusted basis. If you outperform in a bull market by 1% per annum but your beta was 1.2, meaning your portfolio was 20% more volatile than the market (it took on more risk), you've actually *underperformed* on a risk-adjusted basis. Beta measures systematic risk—how sensitive your portfolio is to market movements. A beta of 1.2 means that if the market goes up 10%, your portfolio is expected to go up 12% (and vice versa for declines). So, if you only beat the market by 1% annually, but you took 20% more risk, your performance isn't impressive on a risk-adjusted basis. You should have outperformed by more than 1% to justify that extra risk.

2. During the dot-com bubble (1998–1999), Berkshire Hathaway underperformed the S&P 500 by as much as 50–60%, as tech stocks soared and Buffett avoided internet companies. Critics labeled him "out of touch" and even "obsolete," with headlines like *"Warren Buffett: Lost His Touch?"* appearing in major financial media (Traders Magazine, July 6, 2020). When the bubble collapsed (2000–2002), Berkshire rebounded strongly. While the Nasdaq fell nearly 80%, Berkshire delivered stellar double-digit outperformance over the next three years, vindicating Buffett's disciplined approach. Even the most skilled investors are likely to underperform for years when the market is in the thrall of a speculative boom, but in the end, prudent capital allocation typically wins out. The time horizon, however, for this to unfold is much longer than many people can tolerate.

3. John C. Bogle Quotes. BrainyQuote.com, BrainyMedia Inc, 2025. https://www.brainyquote.com/quotes/john_c_bogle_1119969, accessed July 29, 2025.

4. SPIVA® U.S. Scorecard, S&P Dow Jones Indices, Ganti, Anu R. https://www.spglobal.com/spdji/en/documents/spiva/spiva-us-year-end-2024.pdf
5. Ibid. p. 10.
6. Berkshire Hathaway 2013 Letter to Shareholders, p. 20.
7. https://www.visualcapitalist.com/chart-timing-the-market/
8. Ibid. The Hypothetical Average Rate of Return section displays the portfolio return and the inflation rate used in the calculations.
9. Source: Envestnet © 2024 MoneyGuide, Inc. All rights reserved. When a Retirement Goal is included, the default Confidence Zones are age-based. Younger clients will have a wider Confidence Zone compared to the narrower range for older clients.
10. Bengen, William P., "Determining Withdrawal Rates Using Historical Data," October 1994, *Journal of Financial Planning*, pp. 14–24.
11. See daytonestateplanninglaw.com Limitless Retirement podcast Episode 11: "Why you Shouldn't Use the 4% Rule in Retirement" Gudorf Financial Group.
12. Nassim Nicholas Taleb used the term "black swan event" in his 2007 book ***The Black Swan: The Impact of the Highly Improbable*** to describe rare and unpredictable events such as the 2008 Great Financial Crisis.

Blind Spot 6: "Not Every Asset Needs to Be in My Plan"

1. Herman, Dan. "Introducing short-term brands: A new branding tool for a new consumer reality." *Journal of Brand Management*, vol. 7, no. 5, 2000, pp. 330–340. doi:10.1057/bm.2000.23. ISSN 1350-231X. S2CID 167311741.
2. Hayes, Adam (2022). Tulipmania: About the Dutch Tulip Bulb Market Bubble. https://www.investopedia.com/terms/d/dutch_tulip_bulb_market_bubble.asp
3. Dwivedi, Abhijay. "A qualitative research on the 1630s' Tulip Bubble 'Tulipmania'." *International Journal of Social Science and Economic Research*, vol. 8, no. 8, 2023, pp. 2478–2491, doi:10.46609/IJSSER.2023.v08i08.028. Accessed August 2023.
4. Schreckinger, Ben (2014). The home of FOMO. Boston Magazine.

5. Kunda, Ziva. "The case for motivated reasoning". Copyright 1990 by the American Psychological Association. Inc. 0033-2909/90/S00.75, *Psychological Bulletin*, vol. 108, no. 3, 1990, pp. 480–498.

Blind Spot 7: "I Can Focus on My Wealth Planning After I Sell My Business"

1. US Small Business Administration June 30, 2025, https://advocacy.sba.gov/2025/06/30/new-advocacy-report-shows-the-number-of-small-businesses-in-the-u-s-exceeds-36-million/
2. The United States Small Business Administration (SBA) defines a small business as an independently owned and operated for-profit business meeting the following size constraints: manufacturing companies with 500 employees or fewer, and non-manufacturing businesses with average annual receipts under $7.5 million.
3. US Small Business Administration Frequently Asked Questions, July 2024, https://advocacy.sba.gov/2024/07/23/frequently-asked-questions-about-small-business-2024/
4. Tomlinson, Reese, edited by Micah Zimmerman, **Baby Boomer Businesses Are Up for Grabs — Here's How Entrepreneurs Can Benefit In 2025** Entrepreneur, January 16, 2025, https://www.entrepreneur.com/starting-a-business/why-baby-boomer-businesses-are-up-for-grabs-in-2025/484591
5. 2025 State of Owner Readiness Generational National Report. Exit Planning Institute page 9. Or Rogers, Andrew, 14 July 2025, "The Business Exit Moment" What Every Boomer Owner Should Know About the $84 Trillion Wealth Shift. www.legacykc.com
6. www.advocacy.sba.gov/wp-content/uploads/2021/08/Small-Business-Facts-Business-Owner-Wealth.pdf
7. "New Research from Wilmington Trust Finds Nearly 60 Percent of Business Owners Lack a Transition Plan," https://news.wilmingtontrust.com/New-Research-from-Wilmington-Trust-Finds-Nearly-60-Percent-of-Business-Owners-Lack-a-Transition-Plan, © 2025 M&T Bank
8. Ibid.
9. July 2023 UBS Investor Watch, Wind in Your Sales.

10. "New Research from Wilmington Trust Finds Nearly 60 Percent of Business Owners Lack a Transition Plan", https://news.wilmingtontrust.com/New-Research-from-Wilmington-Trust-Finds-Nearly-60-Percent-of-Business-Owners-Lack-a-Transition-Plan, © 2025 M&T Bank
11. UBS Investor Watch July 2023, Wind In Your Sales.
12. OBBBA, 07/04/2025.
13. https://taxpolicycenter.org/briefing-book/how-many-people-pay-estate-tax
14. Residency transfer is complex and lengthy. You should consult with a tax professional before making any decisions.
15. New York Qualified Small Business Stock (QSBS) and Investor Tax Incentives, June 21, 2020, https://www.qsbsexpert.com/new-york-qualified-small-business-stock-and-investor-tax-incentives/
16. Cornell Law School, Legal Information Institute, Rule against Perpetuities, https://www.law.cornell.edu/wex/rule_against_perpetuities

Blind Spot 8: "I Don't Need to Share My Intentions with My Kids; It's All in My Will"

1. The Great Wealth Transfer Starts with the Great Wealth Talk, Edward Jones Research Finds News release | February 27, 2024, https://www.edwardjones.com/us-en/why-edward-jones/news-media/press-releases/great-wealth-transfer-research
2. Northwestern Mutual's 2024 Planning & Progress Study, p. 10, https://filecache.mediaroom.com/mr5mr_nwmutual/179085/2024%20PP%20Wave%206%20-%20Leaving%20a%20Legacy.pdf
3. The Great Wealth Transfer Starts with the Great Wealth Talk, Edward Jones Research Finds News release | February 27, 2024, https://www.edwardjones.com/us-en/why-edward-jones/news-media/press-releases/great-wealth-transfer-research
4. Charles Schwab HNW Investor Survey 2024 (PDF).
5. Cambridge Trust, Bridging the Gap: The Importance of Estate Planning Through Generations, February 16, 2022, www.cambridgetrust.com/getmedia/f6d7e00f-261b-4cb0-a915-23fef435edbb/Q1-Client-Update-2022-Bridging-the-Gap.pdf

6. Ibid.
7. Ibid.
8. Ibid.
9. Trust & Will 2025 Estate Planning Report, p. 16.
10. Warren Buffett Talks to His Kids About His Will. You Should Too., Wall Street Journal, By Tergesen, Anne; Brown, Dalvin, November 29, 2024.
11. Wells-Fargo-Children-of-Millionaires-Survey-Lookbook, January 9, 2019. https://newsroom.wf.com/news-releases/news-details/2019/Children-of-Millionaires-Want-to-Inherit-Parents-Values-More-Than-Their-Wealth-Wells-Fargo-Survey-Finds/default.aspx
12. https://www.gwi.com/blog/financial-literacy-by-generations; Astre, Kristian.
13. The Hardest Part of Estate Planning: Sharing the Plan, November 28, 2023, BBH Capital Partners.
14. Ibid.
15. Ibid.
16. Ibid.
17. Ibid.
18. Preparing Heirs: Five Steps to a Successful Transition of Family Wealth and Values Hardcover – January 1, 2010 by Roy Williams (Author), Vic Preisser (Author).
19. Generational Wealth: Why do 70% of Families Lose Their Wealth in the 2nd Generation?, October 19, 2018, https://www.nasdaq.com/articles/generational-wealth%3A-why-do-70-of-families-lose-their-wealth-in-the-2nd-generation-2018-10
20. Borrowed from Your Grandchildren: The Evolution of 100-Year Family Enterprises, Jaffe, Dennis T. p. xv.
21. Preparing Heirs: Five Steps to a Successful Transition of Family Wealth and Values Hardcover – January 1, 2010 by Roy Williams (Author), Vic Preisser (Author), p. 36.
22. Northwestern Mutual 2023 Planning & Progress Study, https://news.northwesternmutual.com/planning-and-progress-study-2023, https://newsroom.wf.com/news-releases/news-details/2019/Children-of-Millionaires-Want-to-Inherit-Parents-Values-More-Than-Their-Wealth-Wells-Fargo-Survey-Finds/default.aspx
23. Ibid.

24. Ibid.
25. Page 43.
26. Northwestern Mutual 2023 Planning & Progress Study, https://news.northwesternmutual.com/planning-and-progress-study-2023, https://newsroom.wf.com/news-releases/news-details/2019/Children-of-Millionaires-Want-to-Inherit-Parents-Values-More-Than-Their-Wealth-Wells-Fargo-Survey-Finds/default.aspx
27. "Money blueprint" was popularized by T. Harv Eker, a motivational speaker and author, in his book "Secrets of the Millionaire Mind."
28. Borrowed from Your Grandchildren: The Evolution of 100-Year Family Enterprises. Jaffee, Dennis T., p. 290.
29. Ibid. p. 299.
30. Carol S. Dweck, Mindset: The New Psychology of Success, NY Random House, 2006, pp. 175–222.
31. James E. Hughes Jr., Family Wealth: Keeping in the Family—How Family Members and Their Advisers Preserve Human, Intellectual and Financial Assets for Generations, NY Bloomberg Press, 2004, pp. 73–78.
32. Note that including a Digital Asset Plan is an increasingly important component of modern estate planning. It ensures that your digital life—everything from online accounts to digital files—is properly managed or transferred after death or incapacity. Without a plan, loved ones may be locked out of important accounts, valuable or sentimental digital property could be lost and legal complications could arise due to privacy laws and terms of service agreements. The plan often includes (1) an inventory of digital assets: a list of all accounts and assets, including usernames and access instructions (but not necessarily passwords), (2) access instructions: how and where to find login credentials (often stored in a secure password manager or physical document), (3) legal authorization: language in your will, trust, or power of attorney that gives a fiduciary the right to access and manage digital assets (in compliance with laws like the Revised Uniform Fiduciary Access to Digital Assets Act—RUFADAA), and (4) a designated digital executor: a person authorized to manage your digital estate. While 45 states have adopted RUFADAA or something similar, access to the content of communications (like emails or messages) typically requires explicit consent from the decedent in legal documents.
33. Leaving a legacy: A lasting gift to loved ones. September 2018, p. 21, https://images.em.bankofamerica.com/HOST-01-19-2701/ML_Legacy_Study.pdf

Blind Spot 9: "We're Very Charitable; We Don't Need a Philanthropic Strategy"

1. LendingTree analysis of IRS SOI data for tax year 2021. https://www.lendingtree.com/credit-cards/study/charitable-donations/ 85% of Americans Say Inflation/Economy Makes Charitable Donations Harder, Davis, Maggie, November 18, 2024.
2. Giving USA: The Annual Report on Philanthropy. Giving USA Foundation™, The Giving Institute, and the Indiana University Lilly Family School of Philanthropy.
3. Fidelity Charitable, "Charitable living and the new retirement," September 23, 2024, p. 9.
4. For donations of $250 or more, a written acknowledgment from the charity is required. For non-cash contributions over $500, you may need to have a formal appraisal made and/or file IRS Form 8283 to claim a deduction.
5. https://newsroom.wf.com/news-releases/news-details/2019/Children-of-Millionaires-Want-to-Inherit-Parents-Values-More-Than-Their-Wealth-Wells-Fargo-Survey-Finds/default.aspx, January 19, 2019.
6. What Americans Think About Philanthropy and Nonprofits, chrome-extension://efaidnbmnnnibpcajpcglclefindmkaj/https://scholarworks.indianapolis.iu.edu/server/api/core/bitstreams/b5904a8a-5081-42cd-bd44-56740b98fb67/content, Indiana University Lilly Family School of Philanthropy. April 2023.
7. Bequest Marketing: The Ultimate Guide to Your Most Essential Planned Giving Strategy, https://www.plannedgiving.com/bequest-marketing-the-ultimate-guide-to-your-most-essential-planned-giving-strategy/, Mikaelian, Viken.
8. Furthermore, IRAs are a major source of Income in Respect of a Decedent (IRD), which is taxable to individual heirs but not to charities, making it an ideal asset to bequeath to a nonprofit. IRD is income that a person would have received and therefore would have been liable for taxes on during their lifetime. Heirs must pay ordinary income taxes on IRD.
9. If the donor dies before starting their RMDs, the charity must receive the full distribution to which it is entitled within 5 years. If the owner dies after starting RMDs, the charity can receive distributions over the

remaining life expectancy of the owner. These rules differ from those for individual beneficiaries, who may have up to 10 years before they are required to distribute the IRA.

10. Note that non-grantor CRTs have an additional benefit over CLTs in that they defer capital gains tax. Appreciated assets contributed to a CRT can be sold within the trust tax-free.
11. The IRS views this as a split transaction. There is a Gift Portion which is the value of the remainder that will eventually go to the charity and the Investment Portion which is the value of the annuity payments you receive. Because you've already "paid" for the annuity with your gift, the IRS allows you to recover your investment tax-free over your life expectancy. This is called the "return of principal" or "exclusion ratio."
12. Fidelity Charitable, "Charitable living and the new retirement," September 23, 2024, p. 10.
13. https://thenytrust.org/about/history/
14. Assumes an annual return of 6%.

Blind Spot 10: "I Could Never Leave My Current Adviser"

1. Stay or Stray, PriceMetrix Insights, December 2013.
2. https://www.morningstar.com/financial-advisors/why-do-investors-keep-their-financial-advisors-around

About the Author

1. This Rating was provided on 2/11/2026 by Forbes. It covers the period of 9/30/2021-9/30/2026. There was no compensation exchanged in consideration for or the use of this Rating. For more information, please visit https://www.forbes.com/lists/best-in-state-women-advisors/?sh=64e9af191d11

Acknowledgments

An adviser's value lies not only in the advice they give but in the advice they've been willing—and fortunate enough—to receive. Writing this book has brought into focus the quiet irony that has shaped my career: the most enduring insights I offer often trace back to someone else's generosity. I've been incredibly fortunate to learn from a wide circle of mentors, colleagues, clients, friends, and family, each of whom has shaped my thinking in ways both subtle and profound. This book is, in many ways, a reflection of their wisdom, and I'm deeply grateful for the openness with which they've shared it.

As agent and dear friend, Jennifer Weis has been a superb guide. From our first meeting in college to our constant interactions as adults, your wisdom, intelligence, humor, and grace have been invaluable.

Thank you to Judith Newlin, editor at Wiley, for understanding the need for guidance during the most significant wealth transfer in history and offering me the opportunity to tackle this topic. To Susan Cerra, senior managing editor, and Julie Kerr, development editor, your on-point advice has been instrumental in delivering my thoughts.

Marni Seneker, my coach, editor, and writing guide, I couldn't have done this without you. Your counsel to "invite" the reader to consider alternative ways of thinking set the tone and enabled me to find the path needed to address strongly held convictions. Your experience, conceptual talent, editorial skill, intelligence, empathy, and humor enabled me to, as you so often advised, "trust the process." I am profoundly grateful to you.

Ari Galper, your deep understanding of human communication and insights on how to build trust between advisers and clients have become embedded in my work. Thank you.

I am truly thankful to my clients who have placed their trust in me and my team to help shape the legacies they envision. Over the past 30 years in which I've had the privilege of working with you and your other advisors—estate attorneys, accountants, insurance professionals, and philanthropic consultants—I have gained profound insights that have refined and strengthened my work. Your experience, collaboration, and generosity of thought have enriched my understanding and elevated the advice I am able to offer. I thank you all for the wisdom you've shared and the relationships we have built.

Thank you to my mentors at Morgan Stanley who taught me unparalleled concern for accuracy and attention to detail within a 24/7 environment, to all my Booz Allen colleagues and especially to Lisa Schwartz who taught me the two most valuable words when reviewing an analysis: "so what?," to Don Kerr, former head of the Financial Services Group at Booz Allen, who was committed to helping me continue my career while having a family, a concept yet to be embraced at the time, and to Roger Hertog, former Vice-Chairman Emeritus of AllianceBernstein, who asked the most challenging questions and demanded the most thoughtful answers based on a deep understanding of investment principles.

Acknowledgments

The opportunity to join Stralem & Company; to become partners with my father, Philippe Baumann, Hirschel, and Adam Abelson; and to work alongside my father for 10 years until he passed away has been of lasting significance. My gratitude goes to Leeza and the team who joined us when we merged with Fischer & Company. Their trust and commitment were a meaningful vote of confidence—one I'm honored to have received. To my newest partner, Alan Fischer, your experience, advice, investing talent, and humor help us all make the most of every day. To our combined Fischer Stralem team, broadened by Rodney, Jill, Asher, Lana, and Shelley, I am genuinely thankful for the opportunity to serve our clients and grow our futures together. Thank you to Hightower Advisors for providing the platform on which we are building the next chapter—for ourselves and for those we serve. Special thanks to Barrett Lopez, Managing Director and General Counsel, Dan Berg, Chief Financial Officer and David Work, Managing Director and Head of Estate & Financial Planning, for your unending and sage counsel.

My friends are the oxygen that keeps me going. Girl Chat, my precious PAS community, and so many others from nursery school, Riverdale, Rosey, Tigertown, SOM, Einstein, Weizmann etc., each of you deserves special recognition—not just for your encouragement, but for your patience and understanding during times when my overcommitted life may have made me fall short of being the friend you deserve. For no one is this more apt than Wendy Barasch, who has truly been a sister to me, with all that that connotes. Wendy and Marc, Melissa and Marc, and Elliot and Debbie, your constancy, embrace, and love are deeply meaningful. I am thankful beyond words that we share the journey of life together. Shmuel, thank you for nurturing my soul. Victor, thank you for your wisdom and belief in me.

I hope you, the reader, senses through these pages, the deep influence my family has had on the person I've become, the values

I hold dear, and the character of the advice I offer. I am certain that my great-great-great-grandfather, who founded the Banque Levy in 1810, could never have imagined a great-great-great-grand*daughter* continuing in his footsteps—but I am thankful for his DNA. I am particularly grateful to have had a mother whose brilliance and beauty were always both a compass and a challenge, who showed me that intellect and empathy can—and must—coexist, and who made it clear that pursuing a career was not just acceptable but expected. My father, whose charm, humor, and wisdom left enormous footsteps I've tried to follow, taught me that character is built not just in moments of success, but in how we carry ourselves through the most challenging of times while continuing to care for others. I am also thankful for my brother, my brothers-in-law, sisters-in-law, and nieces and nephews, whose presence and support have added richness, perspective, and continuity to our family story.

And to my three beautiful, talented daughters, each of whom has forged her own path with courage and conviction—you remind me daily that legacy is not something we leave behind, but something we shape forward. You've taught me to adapt to change while honoring tradition. What a pleasure to have you bring my favorite son- and daughter-in-law into the family and witness our happiness expand. The addition of two adorable grandsons and a gorgeous granddaughter has provided the joy and privilege of a lifetime: the ability to pass a legacy down from generation to generation.

None of this would have been possible without the love of my life, Ivan. Your intelligence, self-discipline, kindness, love of family, conviction about how life should be lived, and steadfast ability to handle "*everything*" has been the wind beneath my wings.

About the Author

Andrea Baumann Lustig is Managing Partner of Fischer Stralem Advisors, a wealth management practice within Hightower Advisors. She has been recognized as a Forbes Top Women Wealth Advisor Best in State for five consecutive years (2022–2026).[1] Andrea brings deep experience in wealth and investment management, to help clients create lasting legacies that reflect their values and vision.

Andrea's passion for legacy is in her DNA. She is the sixth generation in her family to lead a wealth management firm, tracing her lineage back to 1810 when her great-great-great-grandfather founded Banque Levy in France. Her grandfather led Banque Asch, Strasbourg's largest bank, guiding French families in wealth management until World War II forced the family to flee to the United States. Andrea's father carried the legacy forward as an early partner in Stralem & Company, founded in 1967 and acquired by Hightower in 2020. Inspired by the enduring success of multigenerational families, Andrea has devoted her career to helping clients build meaningful legacies—sharing insights she has gained to guide them in creating and protecting purpose-driven wealth.

She actively contributes her experience to advancing nonprofit organizations, serving on advisory boards at Princeton University, the Yale International Center for Finance, Albert Einstein College of Medicine, the Weizmann Institute of Science, and Park Avenue Synagogue, where she chaired its record-breaking 2023 capital campaign. Andrea is married, a proud mother of three daughters, and grandmother to three beloved grandchildren.

Index

4% spending rule, 124, 126
5% maximum rule, 148
501(c)(3) organizations, 234
678 trusts, 225
1031 exchange, 175

A
ACAT. See account transfer forms
accountant, 38, 40, 50, 207
account transfer forms (ACAT), 276
active management, 107–109, 118, 132, 133
active risk, 92
ad hoc gifting, 241, 243
adjusted gross income (AGI), 234
advanced healthcare directives (AHCDs), 201, 226, 227
aggressive investment portfolio, 61, 63, 135
AGI. See adjusted gross income
AHCDs. See advanced healthcare directives
arithmetic expected return, 123–125
asset allocation, 47–48, 49, 57–65, 90–91, 271–272
  allocation of specific amount to specific class, 88
  rebalancing, 66–68, 111
  target, 85–88
asset class indexes, 103–104
asset location, 48, 58, 65–66, 91, 288–289

asset retention gifts, 248, 256–264
asset sale, 175
assets under management (AUM), 22, 33, 43
AUM. See assets under management

B
Baby Boomers, 2, 3, 159, 211
Bankman-Fried, Sam, 85
BDIT. See beneficiary defective inheritor's trust
benchmarks, and portfolio performance evaluation, 102–117
beneficiary defective inheritor's trust (BDIT), 224
beneficiary designations, 247, 249
Bengen, William, 124
bequests, 240, 246, 247, 249
Berkshire Hathaway, 290
best interest standard, 20, 25
Bloomberg Aggregate Bond Index, 102
Bogle, John, 60, 107
Bogle Asset Allocation Rule, 60
bond coupons, 126–133
broker-dealers, 18–20, 22, 43, 84
brokers, 18–20
Buffett, Warren, 108, 197, 290
buy-sell agreements, 173
bypass (credit shelter) trust, 218, 222

305

INDEX

C

callability of municipal bonds, 130, 132
capital gains taxes, 116–117, 199–200, 234, 237, 297
capital sufficiency, and outside investments, 145–147
Certified Financial Planner (CFP®), 286
CFP®. *See* Certified Financial Planner
CFTC. *See* Commodity Futures Trading Commission
CGAs. *See* charitable gift annuities
charitable gift annuities (CGAs), 248, 254–256
charitable lead annuity trusts (CLATs), 152, 251–252
charitable lead trusts (CLTs), 247, 250–252, 255, 297
charitable lead unitrusts (CLUTs), 252
charitable remainder annuity trusts (CRATs), 253–254
charitable remainder trusts (CRTs), 178, 181, 183, 222, 232, 247, 250, 252–255
charitable remainder unitrusts (CRUTs), 254
charitable trusts, 183, 250–255
CLATs. *See* charitable lead annuity trusts
closure, role of investors in, 71–75
CLTs. *See* charitable lead trusts
CLUTs. *See* charitable lead unitrusts
Commodity Futures Trading Commission (CFTC), 83
communication. *See also* inheritance, discussion with heirs about
 and business exit plan, 176
 between siloed professionals, 40–41
compensation
 of brokers, 18, 19
 of dual representatives, 25
 of financial advisers, 16–18
 of holistic wealth advisers, 43
 of investment adviser representatives, 22
compounding, 163, 235
concentration risk, 89, 145, 148
confidence interval, 121
corporate structure, changing, 175–176
CRATs. *See* charitable remainder annuity trusts
cross-purchase agreements, 173
CRTs. *See* charitable remainder trusts
Crummey letter, 39
CRUTs. *See* charitable remainder unitrusts
cryptocurrencies, 85
custodians, 275
 regulation of, 83–84
 responsibilities of, 83
 risk of failure, 82–85
Custody Rule, SEC, 82

D

DAFs. *See* donor-advised funds
deferred gifts, 246–247, 249
descendants' trusts, 177–179, 220, 223
Digital Asset Plan, 295
digital assets, 85, 295
disclaimer trusts, 224
diversification of advice, 85–88, 93–94
DNR. *See* do not resuscitate
do-it-yourselfers, 31, 32
donor-advised funds (DAFs), 182, 232, 235, 248, 257
do not resuscitate (DNR), 228
dot-com bubble, 290
DRs. *See* dual representatives
dual representatives (DRs), 16, 25–27, 31–33, 287
 characteristics of, 27, 28–29
 numbers, change in, 33
durable power of attorney (POA), 221, 226, 228
duty of care, 21
duty of loyalty, 21–22
dynamic rebalancing (asset allocation), 67
dynasty trusts, 164–165, 178, 180, 223

E

efficient frontier, 61–64
electing small business trusts (ESBTs), 178, 181, 225
employee stock ownership plan (ESOP), 176
end-of-life
 documents, 227–228
 preferences, 200–201, 226
ESBTs. *See* electing small business trusts
ESOP. *See* employee stock ownership plan
estate flow chart, 48–49, 217–220, 241, 242
estate planning, 162–165, 199. *See also* inheritance, discussion with heirs about
 attorneys, 38, 40, 49, 77, 207
 Digital Asset Plan, 295
 motivations for creating estate plan, 194–195
 overview of estate plan, 217–226
 tools, 221–225
estate taxes, 162–163, 234, 236, 237, 244
exclusion ratio, 297
executor, 196, 200, 201
exit plan, business, 174–176

F

family bank trusts, 225
family foundations, 219, 220
family governance, and pre-sale wealth planning, 168–169
family limited partnerships, 182

family meetings, 168, 197, 214
   end-of-life wishes, 226
   estate plan overview, 217–226
   Q and A session, 226, 229
   reviewing family mission statement, 216
   scheduling, 229
   setting tone and purpose, 216
family mission statement, 208, 214–216
family offices, 30–31
family trusts, 218
fear of missing out (FOMO), 141–142, 144
financial advisers, 9–11, 37–38. *See also* family offices; wealth advisers
   categories of, 16–27
   characteristics of, 21, 24, 27, 28–29
   investor satisfaction with, 13
   relationship of investors with, 4, 14–15, 27–30
   risk of institutional failure, 82–85
   spectrum, 31–33
   top reasons for hiring, 14
financial health management, 155
Financial Industry Regulatory Authority (FINRA), 18, 59, 287
financial literacy, 74, 204
FINRA. *See* Financial Industry Regulatory Authority
fixed-income portfolio, 60, 64, 92
FOMO. *See* fear of missing out
FTX Trading Ltd., 85

G
generation-skipping transfer tax (GSTT), 164, 177
Generation X, 2
Generation Z, 211
gift/estate tax exemption, 162–164, 166, 218–219
grantor CLTs, 250–251
grantor CRTs, 253
grantor-retained annuity trusts (GRATs), 178, 180, 222
grantor trusts, 176–177, 179
GRATs. *See* grantor-retained annuity trusts
growth investing, 110–112
growth mindset, 213
GSTT. *See* generation-skipping transfer tax

H
healthcare proxy, 201, 227
held-away investments, 70
Herman, Dan, 141
HIPAA authorization, 228

holistic wealth advisers, 34–35, 42–45, 52–53, 94, 207, 268, 273
   portfolio construction, 89–93
   searching for, 52
holistic wealth plan, 30, 45–48, 51, 275
hybrid agreements, 174
hybrid RIAs, 25–26, 33
hypothetical average portfolio return, 117, 120–123, 136, 137

I
IARs. *See* investment adviser representatives
IDGTs. *See* intentionally defective grantor trusts
ILITs. *See* irrevocable life insurance trusts
illiquidity discount, 167
inception, portfolio performance since, 123
Income in Respect of a Decedent (IRD), 296
income-related gifts, 152, 177, 247–248, 250–256
income tax, 234, 237, 258, 259
independence of investors, 69–70, 140–141, 143
inflation
   and 100% bond portfolio, 126–127, 129, 131
   and arithmetic expected return, 124
informational interviews, 52
inheritance, discussion with heirs about
   benefits of, 195–205
   concerns of affluent parents, 209, 210
   and family dynamics, 192–193
   and family harmony, 201–203, 205
   family meetings, 215–229
   financial behaviors of children, 211–212
   interest of younger generations, 211
   involvement of teens and young adults, 213
   offering education, 203–204
   parental prudence, 209–213
   perfectionism, 206–207
   preparation, 207–208
   procrastination and paralysis, 208–209
   promotion of clarity, 199–201
   reluctance to, 191–194
   strengthening preparedness, 205
   and three-generation curse, 210
   and transparency, 204–205
installment sale, 175
institutional failure, risk of, 82–85
insurance agent, 38, 40, 50
intentionally defective grantor trusts (IDGTs), 177, 179, 224
Internal Revenue Service (IRS), 165–167, 177, 234, 252, 297

investment adviser representatives (IARs), 16, 20–24, 25–26, 287
　characteristics of, 24, 28–29
　numbers, change in, 33
Investment Advisers Act (1940), 20, 82
investment managers, 41, 57, 94, 109
　changing, 113
　monitoring of, 59, 68, 102
　selection of, 59, 68
investment plan, 47–48
investment selection, 48, 91–93
IRA, 66, 151, 152, 249, 256–257, 259, 289, 296, 297
IRD. *See* Income in Respect of a Decedent
irrevocable life insurance trusts (ILITs), 38–39, 41, 49, 50, 151, 178, 181, 223
IRS. *See* Internal Revenue Service

J
Jaffe, Dennis, 212

K
Know Your Customer (KYC) Rule, 59–60
Kunda, Ziva, 144
KYC. *See* Know Your Customer Rule

L
last will and testament, 221
legal structuring, 167–168
letter of intent (LOI), 167
limited partnerships, 182
liquidity risks, and outside investments, 149–150
living wills, 201, 226, 227
LLCs, 182
LOI. *See* letter of intent

M
Madoff Securities, 85
marital QTIP trusts, 222
marital trusts, 202, 218–219
market conditions, and portfolio performance, 109–112, 118
market timing, and portfolio performance, 115–116, 119
Markowitz, Harry M., 61
MFOs. *See* multi-family offices
Millennials, 2, 3, 211
Monte Carlo–based average return, 120, 123, 125–126, 134–138
Morgan Stanley, 84
Morgan Stanley Trust National Association (MSTNA), 84
motivated reasoning, and outside investments, 143–144
MSCI EAFE Index, 102

MSTNA. *See* Morgan Stanley Trust National Association
multi-family offices (MFOs), 30–31
municipal bonds, 126, 129–133, 149, 289

N
Nevada/Delaware Incomplete Gift Non-Grantor Trust (NING/DING Trust), 224
NING/DING Trust. *See* Nevada/Delaware Incomplete Gift Non-Grantor Trust
nonfinancial spouse, role in wealth management, 73–74
non-grantor CLTs, 250–251
non-grantor CRTs, 253, 297

O
OCC. *See* Office of the Comptroller of the Currency
Office of the Comptroller of the Currency (OCC), 83
One Big Beautiful Bill Act, 219
opportunity identification, role of investors in, 75–76
order of bequests, 249
outside investments, 139–141
　and capital sufficiency, 145–147
　and concentration risk, 148
　and desire for identification, 142–143
　fees on, 153–154
　and FOMO, 141–142, 144
　and liquidity risks, 149–150
　and motivated reasoning, 143–144
　and opportunities for legacy enhancement, 150–153
　and pushback from adviser, 154
　reluctance to discuss about, 154

P
passive management, 107–109, 118, 132
Pension Protection Act (2006), 257
percentage-based bequests, 249
perfectionism, and estate planning, 206–207
periodic rebalancing (asset allocation), 67
personal life, changes in, 77–78
philanthropic strategy, 182–183, 188, 232–234
　ad hoc gifting, 241, 243
　engagement and learning opportunity, 236–238
　goal setting, 239–241
　impact of, 235, 237, 238
　planned giving, 245–264
　sense of purpose and direction, 235–238
　and taxable events, 243–244
　and tax efficiency, 234, 236–238

Index

tools, 245, 246
planned giving, 245–246
  asset retention gifts, 248, 256–264
  deferred gifts, 246–247, 249
  income-related gifts, 247–248, 250–256
play bucket, 147, 153
POA. *See* durable power of attorney
POLST/MOLST, 228
portfolio construction, 57–59, 109–110
  asset allocation, 57–68, 90–91
  asset location, 58, 65–66, 91
  efficient frontier, 61–64
  investment manager selection and monitoring, 59, 68
  investment selection, 91–93
  spending order, 58–59, 65–66
  working with single holistic manager, 89–90
portfolio diversification, 109–112, 148
portfolio performance, evaluation of
  active vs passive management, 107–109, 118
  arithmetic expected return, 123–125
  bond coupons, 126–133
  luck vs skill, 113–114, 118
  market conditions, 109–112, 118
  market timing, 115–116, 119
  Monte Carlo–based average return, 120, 123, 125–126, 134–138
  and performance-chasing behavior, 105–106
  performance since inception, 123
  relative to benchmarks, 102–117
  relative to wealth plan, 117, 120–132
  risk management, 114–115, 119
  short-term performance, 103
  taxes and transaction costs, 116–117, 119
  time horizon for, 111
pour-over will, 221
preliminary valuation for pre-sale wealth planning, 170–171
premium muni ladder vs actively managed muni fund, 132, 133
pre-sale wealth planning, 162, 169
  estate and tax structuring, 176–182
  estate planning, 162–165
  exit strategies and timing, 174–176
  family governance, 168–169
  identification of financial needs, aspirations, and legacy goals, 171
  initial wealth modeling, 171–172
  legal structuring, 167–168
  opportunities for enhancing resources, 173–174
  philanthropic strategy, 182–183
  preliminary valuation, 170–171

  roadmap, 169–183
  and tax efficiency, 165–167
price discovery (bond market), 131
principal erosion, and 100% bond portfolio, 127, 131
privacy of investors, 69–70
private foundations, 248, 258–264
  growth of contributions to, 259–263
  legal setup costs of, 258
  RMDs of, 258–259
  tax savings, 262
purchasing power, and 100% bond portfolio, 127, 129, 131

Q

QCDs. *See* qualified charitable distributions
QPRTs. *See* qualified personal residence trusts
QSBS. *See* Qualified Small Business Stock
QSSTs. *See* qualified Subchapter S trusts
qualified charitable distributions (QCDs), 248, 256–257
qualified personal residence trusts (QPRTs), 222
Qualified Small Business Stock (QSBS), 175–176
qualified Subchapter S trusts (QSSTs), 225

R

rebalancing (asset allocation), 66–68, 111
redemption agreements, 174
Reg BI. *See* Regulation Best Interest
Registered Investment Advisers (RIAs), 20, 22, 25, 26, 33, 34, 35, 82, 84
registered representatives (RRs), 16, 18–20, 25–26, 31, 44
  characteristics of, 21, 28–29
  numbers, change in, 33
Regulation Best Interest (Reg BI), 20
regulatory environment, changes in, 76
regulatory standards for financial advisers, 16–17
reinvestment risk, and bonds, 130, 132
required minimum distributions (RMDs), 66, 256–259, 296
revocable trusts, 41, 72, 217–218, 221
RIAs. *See* Registered Investment Advisers
risk budgeting, 92
risk management, 114–115, 119
risk tolerance questionnaire, 59–60
RMDs. *See* required minimum distributions
Roth IRA, 66, 152, 259
RRs. *See* registered representatives
rule against perpetuities, 164, 177–178

S

Samuelson, Paul, 107
SEC. *See* Securities and Exchange Commission

INDEX

Secure 2.0 Act, 257
Securities and Exchange Commission (SEC), 20–21, 82, 85, 287
sense of purpose, and philanthropic strategy, 235–238
separation of asset custody from asset advice, 82–85
sequence-of-returns risk, 124
SFOs. *See* single-family offices
short-term investment performance, 103
single-family offices (SFOs), 30–31
SLATs. *See* spousal lifetime access trusts
small businesses, 159–160, 292. *See also* pre-sale wealth planning
　purchase offer, 161
　and transition plan, 160–161
SNTs. *See* special needs trusts
S&P 500 Index, 102, 116, 290
special needs trusts (SNTs), 223
spending order, 58–59, 65–66
spousal lifetime access non-grantor trusts, 225
spousal lifetime access trusts (SLATs), 178, 181, 223
spouses/partners, involvement in wealth planning, 72–75
stock sale, 175
suitability standard, 20, 25
systematic risk, 92, 290

T

target asset allocation, 85–86
　departures from, 86–87
　maintaining, 87–88
Tax Cut and Jobs Act (2017), 256
tax(es)
　capital gains, 116–117, 199–200, 234, 237, 297
　and donor-advised funds, 182
　efficiency, and philanthropic strategy, 234, 236–238, 259, 262
　efficiency, and pre-sale wealth planning, 165–167
　estate, 162–163, 234, 236, 237, 244
　events, and philanthropic strategy, 243–244
　GSTT, 164, 177
　income, 152, 177, 234, 237, 258, 259
　and portfolio performance, 116–117, 119
three-generation curse, 210
traditional IRA, 66
transaction costs, and portfolio performance, 116–117, 119
transition plan, business, 160–161

transparency in asset distribution, 204–205
trusts, 176–181, 199. *See also specific trusts*

U

unified credit trusts, 218

V

valuation discount, 166, 167
value investing, 110–112

W

wealth adviser, acting as your own, 56–57, 70–71
　closure, 71–75
　opportunity identification, 75–76
　personal life changes, 77–78
　portfolio construction, 57–68
　privacy and independence, 69–70
　regulatory environment changes, 77
wealth adviser, changing
　focus on your objectives, 273–274
　leaving your current adviser, 275–277
　overcoming guilt when, 271–273
　partial incorporation of current adviser, 274–275
wealth advisers, 3, 48, 169, 183
　client retention rates of, 271
　gaps between needs and advice, 269–271
　holistic, 34–35, 42–45, 52–53, 89–94, 207, 268, 273
　right, characteristics of, 268–269
wealth forecasting model, 45, 47–50
wealth models, 34, 171–172, 207, 240, 241, 244
wealth plan, 34, 35, 97–99, 102–103, 155, 207–208. *See also* outside investments; philanthropic strategy; pre-sale wealth planning
　amendment of, 207
　holistic, 30, 45–47, 51, 275
　hypothetical average portfolio return, 117, 120–123, 136, 137
　long-term return goals, 137
　Monte Carlo–based average return, 134–138
　and portfolio performance evaluation, 117, 120–132
　and small business owners, 160
wire houses, 25–26, 33, 34, 35

Y

Yield to Call (YTC), 130, 131
yield to maturity (YTM), 129, 132
YTC. *See* Yield to Call
YTM. *See* yield to maturity